LYING DOWN TOGETHER

LAW, METAPHOR, AND THEOLOGY

Lying Down Together

LAW, METAPHOR, AND THEOLOGY

BY MILNER S. BALL

THE UNIVERSITY OF WISCONSIN PRESS

Published 1985

The University of Wisconsin Press
114 North Murray Street
Madison, Wisconsin 53715

The University of Wisconsin Press, Ltd.
1 Gower Street
London WC1E 6HA, England

First printing

Printed in the United States of America

For LC CIP information see the colophon

ISBN 0-299-10450-8

FOR ED AND LUCY, FRANK AND LOUISE

The composure, regard for propriety and self-sacrificial courage of a generation have become in them a personal inspiration to me.

[L]aw bends the things which have been towards the things which are to come.
    —Paul L. Lehmann

There is a fishing-station in Breidfjord called the Bjarn Isles; there are a number of islets in this group, and they were very productive. At that time people used to go there in great numbers for the fishing, and many were stationed there all year round. Sagacious people thought it very important that men in such fishing-stations should get on well together, for it was believed that fishing-luck would desert them if they quarreled; and most people were careful to respect this.
    —*Laxdaela Saga*

CONTENTS

ACKNOWLEDGMENTS

The National Endowment for the Humanities along with the University of Georgia School of Law and its Dean, Ralph Beaird, made available to me the financial support necessary for the writing of this book. To Dean Beaird and the NEH, I express my great thanks.

Many people contributed criticism and other kinds of help at one time or another as the manuscript gradually became a book. I am deeply in their debt.

Paul Lehmann was one of the commentators on the manuscript. Except for immediate family, he is the reader with whom I have built up the happiest, oldest, and greatest debt. Next is Coleman Barks who for two decades now has freely shared with me his insights and good works. And beginning about a decade ago with his *The Legal Imagination* (1973), James Boyd White has continued to teach all of us lawyers what it is possible to say.

Within the past decade, and now with this project, I have had the great good fortune to receive the counsel of the following: Thomas L. Shaffer has set an example for me. He also convened a colloquium under the auspices of the Frances Lewis Law Center of the Washington and Lee Law School for the purpose of discussing the subjects addressed in this book. In addition to Professors Shaffer and Lehmann, that discussion included Frank Alexander, Roy Herron, Andrew McThenia, and Buie Seawell (comrade from the ancient wars). Only they will realize how much I benefited and how much the cause was advanced by those days of dialogue. I am grateful for them and the Frances Lewis Law Center. Also from Washington and Lee, Lewis H. Larue gave me a fine, close reading that led to much rewriting. Substantive changes were also the consequence of the thoughtful, useful comments—above and beyond the call of duty and friendship—made by Kent Greenawalt, Bernhard Schloh and Mark Tushnet. The careful criticism of Judith Hatton saved me from many foolish mistakes.

The following colleagues gave good counsel (and in some cases, this was only a recent instance of long-standing friendship): Frederick Ferré, Ellen Jordan, Ronald North, Michael Perry, William H. Rodgers, Jr., Dean Rusk, and Joseph L. Sax.

Acknowledgments

Thanks are certainly due to June, Sarah, Scott, Virginia, and to Marilyn Hibbs who suffered through the hard work of preparing the manuscript without losing her welcome cheerfulness.

Some of the people named above disagree in fundamental ways with what I have written. Their willingness to assist, like that of other friends who find my approach more congenial, is testimony to their kindness and sense of collegiality. There are many ways in which this book is a communal work, but I am fully responsible for its failures and offenses. Do not blame those who helped. They tried. Valiantly.

Some of the material of this book has appeared in earlier, usually much different versions, as journal articles. I thank the following for permission to republish that material as it is now written here: the *Georgia Review* (originally published as *Of Rocks and Dams, PVC and Poetry,* Ga. Rev., Spring 1982, p. 7); the Dean Rusk Center (originally published as *Law of the Sea: Federal-State Relations,* Monograph No. 1, 1978); *San Diego Law Review* (originally published as *Law of the Sea: Expression of Solidarity,* 19 San Diego L. Rev. 461 [1982]); and *Environmental Law* (originally published as *Good Old American Permits: Madisonian Federalism on the Territorial Sea and Continental Shelf,* 12 Envtl. L. 623 [1982]).

PREFACE

In an earlier book, *The Promise of American Law,* I proposed that law may be understood as a performance which mirrors our nature as a people. Critics of that work were generous in their appraisal of it. Time and the opportunity for further mulling over the subject have revealed to me just how generous they were.

Although the present volume takes up a different subject, I continue in the same concerns and struggles. I do hope to have made some gains in clarity.

Chapter 2 of this book examines the necessity for a new conceptual metaphor for law. Chapters 3, 4, and 5 then explore the law of the sea and coast in search of specific possibilities for such a metaphor. The last chapter confronts the constellation of metaphors to which the new one belongs. In that last chapter I shall reconsider the meaning of the natural and of the relation of humans to the created order. It will be necessary for me to do some systematic theology.

The new conceptual metaphor presents law as forming and stimulating an ongoing conversation, as connecting humans to each other, as containing and enriching the cycle of communication. It says that law is a medium for human solidarity.

As you read, you may come to think that my enterprise is fanciful. You may think that it is fanciful at the very best. You may think that we might as well say that law is a flyswatter or a pasta machine or field peas or a brooding omnipresence. Why not? Could not someone familiar enough with the law rummage around in it and come up with the elements of any image of law she wanted to?

One of my responsibilities is to persuade you that it can be plausible to talk about law as medium. I shall try to construct my argument working with the legal materials at hand in such a way that you will be willing to grant that this language is not outrageous, or in such a way that you will be willing to suspend disbelief about its implausibility.

All along the way, never on the page but never very far behind it, I shall be asking the question that Mayor Koch keeps putting to the voters of New York City, minus the arrogance: "How'm I doing?"

You may conclude that I am not doing very well. You cannot vote me out of office. You have a better remedy. You can close the book, put it away and put me out of mind. Or you may find merit in my experiment but think that I am not executing it very well. In that event, I hope you will be moved to construct your own understanding of law and to state a metaphor other than the one presented here and other than the dominating one.

I want to encourage just such activity. I believe that the exercise is important in spite of (or maybe because of) the possibility that you and I will reach different conclusions as a consequence of engaging in it—so long as we continue to be willing to negotiate our meaning. Paradigm shifts cannot be accomplished without some form of conflict. So willingness to negotiate meaning is very important.

This is not an idle game, a form of jurisprudential tinker toys. I am deeply concerned about systemic evil in the law and the victims of the legal system. I believe that fundamental revisions are in order and that one way for me to help bring them about is to stimulate revisions in our conceptions of law. Therefore, I hope you will join in fashioning new conceptual metaphors for law. A joint venture of this sort will be a move toward realizing law that supports rather than stifles human flourishing.

Before I get to all these things, I want first to set the context for my writing. Bear with me a little as I do so with chapter 1.

LYING DOWN TOGETHER

LAW, METAPHOR, AND THEOLOGY

1 INTRODUCTION

I

My son once allowed me the office of companion on his nightly patrol of a stretch of barrier-island coast. He had worked for three summers as a "turtle boy," one of a cadre that keep watch for the now-threatened loggerhead. Female loggerheads return to the Georgia sands on summer nights to lay their eggs. Turtle boys tag them and keep records of their comings and goings. When there is a lay, the eggs are removed to a hatchery—a hidden plot of dune protected by chicken-wire fence—to keep them safe from poachers: ghost crabs, raccoons, possums, people. Six weeks later, hatchlings scramble out of the sand, all action, and are released. About an inch across, they come equipped with a nearly complete program on survival: the direction of the sea, how to get there, how to swim, what to eat.

Turtle boys do not carry hatchlings to the water; that first journey down the beach may be too important. One theory holds that baby turtles receive a chemical imprint from the sand on the trip from hatchery to ocean. The imprint then determines the base to which the females will return in maturity, a quarter century later, to begin their own egg-laying cycles. Hatchlings grow many, many times larger—the few who survive—but their tiny brains acquire little more information than has been stored by the end of their first few minutes. The tape for their long lives is all there, wound on a reel, needing only time to run through.

Tourists sometimes make the early night run along the beach with turtle boys. My son said that he no longer tried to disabuse visitors of their tendency to endow turtles with human thought and feelings. When a shrimp boat lies across a turtle's course through the water, the turtle will ram the boat. If a female loggerhead blunders into a boulder on her way up the sand, she will not lay her eggs. She will reverse direction and head back out to sea even though a few inches to either side lies a clear path to the dunes. Alternatives and diversionary action are not options for a loggerhead. Its ganglia give it no choices. "All the thoughts of a turtle are turtle," said Ralph Waldo Emerson.

Invariably, tourists remark upon turtles' single-mindedness and stubbornness. They ask what turtles are thinking about when they hit stone and turn back toward water. And then there are the tears. Turtles have no blinking mechanism. Their awkwardness on land causes them to throw sand in their eyes. Great tears wash out and stream down their faces. An explanation from my son draws the response: "Yes, but why are they so sad?" There is frustration on both sides of that conversation, just as there is between teacher and student, between one generation and another, between cultures, between, perhaps, any two people.

II

Like other tourists, I had taken instruction from my son in turtle mechanisms of response to sand in the eye. But seeing the event, I could not resist anthropomorphisms of my own. I saw turtle and thought Aeneas, ashore at Carthage, weeping, *lacrimae rerum*, tears for things.

Turtles register one way for me, another for other tourists, yet another for my son. What is to be made of this multiplicity? What are the possibilities for communication across universes?

I had been set up for pondering such questions. On the long drive down to the coast through the oppressive heat and humidity, I had sought distraction from my own wilting by watching visual distinctions dissolve in the stagnant air column's gray wash of haze. Distant forms that lay evaporating across the horizon could equally well be made out as ridges or ocean swells or cloud banks or illusions.

After arriving that night, I had been taken on several dry runs, my son at the wheel of a derelict pickup redeemed from the scrap yard for beach service, sure to be its last tour. Between runs there had been time to lie on the hood, its warmth unexpectedly comfortable in the cool breeze. The fading of distinctions with nightfall was more complete than it had been during the day. In the darkness, boundary lines between land and sea, sea and sky were to be remembered, not seen.

When you and your son are supine on the hood of a battered old pickup, sober, smoking fine cigars relished mostly as a defense against mosquitoes should the wind die, the backs of your heads resting on the windshield, gazing east and beyond, at 2:00 A.M., on the Georgia coast, what you see is universe, and what you think about are many things, including this:

The processes that produced the light we see from the stars took place hundreds, thousands of years ago. Distance and the speed of light are boundaries of experience. But of what kind and of whose making? Are space and time inventions, as some say, that explain and enable much but that constitute self-devised limits? In Shakespeare's day, it was common practice to make music together; it was a way of placing oneself in harmony both with others and with the music of the spheres, a celebration of simultaneity that we now let the speed of light and other limits deny to us. Why do we choose to live without the music of relatedness?

These were the kinds of thoughts I had been entertaining when, around 3:00 A.M., I saw a turtle for the first time. Loggerheads usually weigh two to three hundred pounds. With the tough, powerful flippers that extend from the huge carapace, they oar themselves heavily, inefficiently up the beach, pausing every few yards from the strain. When they reach the dunes, they scoop out neat chambers to receive their deposit of eggs. The laying done and eggs covered with sand by the slow, strained thrashing of body and flippers, the mothers return, heaving and ponderous, to the sea where they have come to be gracefully at home, gliding birdlike through the water.

As many mysteries as barnacles cling to those creatures. When that first one—and others seen since—materialized from the water, a large, solid, organic thing emerging into definition from the dark ebb and flow of the tide, it conjured another time, another place. In India, it is said, a traveler asked a wise man what supported the earth. The wise man said that the earth rode on the back of an elephant, and that the elephant stood on the shell of a great turtle. The traveler then asked what the turtle stood upon. "Ah," was the reply, "after that it is turtles all the way down." I believed. Here was one come up to tell us of it. She had made her way across many boundaries, including those between the animate and inanimate, the waterborne and the landbound, then and now.

Perhaps there is something to the suggestion that the delight infants take in playing peek-a-boo behind a crib is the uninterpreted participation in the appearing of the face,[1] a participation in creating. I wonder whether Stonehenge might be understood in the same way, that is, as the scene for invoking, creating acts of participation in the appearance of the sun. Be that as it may, astonishment at the emergence of the loggerhead into my field of vision and experience left me with a keen sense of having participated in her appearance. The turtle convinced me that what she is, she is, but that what she is also depends on me. After that it was turtles all the way up. Since that encounter, I have come to understand that the nonexceptional, too, especially the nonexceptional, is significantly of our making.

III

I am not a scientist or a philosopher, but I do know that there is a growing literature among both scientists and philosophers which explores the realization that the external world keeps reflecting back what we bring to it. What is out there is not a thing apart. Nature may not be merely a mirror of the mind, but neither is the mind merely a mirror of nature.

There is reciprocity. Even turtle research can affect its subject. For example: It is not known for certain where hatchlings go after they first disperse in the water. A scientist hoped to find out. He attached transmitters to some freshly hatched turtles so they could be tracked. The transmitters proved too heavy for little turtles for whom the burden of survival was enough. The transmitters were then set into small styrofoam flotation devices. When the hatchlings broke for sea, select numbers were fitted out with gear. On came a couple of tracking canoes. They did not have far to go. In violation of every expectation, the hatchlings shrank from the open sea and holed up in the marshes. Later, after publication of the findings, it was learned that the buoyant styrofoam had prevented the hatchlings from making headway against the tide and the onshore breeze. The devices of research had caused turtles to be blown aground. What is discovered has much to do with the preparation for discovery. Werner Heisenberg learned that about physics years ago.

One other turtle research example. It has been suggested that the warmer the sand around the turtle eggs, the higher the proportion of female hatchlings. Hatcheries are located in the upland coastal dunes where the temperature of the sand is warmer than it is in the wetter, more vulnerable sand closer to the water. So turtle boys, husbanding the species, may be creating an excess of females.

The reciprocity between observer and observed has more sophisticated, intriguing dimensions. Astronomers talk of "black holes" in the space they survey and of a universe created in a "big bang." These are metaphors. They are not merely rhetorical devices. They are not simply descriptive. They are conceptual, and they are creative of the reality they embody. I shall take up later the subject of conceptual metaphors. I introduce it now because scientists' use of such metaphors reveals their craft as nonobjective—or to state the matter affirmatively, reveals their craft as creative, i.e., creative in relation to the object studied. Physicists exploring subatomic universes talk of "quarks" and "strange particles." They say that the presently irreducible minimum is not the whirring little balls the old texts used to diagram. Instead there are patterns and relationships. They are recorded as traces of processes on photographic plates. And there are particles that yield energy answers to energy questions about their nature, and matter answers to matter questions. Reality is not necessarily a quantifiable mechanism. What is there is related to the observer, the observer's questions, and the observer's metaphors. What is there—black holes and quarks no less than hatchlings lodged in the marsh grass—is not untouched by the human hand or the human mind.

The Wilderness Act of 1964 says that a "wilderness in contrast with those areas where man and his own works dominate the landscape, is hereby recognized as an area where the earth and its community of life are untrammeled by man, where man himself is a visitor who does not remain." A wilderness is further defined to be an area that "generally appears to have been affected primarily by the forces of nature, with the imprint of man's work substantially unnoticeable."[2] (I am told that a student once defined a virgin forest as one "where the hand of man has never set foot.") A wilderness is thought to constitute a natural area in contrast to an area where the hand of man has left its imprint. But wilderness is a human product, an artificial construct. Roderick Nash has studied the history of the changing concept of wilderness in the American mind. He found that our conceptual relationship to wilderness has varied considerably. Wilderness has been for us everything from a fearful challenge to be conquered to a place of history, wonder, and repose to be preserved. In every case the fact is that wilderness is our idea. With the domestication of animals and plants, a distinction was drawn between that which was under and that which was not under human control. Nash notes: "Civilization created wilderness."[3] In some cultures there is no word and no concept of—no reality to—wilderness. Correspondingly in such cultures there is no bias against and no fear of wilderness. According to Standing Bear, for his people "there was no wilderness; since nature was not dangerous but hospitable; not forbidding but friendly."[4] Our reality "wilderness"—even this reality "with the imprint of man's work substantially unnoticeable"—is a work of urbanized humans. We are active participants in the actuality of "wilderness" just as we are participants in the actualities of outer and subatomic spaces.

Hilary Putnam gives us this metaphor: "the mind and the world jointly make up the mind and the world."[5] His metaphor overemphasizes rationality. Since the body and the spirit figure along with the mind, we might want to add a supplementary metaphor: the heart and the world jointly make up the heart and the world. Notwithstanding its incompleteness Putnam's is a fine, explanatory metaphor that will, for now, nicely serve the point I wish to make. "The mind and the world jointly make up the mind and the world."

IV

The received tradition holds that we are not participants in the creation of reality. It holds that there is an object universe and an objective truth. One of the advantages of this view is believed to be that it supplies a foundation—a grounding, a firm and orienting standpoint. It is thought to provide, that is to say, not only sea turtles and sea turtle truths but also a form of great basic turtle supporting the universe.

The promise of a foundation is fundamentally appealing. Appealing too is the work placed before us by this tradition. It teaches that our knowledge of reality is incomplete. It calls upon us to roll back our ignorance. If the objects of our pursuit, the things-in-themselves, come to us only as representations in the mirror of the mind—like reflections of stars in Mount Palomar's great glass—then we can always follow "the strategy common to Descartes and Kant—getting more accurate representations by inspecting, repairing, and polishing the mirror, so to speak. . . ."[6] In addition, there is powerful appeal here to our immediate need to negotiate our way through one day to the next in reliance upon perception.

A full account of that tradition and of the contemporary thinking that has called it into question would be out of place here. My own conclusion is that it does not provide the promised unshakable foundation and that its insistence that it does so prevents discernment both of its own relativity and of other, potentially fruitful, alternatives. I also think—and to me this is critical—that its dualism leads to a destructive severing of responsibility. Let me briefly explain what I mean.

When observers are regarded as detached—passive, neutral messengers of the reality they report upon—then much remains hidden. We do not see the influence of the observer upon the observed. We do not see the control of the agenda of what will be considered valid questions and legitimate answers. Even what counts as truth has suppressive side effects. Because the measure of truth is thought to be the correspondence of thought and words to an objective, external reality, the avoidance of error assumes constitutive importance. Error is wrong. It is an offensive mar upon accuracy, an essential fault in correspondence. Teaching and learning become organized around the elimination of mistake. Textbooks on earth science, like the one imposed upon my high school daughter, are consumed with having the student reproduce exactly the right answer to the publishing company's questions about its own text. Young people are presumed to be unready for earth until they demonstrate strict trustworthiness by their mastery of an editorial marketing committee's formulae for unlocking the secrets of nature. It is no accident that the class proceeds under a regime in which deportment is emphasized. Behavior figures in the grade, perhaps equally with memorization. The search for faultless rendition of an eternal reality has its political side. Conformity may be the political concomitant of correspondence theory. Social deviation may become, like intellectual error, wrong. Education aimed at eliminating intellectual error may tend to eliminate also nonconformity in life-style and commitment.

The search for truth may then act as a license. The speaker of truth may disregard or assign secondary importance to consequences. If the vocation of the detached reporter is to describe truth, then duty is exhausted in accuracy. Once error is eliminated, nothing remains to be done, and responsibility for effects is removed from the person. The burden is shifted externally: to the thing, or the system, or the nature of things, or market demand, or sinister outside forces, or foreign agitators. For example, if research leads relentlessly to nuclear fission, to more destructive bombs, to more sophisticated missiles, then responsibility for these things can be avoided if one believes that truth and reality demand them. The scientist, the engineer, and the launcher may become obedient rather than answerable. And then language may become impersonal so that euphemism and the passive voice take over explanation.[7] For example: The Department of Defense (euphemism) is armed (passive) with nuclear devices (euphemism) that have been made necessary (passive) by the Soviet threat (euphemism).

In the process we lose much, including the human control of our actions and history, a willingness to take risks, the recognition of promising alternatives, and the sense of wonder and delight. We also lose the affirmative possibilities of mistake. Mistakes may be opportunities. Students of computers and artificial intelligence have learned that mistakes are fruitfully revealing of the way minds and computers work. Others recognize that deviants from the norms of society and of mental health are sources of insight and inspiration. Some appreciate how sensory failure may be received with finesse as an enhancement rather than a debasement of communication. The worth of such errors is illustrated by an episode involving the author Henry Green. Green was deaf and "greatly valued the obliquities this disability conferred upon conversation."[8] He reported that, being deaf, he heard things that had not been said: "This enlivens my replies until, through mishearing, a new level of communication is reached." An inadvertent example of what he meant was furnished in the course of a published interview when Green had suddenly remarked:

> "Suttee . . . is the suicide—now forbidden—of a Hindu wife on her husband's flaming bier." He [went] on to say that he [did] not wish his own wife to do this when his time [came]; "and with great respect, as I know her, she won't." What the interviewer had said to provoke this excursion was that some people regarded Green's novels as too subtle. He explained this. "Oh, subtle," [said] Green. "How dull."

We would not want to lose suttee divertissements through stale antipathy to error.

In sum, the notions of objective reality and a correspondence theory of truth do not provide a determinative foundation, they conceal alternatives, and they are not sympathetic to mistake and adornment. The greatest loss is a loss of responsibility for consequences.

V

I do not have full-blown alternatives to beliefs in an objective reality and a correspondence theory of truth. I do know that abandoning them does not reduce us to chaos and does offer the promise that each of us may be able responsibly to participate in the creation of realities.

I have noted how my son made one thing of turtles while I and the rest of the tourists made others. Our various turtles were not of equal weight. Mine and my fellow tourists' were the less weighty. They were like the opinions of those people who are unfamiliar with computers and so are prepared to attribute understanding to them: "they can explain the computer's intellectual feats only by bringing to bear the single analogy available to them, that is, their model of their own capacity to think. No wonder, then, that they overshoot the mark."[9]

Such views may have worth in several respects and are certainly not to be despised. I can imagine that overshooting turtles may be good. If enough people think of loggerheads lying on the beach brokenheartedly sobbing—Rachael weeping for her children—then they will be more aware of turtles, feel more sympathy for them, and help reduce the likelihood of our sending the species to extinction.

Nevertheless, my son's understanding of turtles is the better one. He has more and richer experience with them. And, of primary importance in my view, he has been more responsible for them.

Knowledge is one of the factors giving greater weight to my son's understanding of turtles. Knowledge is not necessarily to be equated with accuracy and with quantity of fact. Knowledge may also be a function of relationship, discipline, and experience. We may think of knowledge after a fashion that made sense also to the authors of the Bible. They put down "Adam knew Eve" as a satisfactory, natural way of writing that Adam had sexual intercourse with Eve. Knowing may be relational and fecund. Annie Dillard uses the word *knowledge* this way, in association with love. "The lover can see," she writes, "and the knowledgeable."[10] She then gives this example of someone in the know: "The herpetologist asks the native, 'Are there snakes in that ravine?' 'Nosir.' And the herpetologist comes home with, yessir, three bags full."[11] Knowledge is not so much reflective as generative, filling up snake bags where snakes had not been seen to exist. Can we say that the more we are party to, the more we know? As audience, do we know more as we are more participant-producer in the show?

Knowledge does give weight to our realities. My son's turtle is the weightier because my son is the more knowledgeable. This is so not because his knowledge has brought him into greater correspondence with reality. Nor is it so because a veil of ignorance that blocks a view of reality has been lifted higher in his case. It is so because his knowledge produces livelier, richer realities for which he is the more responsible.

Responsibility is a kindred, more important weighting factor. I do not know all that drew my son to the coast and the loggerheads. It couldn't have been the meager pay and certainly wasn't the working conditions—sundown to sunup seven days a week. Nor could it have been the gratitude of the turtles. I hazard this guess: Those are his

beaches and his turtles. They are "his" in a sense that makes possession and acquisition irrelevant. After a turtle boy wrestles a loggerhead expertly, reading data off old tags and applying fresh ones when
needed, or after he extracts a stranded turtle from a potential grave
that she has accidentally dug for herself, or after he has released
hatchlings—after he has performed these operations and launched
his charges out to sea, there is an air of congratulation, of bringing
forth, of love. It arises not from retaining turtles, not from reducing
them to property, not from bringing them to a stop within a domain,
but from letting go, from sending the turtles on their way, from re-
turning them to the sea, from sharing them with the world of the
ocean and the worlds of the tourists, from keeping the cycle going.
Turtle boys make turtles theirs by these acts, which I describe as acts
of responsibility.

There are related phenomena in my experience of the Georgia
coast.

The scientist Eugene Odum made the salt marshes his through
years of research and imagination, and he transvalued them for us.
Formerly the marshes were pestilential swamps to be drained of their
bilious tidewaters. Odum made them out to be fascinating, complex
ecosystems. By suggesting a comparative measurement of carbon
production, he started us thinking of salt marshes, left alone, as more
productive, acre for acre, than cropped Iowa farmland. He also suggested that marshes were great launderers of pollutants, and we began to comprehend them first as natural resources and then as goods
and services of nature. So the marshes have not been destroyed, and
we have been enriched.

My wife is a painter. She made barrier islands hers executing a
series of paintings of the coast and marsh for the national Sea Grant
program. Her visual absorption in the subject produced studies of
the interplay for horizontal form, light, and color. They are land and
sea scapes, but their proof does not lie in their correspondence to an
external, natural referent. Their success lies in the fact that they work
aesthetically. Within their own terms of reference (paint brushed on
canvas), they are disciplined and painterly. They exhibit clarity of
personal vision. They share the islands with us and entice viewers to
create and compare their own coastal prospects. The marshes and
barriers are passed on, and perception of them is augmented and
diversified.

Ebo's Landing on Sea Island, Georgia, is another example. The Sea
Island Singers, Frankie and Doug Quimby, tell the story and sing the
old song about the Ibos who were brought across the Atlantic in

slave-traders' boats. When they arrived in the New World, they refused the life that lay before them. They would not enter slavery.
Ebo's Landing is said to mark the spot where they turned toward
home in Africa and walked into the sea until they drowned. That
place has belonged to them ever since, and the Sea Island Singers
have inherited it through a kind of narrative chain of title, although
legal title is held by others. Frankie and Doug Quimby refresh their
claim by passing it on to others, allowing its message to bring to mind
the courage of some and the crime of others.

My son, Eugene Odum, my wife, and the Sea Island Singers make
a turtle or a salt marsh or a barrier island or Ebo's Landing theirs by
acts that are not a reducing to ownership. In each case the terms are
different, but there are typological resemblances among them all. The
chief of them is the circulation of the subject matter. It is the characteristic of a gift economy.[12]

When nature is appropriated in the production of commodities, it
is reduced to ownership. An object is brought to a stop. It is consumed. The market exchange leaves no trace of personal tie.

Gifts, on the other hand, both increase and establish human relationships. A gift is given rather than consumed. It moves and grows
as it does so. Ideally, it circulates among a number of people so that
it leaves not one but a whole network of bonds of gratitude and obligation.[13]

In the coastal examples I have given, the transaction is one of a gift
cycle. The turtles, the marshes, the islands, Ebo's Landing are passed
on. Instead of being consumed they are enriched, as are the giver
and the recipient. In a gift economy, Lewis Hyde observes, "satisfaction derives not merely from being filled but from being filled with a
current that will not cease. With the gift, as in love, our satisfaction
sets us at ease because we know that somehow its use at once assures
its plenty."[14]

This is specifically and physically true in the case of my son who
was surely not engaged in producing and capturing turtles for a market. It was exactly to keep the turtles going that he was there and that
gave him the satisfaction that I suspect kept him at his labor, ensuring
that the females returned to sea after laying, that their eggs were not
made commodities and consumed, that the turtle population will be
enlarged. The more turtles he could pass on, the more fulfilling for
him. This was not capitalistic pride in productivity and piece goods.
Nor was it in Marx's sense "appropriation of nature."[15] Neither nature nor people were exploited.

Eugene Odum's case is similar. His marsh is not a commodity. He does not develop it for consumers. His use of it as a laboratory is nonconsuming and produces, instead of marketable goods, understanding and appreciation of the marsh as an ecosystem. The reality of our marsh is enlarged. There is a dilemma here that I note without attempting to resolve. When Professor Odum calls our attention to the value of the marsh as carbon producer, shrimp nursery, and launderer, he invites us to think of it as a commodity—the commodity marshland as more valuable than the commodity Iowa farmland. To subject the natural world to cost-benefit analysis does provide a mechanism for protecting it but at the same time renders it vulnerable to market analysis and hence to marketing.

There is a similar dilemma for my wife: "the idea of art as gift and the problem of the market."[16] Inspiration is an inner gift that requires outer acceptance and circulation as a gift for its nourishment. Nevertheless paintings circulate in a market and become commodities. This can be said: My wife's inner gift yielded outer gifts in the form of evocative images that share without consuming the beaches. The islands contained in those paintings circulate as suggestive gifts rather than as commodities.

In the instance of the Sea Island Singers, the story of Ebo's Landing protests the marketing of slaves, the making of people into commodities. The sharing of the story and the place, freely passing them on, is itself a gift in judgmental contrast to the slave trade described. Histories like that save their subjects from oblivion and keep them in the circulation of memory.

In each of these cases, the gift acts are acts of what I mean by responsibility. Perhaps our understanding of responsibility has been subtly corrupted by assimilation to the practice of ownership. The word *responsibility* may have for us some connotation of unilateral control over a static object, usually the bearing of a burden: "I am responsible for my sick uncle"; "I am responsible for this automobile." This unilateral control of a burden under my jurisdiction may carry with it the threat of a penalty upon default because I am under the unilateral control of a party with jurisdiction over me, for whom I am burden. And so on up the line of hierarchy until we get to the top, the owner of all.

Etymologically and as I now use the word, responsibility has the connotation of reciprocity, of mutuality of response. To be responsible is to be in a certain kind of relationship, a mutually beneficial relationship like that typical of a gift cycle. In the coastal examples I have given, the person is held in a relationship that includes both the natural world and its human inhabitants. There is mutuality of response involving both nature and other persons. There is no exploitation of humans or of nature and no appropriation of nature treated as inferior order.

What I have been talking about comes down to this: The new physics recognizes that scientists do not merely unlock the secrets of nature. They are creative and responsible. This reinsertion of the human is a general phenomenon and is not confined to science. Putnam's metaphor embraces us all: the mind and the world jointly make up the mind and the world. For us to live in a world in which even the boundaries are of our making is not so bad. If we had a foundation or objective boundaries, they might even get oppressively in our way. "When we discover that we have in this world no earth or rock to stand or walk upon but only shifting sea and sky and wind," writes James Boyd White, "the mature response is not to lament the loss of fixity but to learn to sail."[17] Because of our creative role, we have limitless possibilities for creating gifts and networks of gift giving. We are oriented in our sailing by dynamic relationships rather than by static boundary lines.[18]

On that night at the coast I have told you about, when the boundaries had dissolved in darkness and astonishment, I was not lost. I was happily located by both son and turtle. I was in a nexus of responsibility, where the boundaries for universes of meaning tended to break down in the process of negotiating between them.[19]

I will elaborate further my understanding of responsibility in the last chapter of this book. Let it suffice for now to align it with the circulation, increase, personal connection, and response to others that are found in gift economies. Taking responsibility is not at all like taking possession.

VI

Law is not a turtle. It does not exist as a turtle may be said to exist. Some people do think the law exists, like a turtle. For some it may even have a kind of superexistence in the form of the law of nature or the law of God to which God himself is subject. For others law exists although it is not natural law or divine law. Chief Justice John Marshall said we are a "government of laws and not of men."[20] The law for him stands over and over against us even though we make it and see it in the making. More recently there has been a tendency to attribute suprahuman qualities to the law but to do so by speaking of it as a legal system, or as rules or principles.

Christopher Columbus Langdell discovered the American casebook/case-method approach to the teaching of law. He believed that law was a science all of whose materials could be found in books. Like scientists, some lawyers and judges believe themselves to be detached, neutral observers doing what God or nature or necessity demands. However, if law is a science, then it is a science like the new physics, i.e., a creative enterprise. Far more than turtles and black holes, law is our creation. There is no external, objective law or legal system for which we are the mere messengers and instruments.

If I thought law exists in the same way a turtle exists, I would nevertheless argue in behalf of taking responsibility for it. Like turtles, law would still be, in significant part, our creation. There is no disputing our responsibility for it.

The law is ours and we must reckon with its consequences. Most of us, most of the time, find law protective and satisfying. It may on occasion uncomfortably constrain or penalize us, and we may know instances in which it has inflicted wrongs upon individuals near at hand. But we are indulgent of these apparent exceptions to what we think is the basic justice achieved in the American legal system. We believe it has a generous core of advantages. We are especially loath to abandon it for the alternatives presently on display elsewhere in the world.

However, if our legal system inflicts unjust and uncalled-for suffering upon the innocent, then we cannot claim that we are uninvolved or that we are powerless to alter cases. Scientists cannot claim to be unlocking the secrets of nature. They cannot disclaim answerability for consequences. Neither can lawyers. We are answerable for the consequences of the legal system.

A decade ago, William Stringfellow asked whether the law is systemically victimizing. The American legal system had seemed viable to him, "a white, middle class, Harvard-educated lawyer."[21] Nevertheless he wondered how it must appear to blacks and others who are subject to abuse under the guise of legality. He questioned: If American law seemed viable to him but was not so for others, "then how, as the dual commandment would ask, in the name of humanity, can it be affirmed as viable for me or for any human being."[22] Are not blacks, who suffer the "aggressions of the legal system against human life," at once both immediate victims and representatives of us all?[23] Is the generically racist legal system not as threatening to whites as to blacks? And is blindness to this danger not itself a victimization? Law does make victims.

This book is one of the ways in which I attempt to take responsibility for law and its consequences and therefore also for its cure. Because much else—including victimization—may flow from our fundamental conception of law, my particular concern here is to take responsibility for the way we think about law and to help change that thinking. Karl Barth observed that "transformation of thought is the key to the problem of ethics, for it is the place where the turning about takes place by which [we] are directed to new behavior."[24]

I hope to participate in the transformation of thought by giving currency to conceptual thinking about law in the terms of metaphor. Conceptual metaphors for law can circulate, diversify, increase, stimulate the creating of other metaphors, and challenge the hegemony of monolithic conceptual thinking. If we can get the hang of it, law itself can be made a helping part of the cycle—keeping a gift moving, keeping a conversation going, establishing connections, breaking through walls.

VII

I am going to be working with metaphor. There are hazards in an undertaking of this sort. Of many warnings that I might post here at the start, I choose two.

The first is a book review written by Thomas Reed Powell in 1925 under the title "Constitutional Metaphors."[25] The book which earned his justly devastating review had been written by one James Beck. The book was entitled *The Constitution of the United States.* I quote portions of Powell's review at length. I do so because they reward the reading and because they give a pointed, if implied, warning. Here is some of what Powell wrote:

> I never knew what the Constitution really is until I read Mr. Beck's book. He says that "it is something more than a written formula of government—it is a great spirit. It is a high and noble assertion, and, indeed, vindication, of the morality of government." It is splendid to have a Constitution like that and to know, as Mr. Beck tells us, that "to the succeeding ages, the Constitution will be a flaming beacon." This is not all that it is, for Mr. Beck says also: "I have elsewhere likened the Constitu-

tion to a Gothic cathedral, like that of Rheims. Its foundations seem secure, even though some of its buttresses may be weakened and its statuary mutilated . . ."

It helps us to know what the Constitution is if we know what it is not. It is a beacon and a Gothic cathedral, but it is not a rock and it is not a beach. Instead of these things, it is a floating dock. Mr. Beck puts it very beautifully when he says:

"The Constitution is neither, on the one hand, a Gibraltar rock, which wholly resists the ceaseless washing of time and circumstance, nor is it, on the other hand, a sandy beach, which is slowly destroyed by the erosion of the waves. It is rather to be likened to a floating dock, which, while firmly attached to its moorings, and not therefore at the caprice of the waves, yet rises and falls with the tide of time and circumstance."

You might think that a Constitution which is all these wonderful things would be sure to last forever without any help from anything else. But this is not so. Mr. Beck says that it would not have lasted so long as it has if it had not been for the Supreme Court which he says is "the balance wheel of the Constitution." He has a whole chapter which he calls The Balance Wheel and this chapter ends up by saying:

"But always the Supreme Court stands as a great lighthouse, and even when the waves beat upon it with terrific violence (as in the Civil War, when it was shaken to its very foundation), yet after they have spent their fury, the great lamp of the Constitution—as that of another Pharos—illumines the troubled face of the waters with the benignant rays of those immutable principles of liberty and justice, which alone can make a nation free as well as strong."

It makes you see how marvelous the Supreme Court really is when it can be a balance wheel at the beginning of a chapter and a lighthouse at the end.

Even if you are not interested in the Constitution for its own sake, you will like to read what Mr. Beck says about it because he is such a lovely writer. He is the kind of writer who likes to write just for the sake of writing. He shows how he loves his work. He is not one of those writers who have to stop in their writing while they are making up their minds what to say. You can read him right along because he is so simple in his thoughts. He does not get you all mixed up the way so many writers do, but he brings up in your mind beautiful pictures of the Constitution as a temple and a beacon and a floating dock and he lets you see the Supreme Court shining and balancing in a very wonderful way. I have read a great many books about the Constitution, but there is no other book that has given me just the same kind of pleasure that this one has.[26]

We are well warned by Powell that metaphors require integrity and the discipline of good writing. Not every metaphor will do. I will have to stop in my writing to make up my mind what I want to say, and you will have to stop in your reading to decide what to make of it. I shall try not to give you a Brunswick stew of images.

The second and more serious warning is that of W. H. Auden's poem "Law Like Love."[27] In the opening stanzas of the poem, various parties describe law in the terms of various metaphors unrecognized as metaphors by the speakers. For gardeners, law "is the sun"; to grandfathers, it "is the wisdom of the old"; to the priest, law "is the words in my priestly book"; while others "say, Law is our State"; etc. In each instance the occupation or preoccupation of the speaker is projected as the definitive statement of law. Finally, the poet, "thinking it absurd / To identify Law with some other word," confines himself "To stating timidly / A timid similarity": law is "Like love."

The poem warns us about solipsism. We may not claim as always, everywhere authoritative for everyone a metaphor formed by our own experiences. And then we may not broadcast a metaphor as though it were a statement of natural, necessary fact. Our guesses and particular position are to be conscious. And self-effacing. Offered experimentally with delight like analogies to love.

VIII

John Calvin and Karl Barth believed that the starting point for wisdom is theological. They also believed that, because God came first in their thinking and being, He ought to come first stylistically in their writing as well.

In wrestling with jurisprudence, responsibility, metaphorical thinking, the created order, etc., I have been reminded once again of the truth of Calvin's observation that we can have no wisdom, no knowledge of ourselves "without having first contemplated the divine character."[28]

Even so, I depart from the Calvinistic order stylistically. I raise the theological point now at the end of this first chapter and wait until the last chapter of the book to elaborate it. There are reasons for my

Introduction

doing so. One of them is what Paul Ricoeur said: the "beginning is not what one finds first: the point of departure must be reached, it must be won."[29]

I have wanted to acknowledge my priorities with this brief word and also to distinguish my own beliefs and methods from those of assorted religious enthusiasts who sock it to you in the end believing themselves to be following the example as well as the will of God.

2   CONCEPTUAL METAPHORS

FOR LAW

In early Iceland, the Althing assembled on the summer plain at the Thingvellir for a judicial-legislative-social celebration and the annual recitation of one-third of the Law Code. A Law Speaker mounted a rise in front of the Law Rock, which may have acted as a sounding board, to address the crowd below. The Law Rock is one segment of a long, dark face of basalt where the plain is divided by a geologic fault, and one level drops sharply to another. From the lower level and below the Law Rock, the wall of stone appears to be an enormous bulkhead, an effect heightened by the nearby waterfall where the Oxar River spills over from above.

I do not know whether the Icelanders at the Althing in session before the Law Rock had the feeling that they were gathered under the shadow of a dam, but the clear sense of *Njal's Saga* and its portrayal of the Althings is that to breach the law is to let loose a flood of social chaos. "With laws shall our land be built up," said Njal, "but with lawlessness laid waste."[1]

Our own version of law has little conceptual distance from that of Njal. For us also law, or *the* law, is an adamantine structure protecting a space for order and life. Without it we would be engulfed in a sea of increasing entropy, overwhelmed by a Hobbesian state of nature and the war of all against all—or so we think. I believe that other notions of law are possible and necessary. The received one has turned to stone.

I

In their provocative study *Metaphors We Live By,* George Lakoff and Mark Johnson successfully argue that the ordinary conceptual system which governs our daily thought and action, although we are frequently unaware of it, is metaphorical in nature.[2] Metaphor (imaginatively identifying one object with another) is stock in trade for sportcasters as well as poets. Howard Cosell was a factory of metaphors on "Monday Night Football." A few minutes of listening to his broadcast gave you a week's worth of metaphors: "He threw that ball on a rope" (a hard, straight pass); "He was really hammered" (tackled hard); "He put a lot of air under it" (a lofty punt); "He got a lot of hang time on that one" (another punt). (That last one has possibilities for life: "O Lord, give me a little more hang time.")

Lakoff and Johnson hold that metaphor is not merely a matter of language or description, the tools of sportscasters and poets, but a kind of fundamental sense whereby we understand the world, perceiving one experience in terms of another. As they say, we live by metaphor (e.g., time is money, life is short, the days ahead, inflation).

Inasmuch as social and physical reality is understood in metaphorical terms, metaphor is instrumental in shaping reality. The reality of Monday night football, whatever it may be, was dependent upon Howard Cosell's metaphors. However, in helping to determine reality, metaphor also restricts or eliminates or conceals.[3] For this reason an adequate conceptual system requires alternate, even conflicting, metaphors for a single subject, and our daily living requires shifts of metaphors for fullness of thought and action.

Preemptive metaphors may be imposed upon us by those in power or may simply have ascended through an undetected evolutionary cultural process. When such colonization of the mind occurs in conjunction with adherence to the belief that truth is objective and absolute, then the ruling metaphors—more dangerous because unrecognized as metaphor—come to define what is considered to be true, and we have what Richard Rorty refers to as the "freezing over of culture."[4] Without access to alternate metaphors, we act and think on the basis of limited comprehension masquerading as the whole truth. In politics, metaphor can thus lead to human degradation. The example given by Lakoff and Johnson is the metaphor "labor is a resource," which fails to distinguish between meaningful and dehumanizing work. If labor is viewed only as a resource, then exploitation is masked by neutral-sounding economic statements (e.g., the costs of labor, like that of all resources, should be held down; cheap labor is good) which hide human misery behind an unexamined metaphor.

I believe that there is a reigning, unrecognized metaphor in jurisprudence. While this metaphor discloses some things, it conceals others. To think and act exclusively in terms of this metaphor presents dangerous risks to authentically human justice. It must be supplemented, or likely replaced, by other metaphors.

Of course metaphor is a traditional device of law just as it is of sportscasting and poetry.[5] Lawyers daily employ metaphors like chain of causation,[6] corporate speech,[7] statutory rape, constructive notice, and quasi contract. Lawyers also create histrionic metaphors when they produce their cases in the courtroom. A trial is a theatrical performance in which each side seeks to persuade the judge or jury by means of a play which passes from fact to metaphor.[8] In addition to using metaphor, law may itself be a metaphor. We sense about legal arguments, even when the battle is over an abstruse point of tax law, that everything is at stake.[9] Chief Justice Marshall discerned in "the power to tax . . . the power to destroy."[10] When we speak the language of law, including tax law, we may well mean everything; we may be making a metaphor of death or of life.

Then, too, there are numerous metaphors for law. Among others, law is an ass (Dickens), a brooding omnipresence (Holmes), a jealous mistress (lawyers who wish for the real thing), and a single-bed blanket on a double bed with three folks and a cold night (Robert Penn Warren's Willy Stark). Such metaphors are obvious and obviously lacking in destructive power.

The controlling conceptual metaphor that rules us largely unremarked—and that is destructive to the degree that it exercises a monopoly in jurisprudence—is: law is the bulwark of freedom.[11] According to this metaphor, "we" are preserved from "them" or "it" by law. Law is a defensive works: the walls of Troy, the Maginot Line, a dike, a dam. The assumption is that law must first be ensured before the establishment of justice can begin. Law is thought to be essential to preservation of the space—temporarily reclaimed from base nature—in which, as luxury allows, we can labor at such improvements as justice.

Above the entrance to the United States Supreme Court there is chiseled the motto: "Equal Justice Under Law." Those who enter the constitutional citadel thereunder seem seldom to remember that, at least since the days of the prophet Amos, others have thought justice has priority over law and that equal law under justice is the more fit order. They seldom remember those alternate possibilities because of the acceptance of a conceptual metaphor that hides them.

Courts, legislatures, and administrative agencies make various contributions to the maintenance and reinforcement of the ascendant metaphor. One way in which they do so is by assuring a continued supply of construction material.[12] Endless extrusions of statutes, judicial opinions, and regulations are collected in volumes about the size and weight of a common variety of concrete block. Lawyers, legislators, and judges instinctively prefer photographic portraits of themselves posed before a wall of shelves packed solid with these books. It is the iconography of stability, a visual appeal against change (après moi, le déluge).

Law schools with their casebooks and case-method courses are contributors. Even the innovative educators among us still refer to the need for basic "building-block" courses in the curriculum, as though legal studies were training in a construction trade. And jurisprudents continue to think of law as composed of rigid rules and principles—an unyielding edifice of noetic brick. They think of law as something that actually exists. Like a turtle.

The subtlest variation of the ruling metaphor is one struck by Archibald MacLeish, a graduate of the Harvard Law School. Upon MacLeish's reincarnation in Cambridge as professor of poetry, his alma mater invited him over to provide an explanation for law students: How could he have lapsed into poetry from the legitimacy which had been settled upon him with the LLB? His response was to propose that the difference between law and poetry was not so pronounced as might appear. The business of both is to make sense of the confusion of human life: "Without a credible structure of law a society is inconceivable. Without a workable poetry no society can conceive a man."[13] MacLeish then quoted a poem he had written for another law-school graduate, Wallace Stevens, and hazarded the suggestion that its metaphor might contain the life of both poet and lawyer. The poem, "Reasons for Music," reads in part:

> The labor of order has no rest:
> To impose on the confused, fortuitous
> Flowing away of the world, Form—
> Still, cool, clean, obdurate,
>
> Lasting forever, or at least
> Lasting: . . .
>
> Why do we labor at the poem?
> Out of the turbulence of the sea,
> Flower by brittle flower, rises
> The coral reef that calms the water.
>
> Generations of the dying
> Fix the sea's dissolving salts
> In stone, still trees, their branches immovable,
> Meaning
>   the movement of the sea.[14]

I have lived with this metaphor of the reef calming the waters, been convinced by it, been enriched by it, and commended it to law students for well over a decade. Now I have come to believe that MacLeish and I were wrong—or at least not completely right. The reef is just another, although richer, version of the bulwark.[15] I am not licensed to practice poetry and so cannot speak for poets. But I am licensed to practice law, and I no longer believe that this metaphor can be said to contain my life as a lawyer, any more than my crypt will contain the life of the body that lies within. A coral reef, after all, is a heap of skeletons, dangerous to the touch.

MacLeish's variant metaphor of law as bulwark discloses the end of law to be the protection of life, but the metaphor conceals too much death. To be sure, within our country law has been a necessary protection for powerless minorities, and there is some truth in Justice Hugo Black's opinion that in our system "courts stand against any winds that blow as havens of refuge for those who might otherwise suffer because they are helpless, weak, outnumbered."[16] In any event, that image has shaped the actions of those courts who so view themselves, as witness *Brown v. Board of Education*.[17]

On the other hand, the controlling metaphor also masks much aggression against the powerless. For example, the achievement of the Bill of Rights—a barrier against governmental encroachment—glossed over trespasses against slaves, Indian nations, and women. The law-as-bulwark metaphor also allows injustice to harden into law which then commands obedience. To cite but two of many obvious examples: maldistribution of wealth is codified in tax laws, and class-economic-racial oppression in exclusionary zoning laws. Such evils are practically invulnerable to reformation. Slavery had to be cured by war. When concrete has set, especially as a dam holding back floodwaters, reinforcement may be a welcome possibility, but extraction of impurities and basic structural alterations are essentially impossible.

Moreover, any breach of law so conceived may evoke desperate response. To "break" the law is to open a breach in society's defensive works, a crack in the dike threatening crime waves in the streets. All crime is then invested with the potential of treason or violation of national security or assault on civilization, and the severest retribution is warranted. So we indulge in the Dantean symmetry of modern punishment: criminals have breached the walls protecting civilized society and so are consigned to uncivilized life behind unbreachable prison walls. This practice in turn satisfies and enlarges our belief in the need for law as a protection and in the horror which would flow from any fissure. Perhaps it also helps to explain why police in this country are a paramilitary force instead of simply an administrative agency. (Yesterday's flatfoot and Mack Sennett character become today's law-enforcement officer and "Strike Force" and SWAT unit. In the instructive synecdoche of the streets, "the law" is the cops, i.e., the chief feature in perception of law becomes its armed enforcement.) But the entire notion of law enforcement is a recent and singular bit of ideology. Within this ideology there is little distinction between armed guards on prison walls, armed police enforcing the law, armed patrols tending the borders, and armed troops protecting the perimeters of national interest.

If the figure of a legal system that fits and fortifies the land has consequences for American thought and action domestically, it is also determinative in our relations with the rest of the world. Beneficially, it allowed us the fruitful understanding of ourselves as protectors of the persecuted.[18] We supposed that within the jurisdiction of the American constitutional system lay protection for refugees. To our credit (and ultimately to our advantage), we took this self-image seriously for many years and sheltered outcasts from abroad. Both image and practice, however, have been strained beyond credibility in the past decade or so by the equivocal receptions accorded Mexicans who crossed the border, deportees from Cuba, and escapees from Vietnam and Haiti.

The same beneficial impulse that prompted us to admit refugees to the protection of our constitutional system also led us to extend abroad defense to those confronted by totalitarian oppression. It is to be remembered that this defense was not construed as successfully concluded after World War II until the military triumph was capped by the installation of an American-exported constitutional legal system among the defeated and by a United Nations whose charter bears the impress of our Constitution. We sent troops; we also sent the law. The latter was the only way to consolidate for the future the advances achieved immediately by arms.

However, under cover of the selfsame image of law enforcer to the world, we have visited economic and military imperialism upon other nations, including the unforgettable recent examples in Southeast Asia and Latin America. Cold War realist mentality is altogether too well served by the dominating metaphor for law. We celebrate Law Day on May 1—the same day they parade arms before their Kremlin. We are protected by noble ramparts o'er which the Stars and Stripes gallantly stream; they are sealed in by an Iron Curtain. We are the Free World; they are the Communists. The fortifications of the

Free World include outer defensive works that must be shorn up lest their downfall precipitate ours like a ripple of falling dominoes. We do well, it is thought, to support friendly regimes, outposts of legality carved out of the jungle brutalities of the real world of international confrontation. Guns, law, stability first. Business and banking next. Bread to follow. Cessation of torture, human rights, justice . . . later.

The conceptual metaphor of law as bulwark of freedom, formative of both our domestic and foreign activity, is an expression of the natural, understandable impulse to save ourselves from danger. However, the impulse is ill served by the metaphor. Uncorrected, the metaphor is productive of the very destruction we seek to avoid.

Law as a protection against chaos hastens the advance of what it is meant to defend against. Prisons, for example, have been correctly described as "breeding places of crime." The more people our criminal law consigns to them under present conditions, the more crime we produce. Similarly, as violent crimes increase, we accelerate resort to arms, larger law-enforcement expenditures, and vigilante groups. It is the same progression as that in Rome, which in A.D. 403 led to the decree authorizing all persons "to exercise with impunity the right of public vengeance against the common enemy."[19] Capitalized by seemingly limitless access to our tax dollars, the military's technology and techniques inevitably demand provocative testing grounds abroad and invite the challenge of a viciously cyclical, destructive arms race. We witness a replication, greatly magnified, of the irony of self-destruction by self-protection.

Law as bulwark of freedom is a metaphor. As such it creates a reality that has to be taken into account. To identify the metaphor with objective truth-in-itself is a mistake. Understanding and action predicated upon the metaphor as though it exclusively were reality are dangerous. What troubles me most about serious commitment to law and order as precedent to justice is the risk, approaching certainty, that it settles for order, with justice deferred. In the absence of pervasive justice, law becomes the systemic, degenerative brute force of the powerful.

II

By the dominant metaphor, law is defensive, adamantine, preterhuman, static, pretentious. It is all limits and divisions and bringing to a halt. Are there not alternate metaphors that can produce more fit legal realities? Something humbler, decalcified,

allowing movement and circulation, connecting rather than disconnecting? A promising area to explore for such metaphors is water and
the hydrologic cycle.[20]

The metaphor of law as bulwark is buttressed by fear of what lies
on the other side of the present order. Hydrologic metaphors could
feed that fear and turn us back to the bulwark. The sea and floodwaters lend themselves all too well to deployment as images of death
and chaos, terror to be kept out at all cost. At the same time, however, there is the image seen in all rivers and oceans—and celebrated
in the opening pages of *Moby Dick*—of "the ungraspable phantom of
life." The organically rich primordial sea was mother of us all, and
she continues to exert upon us the pull of a great matriarch drawing
us home. The waters can be as evocative of life and love as of fear. If
so, we want no dam to keep them out. Also there are the possibilities
of dynamic images to counter the static notion of an ossiferous structure. We need naturally to participate in the hydrologic cycle. What
becomes fearful is its interruption. We try to assure rather than arrest
the circulation. Given a drought, for instance, we seed clouds.

I have been looking for a conceptual metaphor for law that would
capture this dynamic sense. The hydrologic cycle, as I have noted,
could supply images to suit the dominant conception of law as well
as an alternate. There is nothing inherent in the natural world that
determines what we make of its figurative possibilities. This is another way of saying again that there is not an objective truth-in-itself
out there to which our words are to correspond. Then why, or how,
make one thing of nature rather than another? What is to guide our
selection, what determine the mind and the world that the mind and
the world jointly make up? How come I to be rummaging around in
search of possibilities for an alternate metaphor? I raise these questions because they cannot be avoided. I postpone grappling with
them until the last chapter of the book. I put them aside for now and
hope that you will be willing to do so also.

My search for a figure from the hydrologic cycle led me down some
forty iron steps to a cabin deck in North Georgia where a friend of
mine read me a prose poem he had been working on while also working on living close, too close perhaps, to a boisterous filament of the
hydrologic cycle called Fightingtown Creek. The central image of the
poem has possibilities for being plundered from its original context
and worked into a fresh jurisprudential metaphor.

Fightingtown Creek*

for Johnny Thrasher

Five weekends now I've come up here, been told the water's
fixed and five now it's busted, five, or fifteen, minutes after I've
crawled up under the house to turn it on, this time only a quar-
ter-turn, I hear a whang and it's broken loose somewhere else.
I crawl back and turn it off and then spend the weekend, again,
without facilities. I know what's worth writing about. What the
heart—and I know we can't use that word very successfully any
more to mean the loving the self has in it—let's say it anyway,
what the heart remembers, what the mind is sometimes so at-
tentive and attuned to that it carries it off and keeps it in its
pocket, from then on. Anything might be reduced to that handy
size, the Matterhorn, for example, a cameo of Confucius. I don't
deserve to get mad about this water business. I've never
plumbed a house. I call Johnny Thrasher and say this water's
broke loose again. He says *Ain't that a shame. I'll git up ther Monday after work.* He does good work. I've just got some trashy
cheap piping under there, garden hose he calls it, put in by the
previous owner. *I'll put some PVC in ther fer ye, new fixtures in the
kitchen and bathroom. It's all jist rotted to rust and crumblin. Two
hunnert and fifty dollars, and I'll garantee it.* He doesn't want to
mess with what I've got any longer. I might try crawling up
under there to see what I could do, after watching him a few
times, a few hundred times. I might buy a chemical toilet and
bring in drinking water in water bags, not take baths and t'hell
with it. I tell him. Let's tear it out and go with PVC. He's a great
buddy now, drops in on Saturday morning, already glowingly
drunk, 11 a.m., with his wife Ruth, whose grandmother was a
full-blooded Cherokee. *Works perfect, don't hit. Looky here, wash-
erless fossets. I tole you we could git it right.* I am very thankful for
Johnny Thrasher. I have plenty other things I can do here by
myself—other than writing I mean—physical, survival work for
the precarious fleck of consciousness that is this house: Hauling
rock in the wheelbarrow to bolster two concrete block piers that
the stream is beginning to lick underneath when it rises. I can
spend the entire summer hauling rock to make that bank secure. The work here is watching water, containing it some. The
movements and sound: Thrummings exactly like a bass drum,

a low, dragging noise like a heavy glass door sliding open. One night I heard a married couple arguing in the water. Each hour, at least each hour, I return to the deck and look through the intricate presence of Fightingtown Creek, named for the Cherokee chief, Fightingtown. Ruth says, *They's suppose to be gold and Indian things buried along this creek. Maybe you'll find something, if you keep digging up rocks.*

—Coleman Barks

The critical image for my purposes is that of containing the water some: "The work here is watching water, containing it some." "Contain" means enclose, hold back, keep within: The enemy has been contained; we pursue a policy of containment; the bottle contains milk. And in this sense, containing is what law as bulwark does.

But Barks's "watching water, containing it some" has other senses. When I first heard the poem, I thought of the human body, participating in the hydrologic cycle, containing water some. And I thought of myself containing life some. In the poem, containing is not enclosing or keeping out or holding in. And the containers are not closed like casks or caskets or cups but open-ended conductors like tubing, culvert, and PVC. Law may be a container the way PVC and poems are. Appropriated in this fashion, the poem allowed me to begin conceiving law in a way that yields a certain equivalence between plumbers, poets, and lawyers.[21]

A plumber works with pipe that, containing water, delivers it to users in kitchen and bathroom.

A poet works with words and images. The words of the Barks poem contain Fightingtown Creek and deliver it to the reader.

A lawyer works with arguments which contain people's grievances, delivering them for response to courts and legislatures or simply to an ongoing performance in which they may be, perhaps, transcended. A lawyer also draws instruments of exchange, contracts, and wills that contain people's promises and dispositions and deliver them to intended recipients for legal effectuation. Lawyers also make statutes that contain temporary compromises and deliver them to agencies for administration.

Water that breaks loose under the house is unlike water that breaks through a dam. It does not represent an apocalyptic crisis of Western democracy, just a weekend without facilities. A plumber called in for repair thus has the leeway granted by humility. He can reconnect and replace pipe until he gets it right and it works perfect. And he can replumb the whole house again, if need be, or scrap the garden hose if he finds something better. There are always chemical toilets and water bags in reserve.

Poetic license also permits the arranging and rearranging of pieces until they work in a poem as a whole, recreating the world out of its parts until it is gotten right.

If they are like poets and plumbers and unlike soldiers and engineers, lawyers are also free to rearrange and recreate. They can replay cases, revise statutes, recast rules and legal terms until the parts fit together in arguments, codes, and documents that work and get it right, for the present moment.

When a plumber gets the water system right, his achievement is not a terminal event. For one thing, no plumbing job lasts forever. "Works perfect" and "git it right" are not synonymous with "end of the matter." Calls to the plumber will always be with us. Another and more important reason is that completion of the job is occasion for a fellowship of continuing celebration. A good plumber is gifted, and his plumbing can be the initiation of a gift cycle. Connecting water systems establishes human connections. The contract comes with a great buddy as well as a guarantee. There is more than a PVC and cash nexus with Johnny Thrasher, who drops in now of a Saturday.

Poets, too, make human connections. The early lines of the Barks poem speak of what the heart remembers, what the mind carries off and keeps in the pocket. The poetic reduction to palm-size word images—like Lincoln on a penny—is a minting for circulation. The images are only temporarily tucked in the pocket. Their value comes from exchange.[22]

Law may also be humanly, dynamically connective. In Roman times, for example, the *jus gentium* or law of nations was relational. It brought aliens within law and governed commercial intercourse between Roman citizens and members of nations subject to Rome.

If it is a sufficient aim for philosophy to keep a conversation going, as Richard Rorty argued,[23] then it may be a sufficient aim for law to keep conversation, negotiation, argument, dialogue, and conflict going. This facilitation has both a preventive or defensive aspect and a positive, creative aspect.

Defensively, talk may prevent the use of force and may actually provide better protection than force—a cycle of words more satisfying than a cycle of vengeance. I once visited in a Maine summer home built by a person whom experience had taught that the casement windows in such a place could never be completely sealed against rainstorms blowing in from the Atlantic. He had devised a means for both accepting the inevitable and simultaneously protecting the interior from water damage. Fixed to the inside wall under each window, starting from the bottom corners and dropping in a flattened V, were small lead troughs he had fashioned. At the vertex of the V, a hole had been drilled in the wall, and the troughs joined at a small spout emptying to the outside. The apparatus caught and returned the vagrant, invading runnels of rain that blew in. It was a fit defensive works. For protection we may not need law-enforcement officers and uniformed troops. We do need ingenious plumbers and gutterers in overalls—poets, philosophers, lawyers, and gift givers of all sorts who keep the flow going.[24]

Positively and creatively, law in the dynamic sense in which I have begun to think of it augments as well as defends our common life. Our modes of thought have social origins. Truth is not an alien ideal disjoined from perspective and agreement. Truth is relational. It is grounded in and tested by experience in interaction with other people and with the physical as well as the social environment. Across cultures—between people with different bodies of truth— understanding and the extension of horizons[25] come through "negotiation of meaning."[26] Appropriate action, even coping, depends upon the success, expansiveness, and inclusiveness of these interactions and negotiations. Law, by carrying them forward, is a channel of communication.

One of the advantages to understanding law in terms of an image belonging to the dynamics of hydrologic circulation is that it exposes for the old metaphor—law as bulwark—a redeeming if altered context. I have delayed until now noting that the Barks poem deals in stone and concrete as well as pipes and hose. With a summer's worth of rock, the laborer thinks to manage the survival of "the precarious fleck of consciousness" that is his house. But he has not held the water back, does not want to, and cannot. Did he not pay Johnny Thrasher $250 to ensure its coming in? The thrummings of the creek, like an opening glass door, break down the distinction between inside and out. They establish the presence of the creek inside and draw the occupant out. From the house, the poet watches, i.e., becomes absorbed in, the creek. If the deck is preserved, it will be for that distance across which it becomes possible to establish a relation to the water below. The ultimate purpose of the rock in bolstering the concrete-block piers is to unite rather than to separate homeowner and creek. To this end the rocks do not form a dam across the flow of the creek; they are parallel to it. The stone forms, with the natural embankment, a channel, the larger outdoor equivalent to PVC.

The real survival work of those stones, however, has less to do with securing the bank than with the poet's digging them up. The poem contains Fightingtown Creek. And Fightingtown Creek in turn contains us: arguing couples and a Cherokee chief. Digging up rocks along the creek is a release of contents, exhumation of the buried past, and a present adventure in self-discovery. "Maybe you'll find something, if you keep digging up rocks." The excavator, opening graves, opens a way to the past and so to the future.

I am not sure that any form of petrology has a place among lawyers. But if it does, then it will be like the poet's digging up stones and laying them down. Unearthing law rocks—the stone tablets, steles, codes, regulations, rules, principles, reports of opinions, and casebooks—may be fruitful survival work if turning them up leads us to find something: the *corpus juris* or our own buried life. And laying down the law may prove promising if the law laid down is not like rocks for a dam in opposition to life, but like stones on a creek bank along the axis of revolutionary movement. The end is not stasis but circulation.

III

"The work here is watching water, containing it some." This line led me to understand that law need not be a bulwark—containing in the sense of holding back or enclosing. It may "contain some" like the watching poet, or the PVC, gutters, a stream channel, a poem containing a creek, and a creek containing a chief. I began to see how law might be thought of not as a hydrokinetic obstruction but as a medium enhancing the flow, a medium for letting "justice flow like water, and integrity like an unfailing stream."[27] Or, at least, as a medium for responsible human intercourse.

In the next three chapters I shall be telling a story of the law of the sea and the coast, a field of law that allows me to fix the metaphor—of law as medium—to specific possibilities. That story is my way of elaborating and anchoring the metaphor. But there are some other possibilities, preliminary possibilities in addition to the Barks poem, that help a little to concretize "medium."

For example, in the Hebrew cosmology, the firmament held back the devouring waters of the deep. Law as bulwark is sympathetic with such a vault. I am told, however, that the Hebrews incorporated an additional element: holes that allowed life-giving water to pass through. These were openings of just the right size and number in the heavens above (stars) for rain and in the earth beneath for springs. As it turns out, the firmament—a defensive device keeping the monster at bay—was also a medium of domestication and delivery. It regulated and guaranteed the vital flow to the inhabitants of a dry and thirsty land. We could focus our attention upon those apertures in the firmament. Is the medium law like those media? Law as stars and springs? Probably not. Also, any thought of openings (doors, gaps, holes) depends upon the image of bulwark. You have to conceive the wall before you can conceive the openings.

Better is this image, a translation of two lines by the Sufi poet Rumi: "Words let water from an unseen, infinite ocean / Come into this place as energy for the dying and even the dead."[28] The image of words as medium of water/energy/life is rendered more provocative by the translators' explanation that Rumi's work is "the clear, watery medium for a condition of incarnation."[29] What causes me to draw back is the religious content, the mysticism entailed in "incarnation." But imagine the possibilities if words of law could be said to be Rumi-like media.[30]

Perhaps more serviceable is the dominant way in which artists think of "medium": both the liquid (oil, water, acrylic) used as a binder for pigments and the resulting paint. My wife's medium is acrylic. It is her mode of expression. Law may be said to be a medium in the related sense that it is the medium of the human community as community.

Other liquid associations are more unusual but still helpful. The *Oxford English Dictionary*, for instance, cites from one Hamerton in 1873: "The general talk, which is nothing but a neutral medium in which intelligences float."[31] And Lakoff and Johnson recount the following episode:

An Iranian student, shortly after his arrival in Berkeley,

> took a seminar on metaphor from one of us. Among the wondrous things that he found in Berkeley was an expression that he heard over and over and understood as a beautifully sane metaphor. The expression was "the solution of my problems"—which he took to be a large volume of liquid, bubbling and smoking, containing all of your problems, either dissolved or in the form of precipitates, with catalysts constantly dissolving some problems (for the time being) and precipitating out others. . . . [His metaphor] gives us a view of problems as things that never disappear utterly and that cannot be solved once and for all. All of your problems are always present, only they may

be dissolved and in solution, or they may be in solid form. The best you can hope for is to find a catalyst that will make one problem dissolve without making another one precipitate out.[32]

That wondrous liquid is a medium, and such a bubbling, smoking brew might make a wondrous image of law.

Very different but also instructive is the rendering of 1 Corinthians 13:12 in the King James Version of the Bible: "For now we see through a glass, darkly; but then face to face: now I know in part; but then I shall know even as I am known." We see ourselves and each other through the medium of law. We see through law but only darkly. There is the promise that "then" we shall see face to face. At the end of his lectures published as *The Ages of American Law,* Grant Gilmore said that "[t]he better the society, the less law there will be. In Heaven there will be no law, and the lion will lie down with the lamb."[33] I am not so sure. The lion and lamb will lie down all right, but is there no law between them? Is law a function of social pathology? Is it only a response to evil and evil tendencies? Would a saved humankind rise above law? There will surely be no law as bulwark. But what of law as medium? May it not be welcome and animating? The better the society, the more law as medium. In heaven, law will become plentiful and, like the agreeable medium air, utterly transparent.[34] May we not see face to face through law?

I turn to the law of the sea for the real work of testing how and in what more credible, specific terms law as medium may be elaborated. I have chosen the law of the sea and coast for numerous reasons. For one, it provides a comprehensive core sample, from international law at the top layer through federal law to state and local law at the bottom. While my chief concern lies with American law and American conceptual metaphors for law, neither of them can be examined successfully without some consideration of the international developments with which they are closely and affectively associated. The law of the sea gives opportunity for such consideration.

Also, the sea and coast are focal points for those critical conflicts which typify an epoch of exploding needs and shrinking means or shrinking will for meeting the needs of others. It may be that what turns up in the law of the sea and coast will have wider meaning in areas of larger conflict.

Lastly, the law of the sea and coast is fascinating. Like the sea and coast themselves, it is irresistibly seductive. The figurative potential alone has a powerful pull.

Conceptual Metaphors for Law

What I hope to discover in and through this story of the law of the sea and coast is whether talk of law as medium is merely foolish or is utopian and so has a future.

I must append two caveats.

One is that "medium" may be inadequate or faulty. Successful conceptual metaphors are not the product of individual effort. Hard and skillfully as I might try, I could not make one by myself. They are a collegial accomplishment. Sometimes they appear to be collectively achieved unaware, developed well beyond the embryonic stage before their presence is recognized. A new metaphor is due. "Medium" may not be the one. But maybe I can give "medium" a start inviting enough for you and others to help give it the content necessary for passage from abstraction to conceptual metaphor.

The other caveat is that the evidence for law as medium should not be misread or overread. My account of law as medium in the law of the sea and coast will be descriptive. I shall be talking about what is and not about what ought to be or could be. However, hope has much to do with my description. My saying what is really going on in what is happening is like the believer's discerning the body in the sacramental breaking of the bread. The medieval theologian Anselm sought to prove "by reason alone" what he held by faith.[35] He wrote as if readers accepted the truth he wished to convince them was true. He assumed that he shared the ground of theology with the disbelievers whose very disbelief he was addressing. Anselm's assumption led a modern theologian to observe that "divine simplicity and the way of the most incredible deception have always run parallel, separated by the merest hair's breadth."[36] Law as bulwark, or something very like it, is the present, predominate conception of law. I think I can discern law as medium in and through law as it is. In taking delight at the findings, I shall try, like Anselm, to keep at least a hair's breadth away from working an incredible scam. Nevertheless, you are appropriately advised that my reading of the evidence for law as medium is an exercise in hope, not optimism.

3

LAW OF THE SEA

AMONG NATIONS

Most maps have a way of disguising what photographs from space make plain: Earth is dominated by ocean. The land on which we take refuge breaches the water for only two-sevenths of the world's surface. And then it depends upon the seas for its viability: The rain that waters the farms and forests of Georgia is drawn largely from the Gulf of Mexico.

The sea, in turn, is dominated by vastness and mystery: powerful currents stacked on top of one another and flowing in opposite directions; tides, upwellings and outwellings; superheated geysers erupting from vents in the ocean floor to the silent welcome of giant undulating worms; risings and fallings in level from one point to another and from one time to the next; subsurface mountain ranges; great stores of minerals and energy; extreme diversity of life, some of it phantasmal; much that is unknown.

"Dear God be good to me," the Irish prayer runs, "the sea is so wide and my boat is so small." Countless lives have been lost to the sea, and the sea and floodwaters are figures for death, terror, chaos. At the same time, there is that image of the oceans as the "ungraspable phantom of life." The sea was the matrix of life.

In spite of all, the immensity of the sea has more enticed than deterred humankind. Humans may not dominate the sea, but we have not shrunk from a partnership with her: anciently, the Doge of Venice annually cast a wedding ring into the Adriatic, a ritual of marriage. Another ancient, King Canute, took his lords and minions to witness his fruitless command to the tides to halt. He was not railing at the sea. He was reducing it and its inexorable tides to a lesson of obedience to his court: it is no less futile to resist the inevitable force of sovereignty than the tidal force of nature. If the oceans are an "ungraspable phantom of life," then by saying so, we fix them in our imagery and fill them with our gods.

Since time out of mind we have gone to the sea in ships for commerce, for food, for travel. The sea was a means of trade for the

Phoenicians; of war for Persians, Greeks, and Romans; of faith for Irish monks; of adventure for the Vikings; of exploration and conquest for the Spanish, Portuguese, Dutch, and English. For Americans it is recreation, laboratory, food store, mineral source, and garbage dump.

In time law was made for the sea. Mostly this law has been an exercise in dominion, reducing the sea to commodities possessed by nations. It is law as bulwark. But it has not been exclusively so. There are exceptions, and it is these that will help me to say what law as medium might particularly be in international law, the uppermost level of my core sample.

I

What we now identify as law of the sea is only some four hundred years old. And it is this so-called modern period of the law—beginning with Hugo Grotius and extending to the United Nations Conference on the Law of the Sea—that holds the greatest promise for my undertaking.

There were some forms of maritime law long before the modern period. The first law having to do with the sea was designed early in Mediterranean civilization to govern the practices of carrying goods and passengers by water. This transport-business law developed into the present body of admiralty law. I am not going to address this law of the transport business. My subject instead is the public law of the sea.[1]

Public international law of the sea may also have arisen in the Mediterranean. In Roman law the sea, the coast, and the fish were common to all. They were either *res communes* (property of all), or *res nullius* (property of no one), or *res publica* (public property). Because Rome's principal maritime interests were confined to the Mediterranean Sea and because that body of water had some of the character of a Roman lake, it is uncertain whether Roman law can be counted as international law of the sea in our sense.[2] Certainly Roman ideas of marine areas as common to all were later adopted by international lawyers and adapted to international practice, as we shall see.[3]

Subsequent to the Romans, the Vikings with their superior technology and stout hearts (or rapacious predatory instincts, depending on your point of view) were able to roam the sea almost at will. The Vikings left us a splendid heritage, including the word *law*, but they left us no law of the sea.

After the Viking period, seas were appropriated as force allowed.[4] The most extensive claims were those of Spain and Portugal. A Papal Bull of 1493 and a treaty the following year divided the land and sea of the New World between them.[5] In the next century this regime was challenged by the English and the Dutch, Queen Elizabeth and later Grotius.[6] The challenge produced the modern law of the sea.

A

Right at the beginning of the modern law of the sea, there was a conflict that had the appearance of a clash between law as medium and law as bulwark. My temptation is to make out a correspondence between the two sides of the dispute and my notion of the opposing conceptual mataphors for law. But exactness of fit between a present theory and the facts of the past is not the point. It will suffice to find in the law of the sea some particular real-world content—some acceptable illustrative possibilities—for law as medium. Hugo Grotius is my man. Grotius was on one side; John Selden on the other.

The Dutch had designs on the East Indies. In the great division of the world, navigation around the Cape of Good Hope and trade with the East Indies had been allotted to Portugal. The Dutch need for a legal-theoretical challenge to the partitioning of the world was met by Grotius.

Grotius's pamphlet *Mare Liberum* was published in 1609. It is a taut fabric of legal, theological, scholarly argumentation—some of it ingenious, some of it curious—advocating free trade and free seas. Significant for my purposes is the fact that the staying power of Grotius's argument is its fundamental appeal to the nature of mankind: legally free seas prove and serve fulfillment of human life in community. In the economy of God, according to Grotius, no nation has been supplied with all the necessities of life. Human fellowship is thereby engendered through mutual needs and dispersed resources. Divine justice has established that each nation requires the supplies of others. The necessary mutuality of this order of distribution is to be realized through unrestricted navigation and the open access of each nation to all. By nature and by purpose, the sea is a bond of human fellowship: "The sea is common to all, because it is so limitless that it cannot become a possession of any one, and because it is adapted for the use of all."[7] It seems that Grotius's argument is indeed exemplary of the conceptual metaphor law as medium. And because Grotius's notion of the freedom of the seas was to become law for several centuries, it would appear that we have here law as medium in operation. Perhaps. Reservations about it will be raised in the next section.

The other metaphor, law as bulwark, seems easily read off from the counterargument presented by John Selden. Queen Elizabeth had urged the freedom of the seas before Grotius, but open seas were not to be the continuous policy of England until later. In Grotius's day, English sentiment ran in the opposite direction, and Grotius's work evoked a series of rejoinders defending the Crown's sovereignty over the vaguely delineated "British seas."[8] (I know of no one who rose to the defense of the Portuguese.)

The leading response was John Selden's *Mare Clausum*, drafted in 1618 but not revised and published until 1635. Selden's book is more leisurely than Grotius's but is similar in its mode of reasoning. He deflects Grotius's invocation of social mankind as the ground for free seas and free trade.[9] He counters the argument from the limitlessness of the sea with the proposition that "matter and instruments may be had for distinguishing of its dominions."[10] With respect to the sea's magnitude and inexhaustibility, he makes an observation that has equal appeal to the modern ear: "the plentie of [certain] seas is lessened every hour, no otherwise than that of mines of metal, quarries of stone, or of gardens, when their treasures and fruits are taken away."[11] Selden's basic appeal is that of his two opening propositions; the second explains and limits the first: "The one, that the sea, by the law of nature or nations, is not common to all men, but capable of private dominion or property as well as land; the other, that the King of Great Britain is Lord of the Sea flowing about, as an inseparable and perpetual appendant of the British Empire."[12]

Behind Selden's work lay an old English fervor for "keeping" the sea.[13] According to one supporter of English sovereignty over the sea, the sea was "the most precious jewel of his majesty's crown, next [after God] the principal means of our wealth and safety."[14] This blend of nationalism and commercial ambition was sealed with religion by a parliament that thought the securing of the seas to be a preparation for the coming of Christ.[15]

By the end of the seventeenth century, English claims to sovereignty over extensive seas had begun to give way before a variety of considerations. Military cost was one. If Selden were right, according to one contemporary assessment, then what he advanced could not "be gained but by a longer tool than a pen."[16] So Grotius's argument was found persuasive, and freedom of the seas became England's policy and international law from early in the eighteenth century until not long ago in our own.

There was one addition to the legal regime that bears noting. Freedom of the seas attached only to the high seas. The waters adjacent to coasts were viewed as territorial waters. The arrangement of free high seas with a skirt of territorial waters around land masses could be viewed as a workable compromise between *Mare Liberum* and *Mare Clausum*. Territorial waters need not be incompatible with freedom of the seas.[17]

The conceptual theory supporting territorial waters and their breadth was never agreed upon. Another Dutchman, Cornelius van Bynkershoek, proposed the no-nonsense cannon-shot rule for limits of coastal waters: "the dominion of the land ends where the power of arms terminates."[18] The first official placing of a territorial limit at three miles was left to Secretary of State Thomas Jefferson when, in 1793, he delivered to the British and French ministers notes claiming a three-mile zone.[19] This measure was taken up by the British and, although never universal, was as dominant as British rule of the seas. So for a long time, the high seas were free to navigation, and coastal sovereignty was exercised over territorial waters of varying limits.[20]

B

Selden's argument is informed by the conceptual metaphor of law as bulwark. In his reckoning, the law of the sea effects a division that allows the English to keep their seas (as extensive as ambition and pretense could make them). To keep the sea was to exhibit and defend an acquired jewel of sovereignty. Innocent passage is allowed through national marine territory as an act of charity and not of law. Permitting entry through the defensive works confirms the generosity of the grantor; it is not a recognition of the humanity or rights of the grantee. The practice of dividing the sea and excluding others protects exhaustible resources. Its purpose is to increase the efficiency of exploitation and to slow the loss of profit. So says Selden. (I was not surprised to find that the edition of Selden I was using is in a series styled *The Evolution of Capitalism*.)[21] *Mare Clausum* is a clear early example of the working of the dominant conceptual metaphor in the law of the sea.

Mare Liberum, on the other hand, is a statement of the alternate metaphor, law as medium. Law for the sea realizes the social bond in a regime of free communication among diverse nations. The sea is not a divisible commodity but an aid to the intercourse of nations. The law of the sea is authenticated by its accordance with the nature and purpose of its physical subject. A closed sea is legally because naturally preposterous.

Of greater importance is the fact that Grotius made the law of the sea a question of argumentation. _Mare Liberum_ could not be left unanswered. It had to be taken seriously by princes of nations and princes of commerce. Since Grotius, naval force has been brought to judgment by the force and forms of the arguments that it can muster. Argument, as compared with command or propaganda, is a communal act. When we engage in argument, persuading and being persuaded, we practice mutual dignity. The other person must be convinced; the other deserves to be convinced. Grotius is known as the Father of International Law, largely on the basis of his _De Jure Belli ac Pacis_ published in 1625. He framed no constitutions, wrote no statutes or treaties, and handed down no judicial opinions. He became Father of the Law of Nations by persuasion. Beginning with him, international law—especially the law of the sea—contained arguments rather than fiats. Both in form and substance, the law of the sea acknowledges the bond of human fellowship.

But our euphoria for these suggestions of real-world content for law as medium must be quickly bridled. There are three warning signs.

First, the freedom of the seas did not prevent exploitation of humans. When the Dutch and British exercised the legal rights of free navigation and open access, the trade winds did not carry their ships to other lands for the exchange of gifts and conversation. The freedom of the seas aided colonialism. Grotius may have eyed the economy of God, but a different economy moved the heart of his client, the Dutch East India Company. It used the freedom of the sea to inflict the most acute miseries. Karl Marx quotes from one 1817 report:

> The Dutch Company, actuated solely by the spirit of gain, and viewing their Java subjects with less regard or consideration than a West India planter formerly viewed the gang upon his estate, because the latter had paid the purchase money of human property, which the other had not, employed all the pre-existing machinery of despotism to squeeze from the people their utmost mite of contribution, the last dregs of their labour, and thus aggravated the evils of a capricious and semi-barbarous government, by working it with all the practiced ingenuity of politicians, and all the monopolizing selfishness of traders.[22]

Second, the freedom of the seas did not prevent exploitation when the object of desire expanded to include the sea itself as well as lands and people across the sea. Once the ocean floor was perceived as a source of exploitable minerals then the freedom of the seas became a legal basis for their unilateral seizure. The legal argument that the sea serves communal bonds was stood on its head. The freedom for connection and interchange with others became the freedom to serve the self. As President Reagan is quoted as saying: "We're policed and patrolled on land and there is so much regulation that I kind of thought that when you go out on the high seas you can do as you want."[23]

Third, Grotius's greatest contribution—law of the seas as appeal, as argument—also gives pause. Are legal arguments byplay to the real business of power? Is power more effective when it is legitimated, explained, and disguised by argument?

John Selden, unwilling to play martyr, may have written *Mare Clausum* to appease his king and to compose differences with him—legal argumentation as an act of obeisance. The circumstances of Grotius's *Mare Liberum* were hardly more inspiring.

One of the Dutch East India Company's captains seized a loaded Portuguese trading vessel. The prize arrived in the Netherlands in 1604, whereupon its store was sold and the handsome profits were distributed among company shareholders. Among the responses to this action were conscientious protests lodged by Mennonite and Libertine shareholders.[24] Grotius was commissioned to draft an apologia for the company—legal scholarship to still the conscience.

Grotius's work was not immediately published for reasons that remain obscure. He may have offered too powerful an argument for unlimited access to the sea and other nations. The argument may have outrun Dutch policy in other areas. One chapter from the 1604 work was recast as an independent pamphlet and published separately in 1609 as *Mare Liberum*. Once again the Dutch East India Company needed defending, and Grotius was obliging. The company's directors now thought their interests were threatened by negotiations between the Dutch and Spanish. They wanted conceptual buttressing for their claimed right to trade with the East Indies.

Grotius's arguments for the freedom of the seas were a piece of advocacy undertaken on behalf of a nationalistic client for commercial effect. Moreover, he could argue the other side of the case. He made different arguments at different times depending upon the interests of his clients. He flatly contradicted *Mare Liberum* when he later defended trade monopolies against free trade. (The basic argument favoring freedom of the seas remained intact, and Grotius consistently defended it. He did so, for example, in his great work *De Jure Belli ac Pacis,* a treatise not written for a client.)

What are we to make of these three—freedom of the seas as aid to colonialism, as rationale for grabbing seabed minerals, as argument cloaking power?

They could indicate that Grotius gives us a flawed example of law as medium. Or they may reveal a fundamental flaw in the conceptual metaphor itself and so serve as counterexamples to my proposition. Or they may warn us that no conceptual metaphor for law can be complete in and of itself.

I hold to the last. After all, my conceptual metaphor conceals at the same time that it reveals and so will want supplementary, different mataphors, as I explained in chapter 2. And it may be that what we see is early evidence of the need for such supplements to law as medium.

I also think that there is something else going on here. A conceptual metaphor for law requires more than supplementation. Conceptual metaphors have contexts. They belong to families of related metaphors—for nature, for politics, for society, for the human. Metaphors need their context. (See chapter 6.) I raise the subject now because I think the three warnings are no more than that. I do not think they are counterexamples defeating my proposition.

Something can be said in response to each of the three.

First, Grotius's freedom of the sea was fundamentally inconsistent with the use to which the Dutch and British put it. Ideological or ethnocentric myopia is required to employ the bond of human fellowship as a means of oppression. That this happened is not the fault of the law. Law was wrenched out of context. Montesquieu correctly observed that in any confrontation between law and power, law will always lose. The freedom of the seas, as Grotius understood and presented it, was defenseless against cannibalization. Hope lies in the metaphor's larger, affecting context.

Second, to summon the freedom of the seas as a justification for unilateral national exploitation of a marine treasury of mineral wealth—"when you go out on the high seas you can do as you want"—forces upon freedom of the seas a metamorphosis into its opposite.

Third, to charge Grotius with making arguments, or with making different arguments at different times, or with making weighty arguments on behalf of unworthy clients is to accuse him of being a lawyer. It is not so much his character as the character of law that is placed at issue.

When law is conceived as a structure of principles and rules built upon a monolithic foundation, the task of moral lawyers is to find or describe the law and apply it. One reasons from principle to situation. If contrary principles appear or if a single principle is argued as variously applicable to similar situations, then arguments may appear as trickery; they are tactics for obscuring the solid truth. But if law is a medium as I suggest, then argument is paramount.

Argument—as opposed to command or propaganda—is an affirmation of community. One persuades others and is persuaded by them. Argumentation is an exercise in regard for the dignity of those one seeks to reach. The measure of arguments is not their correspondence to an external, objective truth but their legitimate persuasiveness. What counts is the audience and the substantive manner of reaching them.

On the other hand, argument itself is no guide. Argument as argument does not persuade us that solidarity, conscience, and justice are more appealing than nationalism, self-interest, and profit. The fact of argument does not tell us what is to be convincing. Argument is vulnerable to corruption.[25] I think the question here is one not of principle but of people, the community of persuasion. The Mennonite conscientious objectors whose scruples first necessitated engaging Grotius's talent for argument had an inclusive conception of the community of interest. They evidently thought that the Portuguese had to be taken into account along with the investors in the Dutch East India Company. How much were their consciences responsible for calling up the best of Grotius? What convinced them of the need to reckon with the interests of a weak competitor?

Argument does teach the dignity of the other who must be persuaded but does not teach who is to be counted as the other. Why did it not occur to the Dutch East India Company and the Mennonites that the Javans required persuading? Why were Javans thought worthy only of the force of arms and not the force of argument? Again, it seems to me there is no answer in argument as such or in law as medium. Law is a medium of solidarity only when it exists with a conceptual metaphor for humanity as community. I shall address this question of the context and connection of metaphors in the last chapter.

II

The recent history of international law of the sea begins with steps taken by President Truman in 1945. On behalf of the United States, the so-called Truman Proclamations laid claim to the continental shelf and coastal fisheries. The Truman Proclamations replaced Grotius's arguments. They set off another great division of the sea rivaling that between Spain and Portugal. This time, however, the oceans were to be parceled out to many owners.

By the end of World War II it was becoming technologically possible and economically profitable to exploit familiar marine resources like fish and oil to an unfamiliar extent. Demand cast a devouring eye seaward. The sea now appeared as an end to exploitation and not a means only. Derek Walcott gives a clear sense of the sea becoming piece goods; he writes of the Caribbean, but the story is universal:

> One morning the Caribbean was cut up
> by seven prime ministers who bought the sea in bolts—
> one thousand miles of aquamarine with lace trimmings,
> one million yards of lime-colored silk,
> one mile of violet, leagues of cerulean satin—
> who sold it at a markup to the conglomerates,
> the same conglomerates who had rented the water spouts
> of ninety-nine years in exchange for fifty ships,
> who retailed it in turn to the ministers
> with only one bank account, who then resold it
> in ads for the Caribbean Economic Community,
> till everyone owned a little piece of the sea,
> from which some made saris, some made bandannas;
> the rest was offered on trays to white cruise ships
> taller than the post office; then the dogfights
> began in the cabinets as to who had first sold
> the archipelago from this chain store of islands.[26]

Superficially the triumph of law as bulwark looks complete: legally the sea has become a commodity divided among takers who will jealously guard their goods. A more careful investigation produces a more interesting picture. It offers hope for discerning illustrative possibilities for law as medium even in recent international law of the sea. I particularly want to draw your attention to the third United Nations Conference on the Law of the Sea. First I must attend to the background.

A

President Truman issued his two fateful proclamations in 1945. The first, "Natural Resources of the Subsoil and Sea Bed of the Continental Shelf,"[27] declared that the United States regards the continental shelf contiguous to its coasts "as appertaining to the United States, subject to its jurisdiction and control."[28] The legal character of the superjacent waters as high seas was not to be affected.[29] No definition was given for the continental shelf and its seaward extent, but an accompanying press release set the outer limit at the 100-fathom (600-foot) depth.[30] The Secretary of the Interior subsequently set the limits of the shelf at varying distances from 20 to 250 miles on the East Coast and from 1 to 50 miles on the west.[31]

The other proclamation, "Coastal Fisheries in Certain Areas of the High Seas,"[32] stated that the United States regarded it as proper to establish fishery conservation zones off its shores. The proviso was added that free navigation of the included waters would not be affected. Although reference was made to the creation of "explicitly bounded" areas in the contiguous high seas, no specific limits were set.[33] In 1976 Congress set a fishery-conservation-zone limit at 200 miles.[34]

The proclamations were patently intended to prepare the way for enlarging the nation's inventory of available natural resources.[35] They sought to establish American control over the minerals of the continental shelf and the fish in adjacent waters. They sought to do so in a manner that would cause the least damage to other American interests. The navy and the West Coast commercial fishing fleet wanted the greatest possible latitude for roaming the sea. If other nations were to expand their maritime claims, American freedom to maneuver would be constricted. The United States hoped to avoid setting the precedent for a rush to the sea.

Accordingly, the Truman Proclamations carefully noted that the claim to the shelf did not include any change in the freedom of navigation of the waters above. And the shelf was to be viewed as only "appertaining" to the United States. "Appertain" was a weasel word. The United States wanted to hedge bets. It wanted to claim enough control to take the oil and fish but did not want its claim to raise the provocative issues of sovereignty and ownership.

No one was fooled. The real meaning of the proclamations was not missed, and an escalating series of expansionist seaward claims was shortly registered by other nations.[36] Disputes followed. The United States became embroiled in conflicts with numerous other coastal nations. We have yet to extricate ourselves from some of these conflicts—notably those closest to home with Canada and Mexico.

By 1955 there was a proposal to codify the law, and the United Nations General Assembly called a conference that was held in Geneva in 1958. Who would get what? The seaward movement initiated by the United States was accepted but not clarified. The conferees were unable to resolve a number of contested points even after a second conference in 1960.[37] Among the unanswered questions were those of boundaries.

The first United Nations Conference on the Law of the Sea adopted a series of four conventions (or treaties): (1) Convention on the Territorial Sea and Contiguous Zone[38]; (2) Convention on the High Seas[39]; (3) Convention on Fishing and Conservation of the Living Resources of the High Seas[40]; and (4) Convention on the Continental Shelf.[41]

The Convention on the High Seas[42] defines the high seas as those beyond the territorial and internal waters of nations.[43] The reach of such waters is not indicated. It goes on to provide that the high seas may not be subjected to the sovereignty of any nation. Freedom of the seas is acknowledged as including the freedoms of navigation, fishing, laying submarine cables and pipeline, and flight in the airspace above. These freedoms are to be exercised with reasonable regard for the rights of other nations.

The Convention on the Territorial Sea and Contiguous Zone specifies no limits for the territorial sea, although that had been a dominant issue.[44] It does provide for straight baselines for measuring the territorial sea of whatever width, i.e., the base measuring line does not have to follow the sinuosities of the coast. The convention thereby followed the rule earlier established by the International Court of Justice in resolving a boundary dispute.[45]

The Convention on Fishing calls for negotiated agreements on conservation among nations fishing the same stocks in the same areas of the high seas. It recognizes the special interest of coastal nations in fisheries adjacent to their territorial waters but designates no boundaries.[46]

The Convention on the Continental Shelf does define the extent of the shelf area. It is to be the "seabed and subsoil of the submarine areas adjacent to the coast but outside the areas of the territorial sea, to a depth of 200 meters or, beyond that limit, to where the depth of the superjacent waters admits of the exploitation of the natural resources of the said areas."[47] The 200-meter depth is a fixed measure; exploitable depth is not. Increasing technological capability to exploit the ocean floor at ever greater depths would allow the expansion of national sovereignty over the entire seabed.[48]

Where the continental shelf is adjacent to more than one country and claims are likely to conflict, the convention calls for setting boundaries according to agreement or, absent agreement, according to an equidistant line unless special circumstances justify some other measure.[49] Equitable principles and equidistance have been determinative in disputes resolved since the convention.[50]

Perhaps the best-known dispute about who owned what after the Geneva Conventions was between Iceland and the United Kingdom—the Cod War. Fleets from the United Kingdom had traditionally taken fish from the waters near the coast of Iceland. Iceland progressively extended its claims to exclusive fishing rights to 200 miles. She sent out her two gunboats to enforce her claims against intruding foreigners. After skirmishes between the gunboats and British vessels, a settlement was reached in 1976. The United Kingdom agreed to a substantially reduced catch for its nationals. Iceland was popularly agreed to be the victor.[51]

A major influence on the outcome of the Cod War was the fact that the third United Nations Conference on the Law of the Sea had gotten under way in 1973.

B

The questions and disputes precipitated by the Truman Proclamations and left unresolved by the Geneva conferences and court decisions or treaties had multiplied. The means of war and naval movement, methods for taking and processing fish, marine mining projects, oil spills and other pollution, as well as dreams (some partially realized) such as ocean thermal energy conversion plants "grazing" the seas, building sites on and under the water, fresh water unlocked from icebergs—all of these things conspired to place the sea on the international agenda in a politically charged world.

The third United Nations Conference on the Law of the Sea was convened. A post-Grotian, post-Truman regime emerged and was fixed in a comprehensive treaty: 12-mile territorial seas, 200-mile exclusive economic zones, national continental shelves, free high seas, the deep seabed as the common heritage of mankind, and the International Sea-bed Authority, unique in international relationships.

The sanctioning of national claims to the 200-mile limit legally encloses a large portion of Grotius's high seas. The enclosure is more extensive qualitatively than quantitatively since the bulk of fish and

Law of the Sea among Nations

offshore oil is found within the 200-mile limit. And there is some question whether minerals beyond 200 miles may also be subject to national claims. The nationalistic desire to acquire marine wealth— the real force behind the Truman Proclamations—seems to have reduced all of the great sea to parcel goods.

Undaunted, I believe that the Grotian bond has not been severed, that new elements of commonality are to be discovered, and that materials have been supplied to the possible meaning of law as medium. Before I make my case, I must rehearse some of the evidence that law as bulwark dominates current law of the sea.

Two decades after the Truman Proclamations, President Lyndon Johnson expressed publicly the hope that we would never "allow the prospects of rich harvest and mineral wealth to create a new form of colonial competition among maritime nations." He went on to caution against "a race to grab and to hold the lands under the high seas. We must ensure that the deep seas and ocean bottoms are, and remain, the legacy of all human beings."[52]

The following year, 1966, Ambassador Arvid Pardo of Malta proposed that the U.N. address the matter of the seabed.[53] He urged that the time had come to declare the seabed the "common heritage" of mankind.[54] Here was a promising start.

In response to Ambassador Pardo and his continuing efforts, the U.N. General Assembly created a special committee.[55] In 1971 on the basis of the committee's work, the Assembly passed a resolution adopting a declaration of principles on the seabed. The seabed and its resources were denominated "the common heritage of mankind" as Ambassador Pardo had proposed.[56] At the same time, the Assembly called for the sea conference to convene in 1973.[57]

There has not been anything quite like that conference. It included representatives from more than 150 nations and continued for nine years of intense negotiation. Typically, formal sessions of several weeks' length were held once or twice a year, first in Caracas, then alternately in Geneva and New York, and active informal negotiating was conducted between sessions. Complete failure and total collapse were frequently predicted and were always close at hand as first one explosive issue and then another had to be faced throughout the protracted, mammoth bargaining.[58] In the end, almost subverted by the United States, a complex treaty emerged. It includes 320 articles plus nine complicated annexes and covers all aspects of the sea and its uses.[59] The treaty was adopted in April 1982, to come into force as soon as 60 nations have ratified it. The United States voted against the text of the treaty.[60] (I shall discuss this opposition in later pages.)

As I have noted, the treaty provides for a 12-mile territorial sea,[61] a 200-mile exclusive economic zone,[62] a continental shelf,[63] free high seas,[64] and the international Sea-bed Authority for the common heritage of deep seabed resources.[65]

A 12-mile territorial sea has substantial precedent. This is the distance long claimed by many nations, including Russia and China.[66] The United States had continued officially to adhere to the 3-mile limit, but had always set greater distances for various purposes.[67] (Customs jurisdiction, for example, was placed at 12 miles in the eighteenth century.)[68] In 1966 the U.S. Navy began to withdraw its traditional objections to expanded limits, and in anticipation of the conference, the United States lifted its opposition to the 12-mile limit. Twelve miles seemed preferable to the 200-mile limit asserted by some nations, so long as the change included the right of unimpeded passage through straits.[69]

Passage through straits was the major subject to be negotiated in an extension of territorial seas. There are 140 straits used for shipping. One hundred sixteen are overlapped by the 12-mile measure.[70] The solution embraced by the treaty is "transit passage,"[71] the diplomatic evolution of "innocent passage." Innocent passage through coastal seas is a right of all ships and was the rule adopted by the 1958 Geneva conference.[72] It is something like the permission that Selden long ago conceded to foreign vessels in the British seas and was also the rule followed by the International Court of Justice.[73] According to the 1958 Geneva convention, "[p]assage is innocent so long as it is not prejudicial to the peace, good order or security of the coastal State."[74] American naval interests were not satisfied with innocent passage for the newly overlapped straits. There were uncertainties surrounding military vessels. Moreover innocent passage is defined to require submarines to surface and show their flag,[75] something the navy was not eager to do. The new Law of the Sea Treaty continues the innocent-passage rule for territorial waters[76] but adds "transit passage" through straits to make the treaty palatable to the military.[77] Transit passage is "the freedom of navigation and overflight solely for the purpose of continuous and expeditious transit."[78]

With respect to the limits of the continental shelf, the treaty replaces the 200-meter isobath and exploitability tests. Now the continental shelf may extend to the 200-mile limit—even beyond if "the outer edge of the continental margin" lies seaward of the limit.[79] The "outer edge of the continental margin" is not a geologically precise measure but does break the outermost reach of the shelf short of the deep seabed.[80]

In addition to the revised rules for the continental shelf, the treaty also provides for an "Exclusive Economic Zone" of 200 miles' width.[81] With the exception of fishing, the traditional freedoms of the high seas (navigation, overflight, laying pipeline and cable) continue in these zones.[82] But the coastal nation has the right to exploit the living and nonliving resources of the area, and it has scientific and environmental jurisdiction over it. (The United States had already established a 200-mile fishery[83] and environmental protection zone[84] off its coast.)[85]

One of the original reasons for the conference was also the source of greatest contention there. Potato-sized nodules had been discovered lying on the ocean floor beyond continental shelves, i.e., the deep seabed. According to one estimate—how do you estimate such things?—there are 1.3 trillion tons of them.[86] They are a composition of 95 percent recoverable minerals: cobalt, copper, manganese, and nickel. Although there is no foreseeable shortage of any of these minerals, American industry must import all four.[87] Six transnational consortia report the capacity to mine nodules, some of which lie at depths ranging up to three miles below the surface of the sea.[88] The most sought after nodules are found on the floor of the Pacific.

Management of the nodule-bearing deep seabed—the common heritage of mankind—has been assigned to the singular International Sea-bed Authority, a first attempt at international governance.[89] The function and structure of the Authority determine not only who gets what, but also who gets what right to decide and under which conditions. Understandably, it was the toughest negotiating problem.

The Authority will be made up of an assembly, a council, a secretariat, and the Enterprise,[90] and will have its own courts.[91]

The Assembly, the policymaking "supreme organ," will be composed of all signatories to the treaty, each of which will have an equal vote.[92] The Council is to be "the executive organ" with power to supervise and make specific policy for the seabed's resources.[93] Its membership—hotly contested during the conference—will be limited to thirty-six representatives of different constellations of interest.[94] The Council will have two expert groups with line responsibilities: the Legal and Technical Commission and the Economic Planning Commission.[95] The small Secretariat staff is to be headed by a secretary-general, the Authority's chief administrative officer.[96]

The Enterprise will be the operating arm of the Authority and will conduct the mining and marketing of minerals.[97] In addition, other parties may explore and exploit the deep seabed under certain conditions.[98] Production will be subject to regulations intended to promote participation in mining, to safeguard markets, and to protect the economies of mineral-exporting nations in the third world.[99] Revenues are to be equitably shared, with particular attention to the needs of developing countries.[100]

For judicial resolution of disputes, a tribunal of twenty-one jurists is provided for, elected by the parties to the treaty.[101] Three or more of these judges may form special chambers for "the speedy dispatch of business."[102] Eleven members elected by the tribunal will make up the Sea-bed Disputes Chamber to resolve conflicts concerning the seabed.[103]

The orderly, placid way all these provisions align themselves on the pages of the treaty gives no hint of the great conflicting forces that produced them—the diplomatic equivalent to the movements and collisions of plate tectonics. Shifting coalitions formed, divided, clashed, and reformed as negotiation proceeded from one issue to another. For example, the developing countries were organized as the Group of 77 (shortly numbering more than 100). Within the group were landlocked and coastal nations, exporters and consumers, countries with large continental shelves and countries with scarcely any. Their negotiating goals could be unified and then significantly different. A similar uniformity and diversity of interests drove the major powers together and then apart.

One constellation of sensitive negotiations concerned the central endeavor to turn nodules to account. On this issue there was a reasonably definite, continuous, general division between unified sides. The Western industrialized nations lined up against the poor, developing nations. The former sought the least intrusion upon what they viewed as a market promising profits and continuing supplies. The latter hoped for a planned economy with shared expertise and shared technology leading to a more just redistribution of global wealth. Disposition of the common heritage of mankind was the first real opportunity for developing countries to begin implementing their long-sought New International Economic Order.[104]

One of the issues was access to nodules. A non-Enterprise entity must have approval of a plan of work. The Group of 77 wanted to condition approval upon transfer of the developer's mining technology to the Enterprise. The industrialized nations and private business resisted, wanting to keep their competitive edge. The treaty's negotiated resolution provides for transfer of technology but only if it is not available on the open market and then only on fair terms with resort, if need be, to arbitration.[105] Other conditions include ceilings on production as well as antimonopoly controls and regulation of the number of miners.[106] And then there are the financial arrangements.

Revenue from mining will supply operating funds for the agencies and will also be shared among the legatees of the common heritage. The sums could be sizable. The contract application fee is $500,000, to be followed by a fixed, continuing annual fee of $1 million.[107] After production is commenced, a miner must pay either a production charge or a combination of lowered production charge plus a share of the profits. The latter, mixed system would mean that a miner's payment's over the life of the contract would range from $260 million to $2 billion where the rate of return was from 6 to 24 percent.

Another divisive issue was that of treaty amendment. After such lengthy, painstaking negotiations, should the original accomplishment be vulnerable to alteration or undoing by shorthand means? The treaty provides that the system for managing the seabed can be amended through a review conference twenty years after commercial production begins. The amendments can be adopted by a three-quarters majority vote.[108] Another, more guarded avenue for amendment of seabed activities lies through a consensus of the Council followed by a two-thirds majority vote of the Assembly.[109]

Amendments and votes required for amendment are a subdivision of the more comprehensive matter of the role of voting minorities under the treaty. One-nation, one-vote majority rule gives the few big powers pause. They sought various alternative formulae for governing the seabed. In the Assembly, each member will have one vote; procedural decisions will require a simple majority, substantive issues two-thirds.[110] In the Council of thirty-six, however, although each member will have one vote, the majority required for passage of a measure increases with the importance of the subject, ranging from a simple majority on procedural questions, to two-thirds, to three-fourths, to the much more difficult to obtain consensus on the most sensitive items such as who will have a share of revenues.[111] The makeup of, as well as voting majorities for, the Council was also cause of conflict. Western industrial countries were assured six to nine seats, one of which was finally guaranteed to the United States.

c

Little is left of the commonality of the seas. *Mare Clausum* has become the rule. The law of the sea has become a tool for division and dominion. National jurisdiction has been extended to 200 miles, enclosing the most resource-rich areas for national exploitation. Legal devices like "transit passage" bear no witness to open seas; they are a part of the settlement for enclosure.

The high seas are still free, but they encompass a vastly reduced area. The deep seabed is the common heritage of mankind; however, the concept of common heritage favors exploitation of natural resources, and the system which will implement it constitutes an accommodation to capitalism. The seabed regime's provisions for production and revenue sharing are a partial acceptance by developing countries of the argument that there must be sufficient protection of tenure and retained profit—i.e., enough property law—to attract the investment requisite to ocean mining.[112] In precise senses, the regime divides and secures even seabed areas for nations and industries to exploit to their own benefit.

Further, there are doubts both about how soon the international seabed regime will be actualized and about its viability when it is. The treaty has been signed by 127 countries, but the additional step of ratification has not been taken. Sixty nations must ratify the treaty in order for it to come into force. In the meantime the United States continues to pursue its subversive course, attempting to sign reciprocal agreements with potential seabed-mining countries. These minitreaties would allow development outside the treaty system. In 1980, Congress passed the Deep Seabed Hard Mineral Resources Act[113] that provides for American licensing of seabed mining. Although the act mandates a moratorium on mining until 1988 and arranges for transition to the international treaty, American governmental and business interests are prepared for unilateral action. It may be that mining outside the treaty now will prove to be too risky for private investors. Nevertheless, the nodules lie on the seabed. There are technological means for their recovery. Sooner or later there will be markets for their contents. And a variety of legal justifications can be found for mining them. It can be argued that the concept of common heritage does not foreclose unilateral action or is not law with binding force.[114] It can be further argued that the seabed is legally property belonging to no one and thus subject to appropriation.[115]

In sum, there is indication enough that the commonality of the seas has been critically reduced and that what remains is vulnerable to closure. A quarter century after the publication of *Mare Liberum*, Grotius surveyed the intervening events of his day and ruefully observed that the question had become "not whether anyone can take possession of the sea, but how much of it is to be yielded up."[116] Our generation has answered "how much?" with "practically all."

III

Not everything has been surrendered. Some of Grotius's freedom of the seas as a bond of human fellowship remains and suggests how law as medium may be given expression.

A

To begin with, the International Sea-bed Authority should not be peremptorily written off. It is without precedent. It is an experiment in international government. It might prove more fruitful for the community of nations than we can guess.

And then, too, the notion of common heritage does have broad appeal. Its ubiquitous, persuasive power, like the sound of the surf, cannot be dissipated by nice, little legal arguments or by threats of unilateral plundering of nodules.[117]

Moreover, there are other elements of an order of commonality to be read in the treaty. For the first time, landlocked nations are given a right of access to and from the sea.[118] And, where a nation does not take the entire allowable catch of fish within its exclusive economic zone, it is to permit access to the surplus to landlocked nations and others with inadequate sea areas of their own. In granting this access, coastal nations are to give special attention to needs of developing nations.[119] Moreover, nations are to share revenues from minerals mined from their continental shelves in areas that lie beyond the 200-mile limit.[120] And the treaty provides for transfer of marine science and marine technology not involved in nodule mining.[121]

Perhaps, too, there is recognition of commonality in the provisions for conservation of fish. The 1958 convention established fishing as a freedom of the high seas but specified that the right is subject to the duty to adopt necessary conservation measures.[122] The goal of conservation was a failure. Treaties and organizations and twenty fishing regulatory bodies cover practically all ocean areas, but fisheries are still threatened.

The new treaty continues the goal of conservation in a slightly modified form.[123] It's principal action in support of fishery conservation is the extension of national jurisdiction to 200 miles.[124] I remain skeptical that enclosing a fishery and placing responsibility for it in one nation, thus removing it from the commons, serves fisheries any better than it serves the community of nations.[125] Had fishery conservation for the benefit of all been the underlying purpose of enclosure, there was another option. Each coastal nation could have been designated custodian instead of owner of the enclosed fisheries. Canada made exactly this proposal.[126] It was not accepted. Nevertheless I think it is still possible to identify some communal elements in what was done. Fishery surpluses are to be shared,[127] and scientific information is to be exchanged to the end of preventing overexploitation of fisheries.[128] Also, where stocks like tuna move beyond a national zone, the treaty calls for cooperative measures.[129] While primary responsibility for anadromous stocks like salmon is placed in the nations in whose rivers they originate, the proviso is added that consultations are to be maintained with other interested nations.[130] Last, marine mammals, whales especially, are to be the subject of cooperative conservation.[131]

More immediately promising both for action and for realization of community are the provisions for protecting the marine environment. Major, disastrous oil spills and growing awareness of the endangerment of sea life drew attention to ocean pollution. There are many causes of ecological disruption in addition to oil. Much damage is caused by runoff from land, for example, or airborne pollutants and deliberate dumping.[132] The treaty's environmental sections constitute some recognition of communal responsibility.[133] Nations are to take the necessary measures to control marine pollution from all the many sources.[134] Provision is made for enforcement of environmental controls in shipping by port and coastal as well as flag nations.[135] A right is recognized in coastal nations to take protective actions beyond their territorial seas in the event of major maritime incidents.[136] And, although the text repeats the refrain that nations have the right to exploit their natural resources, this right is associated with the "duty to protect and preserve the marine environment."[137] The underlying sense of the environmental section is the need for communal action in the common sea, within and without artificial legal boundaries.

Despite the general tenor of the new regime as a device for division and dominion, there are these several reflections of an order in which the law of the sea is a medium of communication and communal responsibility. Some confirmation that these reflections are substantial and not illusory may be garnered from the Reagan administration's negative response. The United States was instrumental in the convening of the conference. It had been a leader in the negotiations. And it had forced concessions to its interest. Nevertheless the Reagan administration abruptly reversed course. It first sought to dismantle the seabed provision. It then refused to sign the treaty. And then it set to work undermining it. The explanation may be simple bungling.[138] Or the new administration may not have understood the treaty. Or it may have perceived the treaty "as an alarming threat to the principles of free enterprise."[139] (At one of the conference meetings in 1981, some American delegates wore ties bearing the likeness of Adam Smith.) If this latter explanation bears some truth, and I think it does, then the Reagan reading of the treaty negatively confirms the positive reading I give communal elements. The Reagan administration did not like what it saw, but the sightings it reported confirm my own.

The most intriguing evidence from my perspective is also the most obvious: the conference itself. It is worthy of separate consideration.

B

Grotius's world was relatively intimate. Diplomats and books traveled freely, if slowly, across the Channel. There was a lingua franca. When Grotius made a point on the Continent, it was scored in England. Communication in the contemporary world is more difficult. Information travels faster, but understanding is more problematic. Words have to bridge cultures.

In the book on metaphor that I drew from in chapter 2, Lakoff and Johnson note that different cultures have different conceptual systems. Human realities vary from one culture to the next. Genuine communication among people who do not share the same culture is especially difficult. Understanding becomes possible, they say, only through the negotiation of meaning: "you slowly figure out what you have in common, what it is safe to talk about, how you can communicate unshared experience or create a shared vision." They add that, with "enough flexibility in bending your world view and with luck and skill and charity, you may achieve some mutual understanding."[140]

It is hard enough to achieve understanding through the negotiation of meaning between representatives of two cultures. Complexities are compounded in geometric progression as all the nations on earth are added in. Just to establish contact requires some doing. Grotius did not have to worry about being read. Today, absent a proper patron or access to the electronic media, a writer like Grotius and his potential public might never get together. If they did, they would still face the need to negotiate meaning. One of the present essentials, unnecessary for Grotius, is finding the audience. There is no ready-made surrounding, no forum. Absent a means, something fit to contain it, there can be little more than random, reverberant speech in place of discourse.

The United Nations only occasionally provides settings for the negotiation of meaning. However, the Conference on the Law of the Sea was medium for the shared attempt to create a shared regime for the sea.

Lakoff and Johnson made a casual observation that, brought to bear on the conference, may help to explain how the negotiations cohered so long in spite of the centrifugal political forces at work. They note that each culture has a different conceptual system so that the human aspects of reality will differ from culture to culture. They go on to observe that cultures do have physical contexts, "some of them radically different—jungles, deserts, islands, tundra, mountains, cities, etc. In each case there is a physical environment that we interact with, more or less successfully. The conceptual systems of various cultures partly depend on the physical environments they have developed in."[141] Because the earth is mostly ocean, the conceptual systems of diverse cultures might have the greatest convergence—or least divergence—along the front of interaction with the sea. If so, perhaps international, multicultural negotiations regarding the sea may enjoy some natural, cohesive predisposition to mutual understanding. It may also then prove possible that negotiations revolving around the sea may constitute a further, common basis for attempts at mutual understanding on other subjects. In any event, I draw your attention to the singular shape taken by the conference.

Assessments of the conference's success or failure have focused upon its work product, the treaty. I think the focus ought to be on the conference itself as a significant, instructive event of law. It was a laboratory for experiments in negotiation, multinational decisions, and transcultural discourse. The event itself promises more than its documental outcome for the prospects of a bond of human fellowship.

The most striking characteristic of the conference was its adoption of the process of consensus. The text of the treaty was painstakingly put together without a vote until the end. It was produced by consensus.

Consensus as a mode for decisions is of recent vintage in international bodies. It has rapidly gained acceptance.[142] This is so because of several developments: increasing interdependence among nations, adoption of democratic practices in formal international settings, the coming of age of parliamentary diplomacy, the ability of small nations to express ideological unity, and the growth of hugely destructive military power in combination with the diminishment of the political power of its wielders.

The most complete experience with consensus comes from the law of the sea negotiations. The U.N. committee that prepared the way for the sea conference followed the rule of consensus. It then proposed that the conference also adopt a "Gentleman's Agreement."[143] This agreement called for the conferees to "make every effort to reach agreement on substantive matters by way of consensus" and not to vote "on such matters until all efforts at consensus have been exhausted."[144] The Gentleman's Agreement was accepted, appended to the conference rules of procedure, and followed until, at the end, the United States insisted on a vote on adoption of the treaty.[145]

Consensus is hard to achieve where there are many, divergent, and conflicting interests. In operation, it is intricately complicated. For example, one of the conference rules of procedure provided for matters of substance to be decided by a two-thirds majority. Another then stated that a determination had to be made "that all efforts at reaching general agreement has been exhausted" before a matter of substance could be put to a vote. And prior to making such a determination there were to be all sorts of deferments, including a ten-day cooling-off period allowing time to establish general agreement and forestall a vote.[146]

In practice, consensus was achieved by the passage of time, developing familiarity among the delegates, patience, flexible, and floating negotiating groups, intersessional communication, and the kinds of fruitful chance encounters (at tea, cocktails, and meals) made possible by convening in a genial setting like that of Geneva. Above all it depended upon the tentative mutual trust among those who actually believed that arguments count. Consensus is achieved only by persuasion—countering, altering, mixing, dissolving, waiving, restating, revising, erasing, reformulating, walking, talking.

The conference projected consensus into the future as a mode for decision making by the agencies that the treaty would create. As I have already noted in passing, the Council of the International Seabed Authority will decide the most critical, controversial questions by consensus. The same rule will apply to any amendment conference.

Consensus is not the only voting standard established by the treaty. Depending upon the subject, Council decisions are to be taken by votes that can range from a simple majority to three-fourths.[147] Consensus, however, still forms the core. The system of voting by tiered majorities protects this core by allowing less rigorous modalities for less important, less controversial matters.

Also projected for use in the future of international marine affairs is another mechanism closely related to consensus. There will be problems whose solution involves only a small number of nations. The drawing of a marine boundary line between two nations is an example. The treaty provides that many of these disputes are to be resolved by the new judicial tribunal.[148] But nations, jealous of their sovereignty, have traditionally been reluctant to submit disputes to third-party resolution, especially where the third party is a court. The treaty could not realistically require some of the most politically delicate controversies to be submitted to binding judicial decision. It does bring almost all disputes within the possibility of conciliation. Conciliation is less formal, less time-consuming, and less costly than judicial or arbitral proceedings.[149]

Set down for submission to nonbinding conciliation are certain difficulties arising out of scientific research, fishing by one party in the economic zone of another nation, and the setting of marine boundaries between nations. In these cases, compulsory conciliation may be invoked by any party to the dispute.[150] A conciliation commission will then be formed and report its findings along with "such recommendations as [it] may deem appropriate for an amicable settlement of the dispute."[151] However, the commission's report "shall not be binding upon the parties."[152] The success of conciliation will rest upon the power to persuade and the willingness of the parties to be persuaded.

Conceptually, conciliation is the complement of consensus. It does for problems among a few nations what consensus does for problems among many. It depends upon the same underlying mutual trust and good faith brought down from the level of multilateral negotiation to the level of a concrete dispute between two nations. It is the most consensual means for settling limited disputes.

These conciliation provisions are one of the several ways in which the conference put off resolving certain issues—issues that were either small in scope or very large and politically difficult. Leaving various problems unsolved for the future will generally be characteristic of consensus. A conference which proceeds by consensus is not likely to make precise, determinative legal texts. Achieving agreement on textual provisions by consensus requires that many of them be left open to further negotiation. Some observers think this is a weakness. I count it as a strength because it is an invitation to more of the same, a solicitation to continue the process.[153] A collectively drawn treaty may affirm community as much by what it does not settle (issues open to further negotiation) as by what it does settle (seas open to all).

It is misleading to think that any treaty (or statute) should last for ages. If you think a treaty is forever, then you will find the brevity of its existence disheartening—a sign of the failure of the framers or of the failure of law among their successors. The temptation is great among those who negotiate treaties to believe that the longer and more subtly their product has been cooked, the more substantial should be its shelf life. By that standard the sea treaty ought to be with us longer than the United States Constitution. The sea treaty is valuable, I think, exactly because it was not written for the ages. It says what could be done now, in the present, and leaves much open to be settled in the future. It says that future negotiations will be necessary.[154] That is as it should be. It keeps a conversation going and makes for a kind of conference in continuous session. That may strike terror in the hearts of those who had to participate in the tough years of the third U.N. Conference on the Law of the Sea, but I think it is a promising, fruitful development. It shows what law as medium might mean in international relations.

I have mentioned another characteristic of consensus that also marks its potential for law as medium: dependence upon persuasion. Only once does the text define consensus. In the context of setting out the provisions for the Council's deliberations, it says that consensus is "the absence of any formal objection."[155] (Consensus had long been thought undefinable, its elusiveness being one of the qualities that commended it to use.) What follows this deceptively simple definition reveals something of the subtleties actually involved:

> Within 14 days of the submission of a proposal to the Council, the President . . . shall determine whether there would be a formal objection to the adoption of the proposal. If the President determines that there would be . . . an objection . . . , [he shall constitute] a conciliation committee . . . for the purpose of reconciling the differences and producing a proposal which can be adopted by consensus. . . . The committee shall work expeditiously and report to the Council within 14 days. . . . If the committee is unable to recommend a proposal which can be adopted by consensus, it shall set out in its report the grounds on which a proposal is being opposed.[156]

The last sentence of the quoted passage points us to the motive force of consensus in complex multicultural negotiations. If a consensus proposal cannot be found, the grounds of the objection are to be published. If a formal objection finally blocks consensus, then it is held up to general public scrutiny. The immediate pressure for reaching consensus is exposure. That is all. The sole punitive measure in the Council's repertory is the prospect of having one's consensus-defeating objection brought into the open. Either the objection will be legitimate and have purchase in the international community, or it will not. If not, the objector who has prevented consensus will presumably draw the censure of the audience. Consensus is backed by nothing more than the force which backed Grotius's argument for free seas, i.e., the power of persuasion.[157]

Consensus is not without its drawbacks. During the sea conference it proved vulnerable at several points. It was subject to manipulation by cynical forces beyond the conference table and by representatives at the table acting in bad faith. It was subject to the self-absorption always found at such gatherings: delegates could become their own constituency, or professional conference boosters, or an exclusive elite whose outer circle was a parasitic coterie of knowing academic commentators. Consensus was also subject to oppressive tactics. Dissent by the powerless could be suppressed on the pretext of needing to wrap up a package deal, while dissent by the powerful could be expressed with a fairly easily exercised veto. Moreover, it was subject to diversionary uses. A gradual process occupying attention in Geneva was good cover for those whose real interests were to control the mineral market or to postpone action until seabed mining technology was developed and ready for unilateral deployment.

Also there may be ground for suspicion in the fact that consensus has commended itself especially to the minority of big powers as an alternative to majority rule. Now that so many nations, each with one vote, participate in balloting, the requirement that international actions can be taken only by consensus gives the big powers a discreet veto. It can be made a new device for the old power politics in international affairs.

Questions can be raised about consensus as its U.N. conference history shows. However, that history also shows that consensus has promise and attraction, especially for my enterprise. Presently "in any discussion of international law—which itself is designed to persuade the reader and not to force him to accept a position—[we must] assume equality of states before the law and genuine reciprocity."[158] Because it does embody some reality of mutuality, consensus commends itself as the form for negotiations among those who share an equality of parliamentary dignity.

If consensus and conciliation are to be media of a genuine community of nations sharing equality of dignity, then there must be such a community with the will for mutuality and reciprocity. International law cannot create these conditions in which it serves as a medium; it properly fits within them when they come to be. I shall return to this subject in the last chapter.

IV

International law for the sea began with the papally sanctioned division of the oceans between Spain and Portugal. This allotment, challenged by Grotius and the dispersion of naval power, yielded to a regime of undivided seas. Not until the Truman-sanctioned modern assault on the freedom of the seas did the Grotian regime give way. The acquisitive rush to dominion seems recently to have abated but only because most of the marine store of wealth has already been spoken for.

Selden argued that instruments could be found for distinguishing the dominions of the sea. He meant the instruments of geographers. He could not have imagined the possibility, now seriously raised, that husbandry of fish can be effected by confining them within marine fields marked off by electrical currents. Such electric "fences" are a parable of how far technology can carry the enclosure movement. Law has figured in this movement as a contrivance serving division and defense—a protection of exclusive franchises for exploitation. This is law as bulwark.

The third United Nations Conference on the Law of the Sea may have presided over and legitimated the final stages of the closing of the seas. But such formal ceremonies were not its sole occupation. It also substantively acknowledged the commonality of the seas by supplying the common heritage with specific content. More important in my view, it experimentally realized consensus.

The conference was more than once almost sabotaged by a corporate failure of will or by one of the participating nations. It was almost done in at the finish by the United States. The treaty it produced may have bad results or may come to nothing. Nevertheless the conference does give some evidence of the survival of human solidarity and the correspondent commonality of the seas exhibited in Grotius's appeal to the bond of fellowship. When a single bulb has been made to burn, however briefly or dimly, the possibility of electric light has been demonstrated. The conference gave preliminary demonstration of the possibility of mutual trust, good faith, and belief in the efficacy of argument. Even if only proleptically, it was occasion for impressive multicultural discourse. This is law as medium.

4 THE UNITED STATES LAW

OF THE SEA

The United States exhibits some of the indicia of an island nation. As the bicentennial parade of tall ships in New York harbor served to remind us, the early life of our country was sea-bound. In some respects it still is. We depend upon the sea for fossil fuel, food, trade, military offense and defense, recreation, and garbage disposal. And we continue to perceive the nation as lying coast to coast.

Like an island fortress, the United States regards its coastal waters and continental shelf as though they were continuations of outer defensive works. As against the outside world, our position has been simple, clear, and uniform: the sea and shelf around us are ours. Law sets the boundaries against other, competing nations.

Within the United States, among ourselves, the story is not so simple; the theme is straightforward enough, but the plot keeps dissolving in complexity. The problem is this: the law is persistently bulwark law—dividing up and defending possessable territory. But the bulwark crumbles into incoherent bits as it advances into the politics and nature of the territorial sea. The failure of the law has been compounded as greater demands have been made upon the sea for oil, fish, war, and the dilution of pollutants. Who is to enjoy priority in conflicting uses: coastal states, national government, oil and gas producers, the fishing industry, the coastal tourism trade, environmentalists, others? Who is to decide, and how?

Because the dominant conception and the consequential practices of law are so markedly inappropriate in these matters, you might think that the massive evidence of confusion would long ago have produced fundamental revisions. That it has not done so is testimony to the hold a conceptual metaphor can have upon us. We lose the capacity to see both the negative effects of the prevailing reality and the positive possibilities of alternates. We suffer a kind of ideological blindness.

In this chapter I shall survey some of the areas of confusion in the prevailing legal disposition of the resources of the coastal sea and shelf. After reviewing the sense not made by law as bulwark in the territorial sea, I shall turn to the faint glimmer of another, emerging possibility.

In the previous chapter I suggested that if we thought of law as medium we could discern in international law the shaping of a forum and a language for the dynamics of international conversation. A similar development may be discovered in our national law. I propose that there is some evidence of it where the coastal waters and seabed have recently served as an experiment in Madisonian federalism. I think that Madisonian federalism has a lot to do with political community and very little to do with national-government/state-government relationships. My case for Madisonian federalism and therefore law as medium in the territorial sea will rest upon the much-maligned permit system in effect in marine activity.

I

The basic proposition of existing law is that the first three miles of the sea belong to the respective coastal states and that the remainder of the expanse to the 200-mile limit falls under national jurisdiction.

This simple statement is no sooner made than lawyerlike accuracy requires its qualification. Three miles was the old limit that we claimed for our territorial sea. It is not clear whether or how coastal states may legally extend their seaward boundaries now that international law has moved territorial seas out to 12 miles.[1]

Through the years the 3-mile limit has expanded and contracted depending upon the jurisdictional requirements or resource needs involved.[2] Three miles has remained the territorial limit in its strictest sense, but customs jurisdiction and military defense zones have extended much further, as have claims to the continental shelf and to fishery zones.

The question of whether coastal-state or national jurisdiction would prevail within these limits did not arise formally until after the Truman Proclamations of 1945 laying claim to the continental shelf and coastal fisheries.[3] Two years after the Proclamations the Supreme Court held that the federal government's rights were paramount in the territorial sea.[4] The Court explained its decision in clearly identifiable bulwark terms: Offshore oil might become the subject of international dispute, and "if wars come, they must be fought by the nation. . . . The State is not equipped in our constitutional system with the powers or the facilities for exercising the responsibilities which would be concomitant with the dominion it seeks" over tidewaters.[5]

The states might not be able to man the military garrison but they quickly demonstrated their strength in the political wars. By 1953 they had succeeded in having Congress pass the Submerged Lands Act ceding the 3-mile territorial sea and underlying shelf to the states.[6]

The national government has vied with the coastal states for marine jurisdiction largely for the profits from offshore oil and gas.[7] Although it was not until the oil embargo of 1973 that offshore fuel development was promoted in real governmental earnest, oil had been produced off the coast of California since 1896, and the use of mobile platforms had begun with the drilling of a well off Louisiana in 1947.[8] From 1953 to 1980, national receipts from outer-continental-shelf oil and gas leasing totaled over $41 billion.[9] The coastal states contend that they are entitled to a share of these funds. Congress's response has been to hold onto the money but to create surrogate funding programs for the states. For example, one statute made loans, guarantees, and grants available to coastal states for the preparation and implementation of coastal management plans. Other acts made states eligible for payments and compensation for various deleterious impacts suffered from development of offshore oil and gas.[10] The states continue to press for straight revenue sharing. In any event, the controversy is about money and not about whether the continental shelf should be exploited. The intention all along has been to turn offshore resources to account.

In opposition to the unchecked impulse to exploit, some sentiment gradually developed in favor of preserving a few marine sites. And offshore fossil-fuel exploitation has been selectively opposed by those who make profits from other marine resources. So the long-standing commitment to exploitation continues, but it is played out in a larger arena with a greater number and diversity of contestants representing the often-conflicting interests of fossil-fuel development, fish harvesting, tourism, commercial and military navigation, and environmental protection. The law has attempted to sort out the interests through the conventional modes. It has done so with increasingly less success and greater confusion.

A

The states have never been satisfied with the 3-mile restriction to their seaward aspirations. And the federal government has not been content to withdraw its coastal interests behind a line three miles at sea. The 3-mile division is no more than what it is, a line drawn on water. Even so, the courts continue to pay it lip service.

In 1969, the federal government brought suit against thirteen Atlantic coastal states alleging that they were asserting claims to the outer continental shelf beyond the 3-mile limit. The case was settled in 1975 in *United States v. Maine*[11] when judgment was entered for the United States. The Court reaffirmed its earlier decisions, all of which, like the original case in 1947, upheld federal priority. Despite the Court's consistency, the states have never been persuaded. The resistance is legally as well as politically understandable.

The Court had given two grounds for its original tidelands decision in 1947, *United States v. California*.[12] One was history. The Court said that the national government had been first to accomplish dominion over the territorial sea. The evidence in support of this contention is mixed, and the states were unmoved. So by the time of *Maine*, its 1975 decision, the Court abandoned its argument from history and took refuge in the second argument: national external sovereignty.

National external sovereignty is a technical legal fiction. It tells us what the Court has done, not why. The Court said that because the Constitution gives the federal government power over commerce with foreign states, foreign affairs, and national defense, it follows that "as attributes of these external sovereign powers the federal government has paramount rights in the marginal sea."[13] Even if the national external sovereignty has meaning, it does not have power to part the seas at the 3-mile or any other limit. Let me give some examples.

The first set of examples illustrates that there is nothing about national external sovereignty (whatever that may be said to be) that prevents states from having and acting upon interests in coastal waters beyond the 3-mile limit. By act of Congress, when it is not inconsistent with federal law, the law of the adjacent state applies beyond the 3-mile limit to activities associated with the outer continental shelf.[14] When recovery was sought for the deaths of two workmen killed on a drilling rig in the Gulf of Mexico, the Court said that the case must be decided according to Louisiana law.[15] It said that the rigs were to be treated as "islands" or "federal enclaves" where Louisiana law would act as surrogate federal law.[16] Because over thirteen thousand rigs operate on the outer continental shelf in the Gulf of Mexico, state law potentially applies to a sizable population on the far side of the 3-mile limit.[17]

In this example, Congress acted to give state laws extraterritorial application. State law can also have effects beyond the territorial sea without prior congressional action. Alaska's measures restricting the king-crab season in the Bering Strait have been held to apply beyond the 3-mile limit.[18] And when Maine imposed a license fee on petroleum products transferred over water, this action was held to apply to petroleum terminals and ships within a zone extending nine miles beyond the 3-mile limit.[19]

The legal fictions of national external sovereignty and paramount rights do not cut off state interests at the 3-mile boundary. Correspondingly, they certainly do not prohibit federal interests from being exercised within the 3-mile coastal sea.

When Congress ceded the tidelands to the states it reserved certain rights. The courts have recognized these rights and have said that the federal government has power, for example, to regulate dredging and filling within the area ceded to Florida.[20] A federal statute has also been found to prevent Virginia from enforcing certain of its fishing laws.[21] (Virginia wanted to prohibit nonresidents from catching menhaden in its portion of Chesapeake Bay and to deny commercial fishing licenses to citizens of other countries.)[22] Moreover, federal admiralty law is preeminent in governing surface uses of the territorial sea.[23]

In sum, the states have legally acknowledged interests in the area beyond three miles "owned" by the federal government, and the federal government has legal interests within the three miles "owned" by the states.

B

A line three miles from shore does not satisfactorily distinguish state from federal interest in the sea. Boundary lines, divisions, and defensible territory are apparatus of the bulwark. Because they still appear necessary to the Court, it has tried to devise methods of demarcation other than the 3-mile limit. By one of these methods, the further seaward the contested marine zone lies, the more preponderant the national interest; the closer landward the area, the greater the state interest. According to the other method, where there is need for national uniformity, federal interests prevail; where there is need for diversity and local approaches, then state interests are to dominate.

Both methods enjoy some support in tradition and utility, but neither is any less of an ultimate failure than the 3-mile limit.

The seaward-distance measure sinks before it gets very far. The relative degrees of national and state interest simply cannot be determined by nautical distance. Alaska's interest in preserving king crab does not wane with distance as some national interest waxes. Nor would Washington State's interest in preserving salmon vary depending on whether the fish were at the furthest offshore extreme of their migratory pattern or at their spawning stage in the state's inland waters. The national defense issue works the same way. You will remember that the Supreme Court led off the modern jurisprudence of marine jurisdiction with a national-defense argument. The Court found that the states had to yield their interest in the territorial sea to the national government because offshore oil might become the subject of war, and "if wars come, they must be fought by the nation."[24] The states could not own what they could not defend. California is no better equipped to defend its land than its waters. If wars come, the nation must defend the dry land of the state as well as the sea. If anything, the national-defense interest increases as the focus moves landward. Surely this is no basis for claiming that the federal government should dislodge state jurisdiction within the borders of California.

The other test, uniformity versus diversity, is no more successful than the seaward-distance formula.[25] According to this test state regulation will not be allowed if the situation requires a uniform national rule but will be allowed if the activity is one of predominately local interest inviting diversity of response. The test offered as a solution is plainly a restatement of the problem: which are the circumstances requiring national uniformity and which diversity?

The case of *Ray v. Atlantic Richfield Co.*[26] was a contest about Washington's Tanker Law regulating oil tankers in that state's Puget Sound. The Court, employing the uniformity/diversity test, struck down much of the statute. The state had prohibited supertankers based on its judgment about water depth in Puget Sound and other local peculiarities. This was the sort of judgment, said the Court, that lay within the scope of federal authority preempting local decisions; there was need for "someone with an overview,"[27] "a single decision maker, rather than a different one in each State."[28] The state was forced to yield its judgments about conditions in Puget Sound to the Coast Guard. The local Coast Guard's local navigational practices in local waters were to prevail over those of the state. Factually, the Court's test is a failure because it does not provide for the possibility that the federal agencies may lack the capacity for disinterested, uniform regulation. The Court did not explain how the local Coast Guard unit—or any federal-agency representative—can be thought to have more "overview" than the state legislature. Although the Coast Guard may never have done so, other federal agencies have protected interests far more parochial, bureaucratic, and provincial than any that the state might wish to pursue. Theoretically, the test fails to provide for the possibility that national interest warranting federal priority may lie in diversity rather than in uniformity. Should not the navigation of Puget Sound be expected to be different from that of Chesapeake Bay?

Like the 3-mile limit, the seaward-distance and diversity/uniformity tests try to but do not divide the seas or marine interests.

It should be added that Congress has done no better than the Court. After putting the 3-mile limit in place, Congress has acknowledged the interests of states in the sea to greater or lesser degrees and extents depending upon the changing fortunes of state influence in the political process.

II

The 3-mile limit does divide state territory from national territory for some legal purposes, but neither it nor any of the surrogate rules of differentiation have proved suitable for division of state and federal interest in the sea. If we abandon all thought of boundary lines, dual sovereignty, and divisions for the purpose of ownership—that is, if we cast off bulwark modes of thought—then other realities and possibilities emerge.

A

The apparatus of law as bulwark does not work very well in the context of state-national marine jurisdiction. It fails for two reasons. One is the assumption that the sea and continental shelf constitute a treasury whose riches may be allocated by law. It is true that foreign competitors were effectively walled out by the Truman Proclamations and the ensuing legislation, but there remains an intractable problem of allotment within the American monopoly. The nature of the sea, the limits and interdependence of its contents, the limitless expansionist dynamic of greed, and assorted other considerations render hard and fast marine boundaries physically as well as conceptually problematic. A system of franchises in the sea satisfies no one.

The other reason for failure is the assumption that state and national governments are to be delineated and upheld for their own sakes, like independent sovereignties. This assumption violates the first premise of the original conception of American government that both state and federal governments are, as James Madison pointed out, "substantially dependent on the great body of the citizens of the United States."[29] His correction of the error is important and helps direct us to a reality—the communal reality and communal sense of federalism—in which boundaries between the state and national governments are secondary:

> The Federal and State Governments are in fact but different agents and trustees for the people, instituted with different powers, and designated for different purposes. The adversaries of the Constitution seem to have lost sight of the people altogether in their reasonings on this subject; and to have viewed these different establishments not only as mutual rivals and enemies, but as uncontrolled by any common superior in their efforts to usurp the authorities of each other. These gentlemen must here be reminded of their error. They must be told that the ultimate authority, wherever the derivative may be found, resides in the people alone; and that it will not depend merely on the comparative ambition or address of the different governments, whether either, or which of them, will be able to enlarge its sphere of jurisdiction at the expense of the other. Truth no less than decency requires, that the event in every case, should be supposed to depend on the sentiments and sanction of their common constituents.[30]

For Madison, federalism, or what he carefully described as "a judicious modification and mixture of the federal principle,"[31] connoted a political community that enhanced participation through representation and protected the powerless few through diversity. In this communal, political reality a state-national division was no more than a subsidiary supporting component.

Power is to be spread through state and national governments and further dispersed within government among the executive, legislative, and judicial branches. This dissemination of power protects the people: the "different governments will control each other, at the same time that each will be controlled by itself."[32] Because this system, as compared with pure democracy, can comprehend a vast territory with large numbers of people, it will produce social and political diversity. This multiplicity protects individuals and minorities against the tyranny of the majority: "the society will be broken into so many parts, interests and classes of citizens, that the rights of individuals or of the minority, will be in little danger from interested combinations of the majority."[33]

Extending the experiment in federal government offshore is a greater, altogether different task from extending state and national lines of jurisdiction. The end, what Madison called "the great desideratum,"[34] is to extend the means whereby popular government is preserved at the same time that minority rights are secured. It is a matter of the extension of a political community.

Two related aspects of the Madisonian vision bear repeated emphasis. First, the dispersal of governmental power and the diversity of the people are not occasion for a contentious struggle. The many parts are counterpoised elements of a smoothly functioning whole. One image for it might be a Calder mobile; the components are attached and animated by "that chain of connection that binds the whole fabric of the constitution in one indissoluble bond of unity and amity."[35] A somewhat better image might be body building. Madison wished to provide for the increase as well as control of power. To match power to power—state to national government—is to build in an isometric exercise for the body politic. The parts grow in strength together. The point is that, although it is generally thought of in exclusively bulwark terms of conflict, federalism in Madison's view was not a competition of incompatible interests.

Second, the government is representative—a republic rather than a democracy. People and their opinions rather than interests are to be represented. Electors are not to be passive investors with whom managers of their capital periodically settle accounts. Electors are to be represented in the way that a character is portrayed or represented onstage. The ties of affection that bind the whole especially bind representatives to their constituents within the many decentralized units of the republic. A representative more easily, more naturally acts the part of (represents) those who sent him. Citizenship is refined and enlarged by this representation: "Had every Athenian citizen been a Socrates; every Athenian assembly would still have been a mob."[36] Justice is more apt to prevail when opinion is distilled through stages of representation. We are better acted.

An extension of federalism—and I am talking now about federalism in the Madisonian sense of community, "the social psychology of federalism"[37]—does not mean projecting onto the oceans a struggle of interests. It means extending the forms through which the government of marine affairs is popular at the same time that it protects minorities—the forms for participation, representation, opinion, dialogue, diversity, and fruitful conflict.

These forms could include boundaries.[38] Such boundaries would not have the significance that they do for the bulwark. You will remember that Grotius believed international diversity was fundamentally communal. In the divine economy, dispersed resources and mutual needs cause each nation to require others. Differences become the occasion for affirming interdependence and solidarity. In such a world national boundaries serve the social nature of humanity and not national sovereignty and nationalism. They do not set one sovereign against the other but designate the location from which the community in one place reaches out to the community in other places for reciprocal giving and receiving. Such boundaries are nonessential.

Similarly, federalism, as I have been talking about it, employs boundaries in aid of community. They are a function not of acquisition or sovereignty but of responsibility. For example, state boundaries projected seaward might designate areas of responsibility for protection of the marine environment and its life. The citizens of each coastal state would be trustees for common resources. Boundaries would not be immovable or the outer limit of responsibility. Fisheries provide an example. They are often common to the waters of several states and the federal government. The Fishery Conservation and Management Act of 1976 establishes regional councils to prepare management plans for offshore fisheries.[39] The councils are composed of representatives of each region's coastal states. In this instance, state boundaries and their seaward projection are simply a method for assembling areas of joint responsibility and for making up membership of the acting bodies. The federal Secretary of Commerce then serves as coordinator of the councils and as guarantor for the meeting of minimal standards.[40]

Boundaries themselves currently present an interesting possibility for the practice of federalism. If international law provides for territorial seas twelve miles wide, then the United States may wish formally to extend its territorial sea an additional nine miles from the present 3-mile limit. The principal effect of such a move would be to raise the domestic question of whether the addition would be tacked onto the coastal-state areas. Should the coastal states' seaward borders be extended now from three to twelve miles? By what means (congressional, state, or judicial action)? With what consequences (revenue, state navies)? What, after all, is the sense of marine divisions between one state and another and between coastal states and federal government? Rethinking these issues, informing the citizenry, and making the requisite choices would allow the boundaries themselves to become occasion and subject for federalist dialogue.

So the forms of Madisonian federalism might make use of boundaries and make them into media of the political community. But then physical boundaries and national-state jurisdictional boundaries would be subordinate to communal realities and would always yield to newer, perhaps unsuspected possibilities. One such possibility is already to be found in the practice of leasing the continental shelf for oil and gas development.

The continental shelf is the size of one-third of the United States and may contain most of our remaining undiscovered oil and gas reserves. From 1953 to 1976, about 15 million acres, some 3 percent of the total, had been leased for oil and gas drilling.[41] Another 7.8 million acres were leased in 1976–78, 14.5 million more in 1979–81, and an additional 26 million acres were originally projected for lease in 1980–85.[42] The 1980–85 plan was attacked, litigated, and revised.[43] With certain environmentally fragile or financially unpromising exceptions, the entire shelf is being drawn into consideration ultimately for leasing.[44]

Until the past several years, continental-shelf leasing was conducted in a closed system controlled by oil companies and the Secretary of the Interior. The system bore no resemblance to Madison's picture of government. The lack of resemblance is due not merely to the subtraction of the states from the scheme. The possibility of the atrophy of the states did not trouble Madison:

> If . . . the people should in future become more partial to the Federal than to the State governments, the change can only result from such manifest and irresistible proofs of a better administration, as will overcome their antecedent propensities. And in that case, the people ought not surely to be precluded from giving most of their confidence where they may discover it to be the most due.[45]

The system was nudged toward Madisonian federalism in 1978 by congressional amendment of the Outer Continental Shelf Lands Act.[46] By these amendments, coastal states were finally given formal, structural room in offshore oil and gas leasing. The states have a consultative role. Information must be shared with them, and their approval must be granted before actual exploration and development can begin.[47]

To the extent that the process has been opened to the states in this manner, their presence makes leasing more public and responsive; the system is more of an exercise in federalism. The simple inclusion of states, however, is an incomplete cure. To take but one example, the national and coastal state governments may have the same ambition and a uniformity of interest. This will be so any time a coastal state leases acreage within the 3-mile limit or gains revenue from onshore activities related to outer-continental-shelf drilling. The state and national governments will then share a predisposition to promote oil exploration. In such cases, dissentient minorities—fishermen, for example—lack structural protection and a voice. Power is not effectively dispersed, and diversity is insufficiently enhanced.

B

Another possibility offers some evidence of a medium for fuller, more authentic realization of federalism: the permit system. More than permits is involved, but permits are the chief external feature.

Within the general clamor for deregulation, it has been specifically argued that industrial actors ought not to be subject to environmental permits. The goal would be to make environmental regulation presumably self-executing, like tax law. No permits would be necessary. Industry would act without waiting for outside approval. Permits, it is said, cause delay and unnecessary expense and are an obstructionist tactic of the bureaucracy. So, for example, Congress has been asked "to enact legislation requiring 'fast track' reviews of environmental impact statements and environmental permits to speed the expansion and development of ports,"[48] and the Department of the Interior has sought to promulgate "streamlined" outer-continental-shelf regulations.[49]

A Congressional Research Service study of continental-shelf leasing includes a draft, "Procedural Leasing Flow Chart for OCS Oil and Gas Production," prepared by petroleum-industry representatives.[50] The chart depicts the numerous permit processes that must be completed before oil and gas can be produced on the continental shelf. Even though the chart is abridged and incomplete, it unfolds in sixteen panels to a length of five and one-half feet. To oilmen with fond memories of the prior system of unencumbered access to the continental shelf through the Secretary of the Interior's office, this chart is graphic proof of the blasphemies of bureaucratic irrationality and inefficiency.[51] The stages of such a permit process seem to be nothing but complicating, delaying obstacles to the fulfillment at sea of capitalistic enterprise.

If one is committed to port expansion or continental-shelf drilling, then permits will appear to be costly hindrances to the business at hand. Such an attitude fails to recognize that the permit, and all that surrounds it, is not only a means but also an end. The permit is an integral part of a properly political event. Deregulation, at least in this circumstance, is an assault on the politics of federalism.

The larger potential of permits was seized upon several years ago by the artist Christo when he erected the *Running Fence*, continuous panels of eighteen-foot-high white fabric that stretched across 24.5 miles of rolling hills in Sonoma and Marin counties, California.[52] His project required numerous permits, an environmental-impact report, hearings before fifteen governmental agencies, the permission of many private landowners, and the services of nine lawyers.[53] (One of the required permits was a Coastal Development Permit for the last leg of the fence as it crossed the coast and ended, submerged, in the Pacific. The permit was first issued and then revoked; that Christo proceeded without it was an independent source of controversy.)[54] Even though the expected life of the fence was only two weeks, it took two years to obtain all the necessary permits and agreements. These preliminaries were no diversion. Christo could have built the fence in another country where no permits were required, but he chose the place he did because of the permits.[55] He embraced them. As a commentator observed, "The entire process was the work of art. . . ."[56] Or, as Christo said at one hearing: "It's hard to explain that the work is not only the fabric, steel poles, or Fence. Everybody here is part of my work."[57] The permit requirements allowed Christo to gather maximum public involvement in the act.

Permits for outer-continental-shelf activities—all those stages outlined on the panels of the flowchart—can also generate public involvement. The preparation for and aftermath of permit issuance render the system a continuing political event, as I think it should be. Permits are not simply tickets of entry; they are part of the performance, potentially a performance of federalism.

The use of permits as a political art form is a recent invention, but the permit is an ancient device which has served many purposes having nothing to do with politics. Grotius notes that, among the Romans, for a permanent structure on the seashore, "a permit was wont to be obtained from the Praetor, just as a permit was required for the construction of a building in the sea."[58]

Given a commons like the seashore, or a defined space or limited activity, permits (licenses, tickets) can regulate entry for several purposes, such as making money, limiting access, and controlling quality.[59] Typically, governmental permits implement technical or other standards established by a legislative body, or by an administrative agency with a broader set of guidelines established by the legislature.

The issuance of a permit usually draws no public attention. Drivers licenses, for example, are routinely granted or denied without comment. But the issuance of an ordinary permit may provoke publicity, and when it does it will be for reasons unrelated to the permit: celebrities apply for a marriage license.

Permits may take on a public, political cast in one or both of two circumstances. One is expedience. Controversy, uncertainty, scientific data which are either inconclusive or premature, or a legislative compromise that left hard substantive choices undecided may result in the installation of a permit system. In such cases, what the legislature delegates is not the implementation of standards, but the continuation of the political process. This kind of delegation may be the indirect accrual of a series of statutes bearing inconsistent mandates, or it may be the direct and open intention of a particular statutory provision. The Multiple-Use Sustained-Yield Act, for instance, provides that the national forests "shall be administered for outdoor recreation, range, timber, watershed, and wildlife and fish purposes."[60] According to the statute, the stated interests are of equal weight, and all are to be satisfied. The legislature has refused to make a choice, and there is no standard to implement. Congress delegated the responsibility for politics, providing for the political process to be played out in the agency as specific steps are taken.

The other circumstance which makes permits more than technical devices is a politically charged atmosphere. Permits which would be, in isolation, merely technical may be caught up in the political dynamics of their surroundings. Administrative agencies have changed character in recent years. In part that change has brought to the agencies a certain amount of ventilation, what Pope John XXIII called *aggiornamento*. Agencies are often required to hold hearings before making decisions, to disclose much of the information they hold, to carry out an increasing number of legislative-like tasks, and to justify in court what they have done.

The effect of these changes has been disputed.[61] Joseph Sax thinks that the reforms amount to "about nine parts myth and one part coconut oil."[62] I think he is right only to the extent that all politics is a concoction of myth and coconut oil. In any event, where there previously existed only bureaus of technical expertise, there are now technocratic bureaus plus political forums. The agencies' permitting activities have been drawn into the political arena.

I have said that permits acquire a political cast as a consequence of either legislative expedience or context. Permits for offshore activities are political as a consequence of both.

To take the second circumstance first, the agencies in charge of outer-continental-shelf activity have experienced *aggiornamento*. Many offshore permits serve nonpolitical purposes in the first and narrow instance. Tract leases are a form of permit designed to limit entry and raise revenue. Permits for drilling (issued by the Geological Survey), for erecting offshore structures (Corps of Engineers), for installing navigation aids (Coast Guard), and for discharging pollutants into the water (Environmental Protection Agency) all implement technical standards. Notwithstanding the immediate purposes of these permits, they become political instruments because of the political nature of continental-shelf regulation. So, for example, issuance of the wastewater-discharge permits for operation in the Georges Bank provided a focus for a political struggle.[63] (I shall return to the Georges Bank litigation later.)

Although some technical permits become political by virtue of their general context, other offshore permits have been made political by Congress. Hovering above the outer continental shelf is a mélange of statutes containing a vast array of options, often overlapping or contradictory. Taken as a whole, the statutes are a statement of possibilities rather than a prescription of determinate standards. If most alternatives are possible, choices among them at the agency level will be versions of legislative, political choice. The political process is turned over to the agencies. In addition to this indirect delegation resulting from statutory multiplicity, there are legislative acts specifically calling for some active, political exercise. Title III of the Marine Protection, Research and Sanctuaries Act[64] is an example. Its marine-sanctuaries program involves the states and encourages the public to play an active role. It also calls for sanctuary management accommodating conservational, recreational, ecological, and esthetic values. Like the Multiple-Use Sustained-Yield Act, it offers a broad range of choices inviting political resolution.[65]

The permit system opens the management of offshore areas to the public. Madisonian federalism requires more. Madisonian federalism requires not only the spirit and form of popular government but also the assurance of protection for the powerless.

There is some built-in protection for minorities in that power is divided among permit-issuing agencies with diverse constituencies.[66] Some protection also derives from the permit system's preference for consensus so that individuals and minorities can exercise a bit of a veto over agency action by bringing the "squawk factor" into play.[67] William Rodgers notes that the squawk factor has figured in enhancement of Indian fishing opportunities, modification of whaling policies, revision of strip-mining legislation, and prohibition of DDT.[68]

The powerless also gain some leverage in agency deliberations from the possibility of judicial review. According to the "hard look" doctrine, courts take a hard look at challenged agency action to ensure that the agencies have taken a hard look at alternatives.[69] One of the judges who played a prominent role in development of the "hard look" said that courts and agencies "together constitute a partnership in furtherance of the public interest, and are 'collaborative instrumentalities of justice.'"[70] I think that is saying a great deal too much. But when the courts have been willing to grant it, close scrutiny of agency processes has made them more transparent and amplified the squawk factor.

In the course of such review, the courts as well as the agencies have changed. Starting with *Brown v. Board of Education*[71] and other school desegregation cases, the courts have been drawn ever more deeply into agency activities. The structural remedies granted in response to public-interest litigation require long-term judicial oversight and involvement.[72] There is no terminal point. One purpose of such litigation is exactly to prevent termination and to keep the process open and moving.

Litigation in support of public participation and minorities has led to continued judicial supervision of school boards, hospitals, prisons, and universities. The cases invoking such ongoing, structural remedies have been argued as precedents for judicial oversight of oil and gas leasing. In one case, plaintiffs urged the court "to place the Secretary of the Interior in virtual receivership to make certain that he does not subordinate the interests of the fisheries to the interests of those seeking to tap underseas oil and gas deposits."[73] So far the argument has been rejected: "The Secretary cannot be likened to a municipality bent on violating the civil rights of citizens."[74] The civil-rights-receivership analogy has not provided a winning argument, but it is instructive and may have helped to achieve the oversight of offshore activity that has been granted and that has provided some protection to the powerless.[75]

c

There was no evidence of Madisonian federalism in the old system of leasing. Some evidence of law serving as a medium of federalism can be discerned in the new method, and permits are the place to look for it. Oilmen view government permits as an unnecessary evil; I view them as a possible instrument of the people. At least insofar as they give both the majority and the powerless a voice in the government of marine affairs, they indicate how law might be a medium of federalism. Permits aid in shaping and giving access to effective political discourse. Their potential is both confirmed and denied by their recent history, as the following instances illustrate.

Baltimore Canyon and the National Environmental Policy Act
    After the 1973 Arab oil embargo, President Nixon announced "Project Independence," a program whose key element was accelerated petroleum development on the continental shelf.[76] For years, oil companies had been drilling off the coasts of Louisiana and California with little or no public opposition. Then the rigs moved north on both the Atlantic and Pacific coasts.
    The subsequent story is briefly this: Initially, accelerated offshore-oil exploration led to great expectations. But then opposition to drilling resulted in some partially successful law suits. The absence of any major strikes in the new fields and the downward revision of expectations for offshore reserves had more effect than the litigation in slowing the seaward oil rush. Secretary of the Interior James Watt nevertheless made his proposals for an even greater acceleration of leasing. Many more suits and congressional protests followed. After the departure of Secretary Watt, the pace slowed a little, the grand design was somewhat scaled down, and tracts of the shelf that were the focus of particular concern were removed from the leasing program. Most of the shelf bearing promise of oil reserves will be put up in phases for lease. If the past is any guide, the explosion of litigation ignited by Secretary Watt's grandiose plans will continue, if at a less frantic tempo.
    I shall focus on one theme in the larger and still-continuing story: permits served the emergence of the spirit and fact of federalism. In this sense law did serve as a medium for a communal, political reality.

The United States Law of the Sea

I make no exaggerated claim for the role thus performed by law. Indeed, it may be plainly visible only to those with eyes to see it. I do claim that the permit gives some evidence of what law as medium might in fact mean.

The first major challenge to offshore drilling arose from a lease sale of tracts in the Baltimore Canyon off the coasts of New Jersey and Delaware. In 1977 a New York federal district court enjoined the sale.[77] After several more judicial opinions, the sale was allowed to proceed.[78] Exploratory drilling has resulted in insignificant finds of oil and gas.[79] Additional sites have been leased.[80]

Although the injunction provided only a temporary reprieve to lease opponents, its grounding in the National Environmental Policy Act is worth noting. The Baltimore Canyon sale was enjoined because the Act required an environmental impact statement, and the one filed by the Department of the Interior was legally insufficient.

The National Environmental Policy Act has been used by states and by citizens for impressing their concerns upon federal agencies.[81] The Act requires federal agencies to take environmental consequences into account in their planning and decision making. It specifically requires that federal agency proposals for actions significantly affecting the human environment be accompanied by an environmental impact statement.[82] States and interested citizens may participate in the preparation of these statements and may challenge them as inadequate after completion. Beginning with the Baltimore Canyon case—and in some later instances with much greater success—such challenges have been a major avenue for state and citizen influence upon federal activities beyond the territorial sea. Legal attacks premised upon a failure to comply with the Act have resulted in the delay or halt of numerous continental-shelf lease sales.[83] One commentator has correctly observed that federal agencies proposing outer-continental-shelf actions will eventually succeed in completing adequate impact statements which allow the project to go forward, but the continental-shelf "issue is intensely political, and the chief effect of [the National Environmental Policy Act] may be to give opponents time to build political opposition to block the leasing."[84]

An environmental impact statement is a type of permit required of the permitting agency. It certifies that the agency has evaluated its proposal in light of environmental consequences,[85] and to that extent it is a technical permit. But it is also and more interestingly a political device. It opens agency decisions to political refraction.[86] And, together with the delay which may be provided by judicial review, it provides an opening for the gathering of political forces. Now this is admittedly a long way from realization of the kind of political community that Madison's federalism represents. But it is much closer than the former cozy system involving only oilmen and the Secretary of the Interior, and law is its medium in the form of the environmental impact statement together with judicial review.

Georges Bank and the Outer Continental Shelf Lands Act

Subsequent to the Baltimore Canyon episode, a more recent and controversial Atlantic drilling took place off the coast of Massachusetts on the continental-shelf area known as the Georges Bank, one of the world's largest and most productive fishing grounds.[87] An initial estimate placed fossil-fuel potential for the area at 3.8 billion barrels of oil.[88] The most recent estimate shows only $\frac{1}{31}$ as much.[89]

Oil spills on Georges Bank are a dramatic threat to the fishery. The area potentially affected is considerable: 113 square miles of fishing ground could be displaced by drilling, and 466 square miles could be disrupted if unburied pipelines are laid down.[90] Within this area there is risk of a spill caused by storm or earthquake, and a large spill attributable to human error is statistically a near certainty.[91] Spills are not the only environmental danger.[92] Drilling muds and cuttings will be discharged into the ocean; environmentally disruptive onshore facilities will be built; and an "iron bottom" that could slice and tear fishing nets may form from discarded drill bits, cables, and pipes.

The State of Massachusetts, fishermen, and enviromentalists opposed the introduction of drilling on the Georges Bank. After three years of litigation, exploratory drilling began. Some fishermen believed that they had lost everything except the continuing hope that little or no oil would be discovered. According to one of them, all they were able to wrest from the oil companies was the showing of "movies of colorful fish caught around the oil rigs in the Gulf of Mexico."[93]

However, the limited exploratory drilling undertaken so far has been conducted under the terms of a court-sanctioned settlement. Twenty-two oil companies thought the settlement exacted enough from them to warrant bringing a judicial challenge to defeat it.[94] An oil-industry spokesman said that the settlement "will certainly provide [environmental groups] with more opportunities for litigating the approval of exploration, development and production plans."[95] The environmentalists viewed the settlement as "the first round in an extended series of efforts to force adequate protection" of the Georges Bank fisheries.[96]

The fact that drillings proceeded could be interpreted as a simple clear defeat for the minor parties—the fishermen and environmentalists. And there would be little comfort for them in the court-expressed "hope that the Department of the Interior is not moving faster than technology safely allows."[97]

On the other hand, they have been granted a continuing role as drilling proceeds. Under the terms of the settlement, plaintiffs were to be sharers in the information acquired by the government, and they were given access to and some power in decision making about controls.[98]

In addition, the 1978 amendments to the Outer Continental Shelf Lands Act also now apply to Georges Bank as to all offshore drilling.[99] One of the stated purposes of the amendments is to "assure that States, and through States, local governments, which are directly affected by [offshore activities] are provided an opportunity to participate in policy and planning decisions relating to management of the resources of the Outer Continental Shelf."[100] The amendments identify stages of oil and gas activities that cannot proceed without permits. The permits are occasions for participation and for invocation of judicial review.[101] To begin with, the amendments require the Secretary of the Interior to draw comprehensive, five-year leasing plans.[102] These plans serve as a type of permit required before the secretary can proceed, and they require consultation with representatives of coastal-state and local governments. Next come lease sales, and when they are proposed there must again be coordination with state and local officials. In the next phase, exploration carried out pursuant to any lease may not begin until an exploration plan has been submitted and approved with state concurrence.[103] After exploration, the next stage of development and production may not go forward until a second plan has been submitted by the developers and approved by the affected states.[104] In addition, the amendments note that the major steps from five-year plan to development and production may require environmental impact statements which also involve the public.[105]

And there is the further possibility of judicial review enhanced by the amendments. In commenting upon the revised Outer Continental Shelf Lands Act, one court noted that the Secretary of the Interior retains full supervisory power over leases in that he can disapprove or modify exploration and development plans and can suspend or cancel leases if environmental damage warrants. The court then went on to observe that "Congress provided the judiciary with jurisdictional competence corresponding to this ongoing power of the Secretary," so that the "pattern of comprehensive Secretarial approval and judicial review holds" for the lifetime of a project.[106]

Like the settlement, the 1978 amendments, together with the National Environmental Policy Act and judicial review, draws offshore-oil development into an elongated, open process. The process is shaped by permits which provide political checks and vents at critical stages. The supervisory role of the courts adds some weight to the influence of the public participants, especially the minor parties.

California and the Coastal Zone Management Act

Outer-continental-shelf oil and gas leasing issues on the West Coast during the past several years have developed in a manner similar to those on the East Coast. California's waters were the scene of the country's first offshore production and the first major offshore catastrophe, the Santa Barbara blowout in 1969. More recently, objections by Californians, litigation, and congressional intervention have led to withdrawal of several environmentally sensitive offshore tracts from leasing plans.[107]

One of the means by which Californians have gained some voice in what happens off their shore—in addition to the National Environmental Policy Act and the Outer Continental Shelf Lands Act—is the Coastal Zone Management Act. The express purpose of this act is to encourage states to protect their coastal resources.[108] To this end, the Act employs two inducements. One is economic assistance.[109] The other, the one of present moment, is the "consistency" provision, a kind of permitting power. The consistency provision mandates that federally conducted or supported activities on the continental shelf must be carried out "in a manner which is, to the maximum extent practicable, consistent with approved state management programs."[110] That is, a veto can be exercised by the states over continental-shelf activities. It may be objected that the consistency provision, like the requirement of an environmental impact statement, "allows the States to block plans in the courts instead of joining in the original development of plans in the Federal agencies."[111]

Whether the real value of the consistency provision has been lowered by the Supreme Court is uncertain. The Act provides that consistency with state plans is necessary only when the continental-shelf activity "directly affects" the coastal zone. The Court held that the lease sale of tracts (as compared with actual drilling) in the Pacific off California did not affect the state's coastal zone.[112] The effect of the decision is to promote unilateral decision making by an agency and to shut off an opportunity for the very kind of national-state-citizen dialogue that is an expression of our federalism.[113] Moves were made in Congress to reverse the Court's interpretation and to reopen lease sales to the consistency provision, but no action has yet been taken.

In any event and to the extent of its remaining coverage, the consistency provision is a kind of permitting device that does have some effect in drawing out the process of leasing and bringing it into the open.

Puerto Rico and the Clean Water Act

Fossil-fuel extraction and fishing are not all that is happening offshore. I interrupt my review of oil and gas leasing for brief notice of naval maneuvers and the Water Act.

In the earliest days of the republic, the navy was described in terms which made it an emblem of the federalism I have been talking about. One of Alexander Hamilton's appeals for the adoption of the Constitution was the prospect it gave for a navy. He depicted the formation of a navy in terms reminiscent of Grotius, who envisioned human fellowship achieved by means of the sea in a divine economy where needs and resources are dispersed. According to Hamilton, "different portions of confederated America possess each some peculiar advantage" for creation of a navy:

> The more Southern states furnish in greater abundance certain kinds of naval stores—tar, pitch and turpentine. Their wood for the construction of ships is also of more solid and lasting texture. . . . Some of the Southern and the middle States yield a greater plenty of iron and of better quality. Seamen must chiefly be drawn from the northern hive.[114]

The early promise of the navy as exercise in federalism has given way to the reality of a navy which is a monolithic national military bureaucracy. Its affairs seem more remote from citizen representation than the old system of outer-continental-shelf oil and gas leasing. However, the federalizing politics of the permit system have been brought to bear even upon the navy, as a recent incident off the coast of Puerto Rico illustrates.

The navy owns some 26,000 of the 33,000 acres of the island of Vieques, located in the Commonwealth of Puerto Rico, six miles southeast of the main island.[115] Puerto Ricans make use of the island's agricultural and fishing resources. The navy uses it for training exercises, amphibious landings, and target practice. In 1979, the Governor of Puerto Rico, the Mayor of Vieques, and some fishermen brought suit to enjoin the navy from continuing its maneuvers. They were momentarily successful. The navy lacked the necessary permits.

The plaintiffs were, said the court, "[a]rmed with a battery of federal and state laws."[116] They discharged pleas alleging the violation of eleven federal statutes, two executive orders, and three Puerto Rican laws. The court found violations of three federal statutes, all requiring permits not procured by the navy.[117]

First, the navy had not fulfilled the requirements of the Endangered Species Act.[118] Although its Vieques maneuvers possibly affected five threatened and endangered species, the navy failed to secure from the U.S. Fish and Wildlife Service of the National Marine Fisheries Service the requisite "Biological opinion" explaining the impact of its operations on the listed species. It "side-stepped the administrative process" by failing to secure a permit.[119]

Second, the navy had failed to compile an environmental impact statement. Because this deficiency was cured between trial and appeal, the First Circuit Court of Appeals found the impact statement issue to be moot. The court noted, however, that its conclusion "pertains only to the preparation and filing of an [Environmental Impact Statement], it does not foreclose the Commonwealth from challenging the adequacy of the [statement] or the Navy's response to the [statement's] findings."[120]

Third, the navy's weapons training came within the ambit of the Federal Water Pollution Control Act.[121] This Act prohibits discharges of pollutants into the waters of the United States, including the territorial sea, except as allowed by permit.[122] Public hearings can be made part of the issuance of such permits. Navy training at Vieques sometimes resulted in the discharge of artillery and ammunition into coastal waters. Under the Water Act, such action is a discharge of pollutants and requires a permit. The navy had none.

According to the Court of Appeals, although the trial court had found "that the Navy's dropping of ordnance caused no significant harm to the environment, it erred in failing to consider the judiciary's 'responsibility to protect the integrity of the . . . process mandated by Congress. . . .'"[123] The navy had to stop until it obtained the permit. On appeal, the Supreme Court held that an injunction was not mandatory; lower courts had discretion in deciding whether to enjoin the navy before it complied with the Water Act.[124] The issue is not of minor importance. If a court refuses to enjoin an agency's violation of a statute, it does so in derogation of congressional power and by so limiting a statute limits what citizens can do in the face of overwhelming bureaucracies. The equitable power and responsibility of the courts are then forfeited as a means for federalizing agency processes.[125]

The residents of Vieques did not stop navy operations on their island forever. But they did win a temporary reprieve because of the navy's lack of permits. When the navy seeks permits, it will have to open its process a little to interagency and judicial review, public comment, and citizen participation.

Alaska and the People of the North

Offshore activities, whether military maneuvers or economic exploitation, have their greatest immediate potential for disaster in the waters around Alaska, the site for the severest test of law as a medium of federalism. Failure could issue in the destruction of a people, one of those wrongs that is qualitatively set apart, like a crime against humanity.

When the rigs moved north from California to Alaska, they brought drilling to areas where ecosystems are more fragile and the rights of those whose lives and culture depend upon them are more precarious.

In explaining the details of his Project Independence, President Nixon announced that the Gulf of Alaska would not be leased until the Council on Environmental Quality had completed an environmental study of the possible effects of drilling.[126] The study, released in April 1974, concluded that the eastern gulf posed the highest level of environmental risk among all areas on the outer continental shelf.[127] The gulf is the nation's largest marine-mammal habitat, the most important bird habitat in the world, and a major fishing ground. Its shores are pristine wilderness areas. It is susceptible to earthquakes and frequent, severe storms.[128] In spite of these characteristics, the Department of the Interior offered for bid over one million acres of the gulf shelf in April 1976. In a suit based on the National Environmental Policy Act, Alaska sought unsuccessfully to have the sale set aside.[129]

Drilling has gone forward there and elsewhere around Alaska. One of the subsequent lease sales, for tracts in the Beaufort Sea, was scheduled for December 1979. The Secretary was enjoined from accepting bids in January 1980, but the injunction was lifted in the summer of 1980, and the leases were executed.[130]

The Beaufort Sea, the near-shore portion of the Arctic Ocean, is close to the Prudhoe Bay oil field and the northern terminus of the

Trans-Alaska Pipeline.[131] The environment of the Beaufort Sea is even more fragile than that of the Gulf of Alaska. It serves as the habitat for many wildlife species, including the endangered bowhead and gray whales.[132] The bowhead is in extreme jeopardy of extinction. The Beaufort Sea area is also home to the Inupiat, a people whose life and culture are totally dependent upon subsistence hunting, especially the taking of a now-restricted number of bowheads.

Subsistence whaling by Eskimos was the subject of a special 1979 meeting of experts who concluded that no whales should be hunted if the bowhead stock was to have the best prospects for recovery. They also stressed, however, that whaling is "the most important single element in the culture and society of north Alaska whale hunting communities."[133] The bowhead population is estimated to have been approximately 18,000 before commercial whaling began in 1851. In 1979, the population estimate was down to 2,300 and is expected to decline further into the next century even if none are taken.[134] The International Whaling Commission set a three-year block quota of 45 bowheads for the Inupiat, with no more than 17 to be taken in any one year.[135]

The effects of oil and gas development on whales are impossible to assess, according to the environmental impact statement prepared for the Beaufort Sea lease sale.[136] It reported that developmental activity may remove the animals hunted by the Inupiat: ships may displace whales while land and air activity may displace birds.

The study then turned to cultural impact. It listed as likely occurrences the increase of westernization, reduction in subsistence food gathering, and decline in Inupiat health. It then drew conclusions in language that makes it hard to read the mind of the person behind the words. Is this only the cold style of a disengaged bureaucrat, or is it a distress signal about impending human catastrophe sent in bureaucratic code: "[a] decline in health resulting in death is definitely irretrievable. Further declines in Inupiat lifestyle, values, culture, and culture-related activities may be irreversible. They are definitely irreversible and irretrievable if continued past the collective memory of those activities."[137] In plain terms, even before the possibility of a spill arises, Beaufort Sea fossil-fuel development may destroy a people as well as a species of whale.[138]

In allowing the lease sale and preliminary activities to proceed in the Beaufort Sea, the Circuit Court for the District of Columbia emphasized repeatedly the tentative nature of the actions that the court and the Department of the Interior were authorizing: "Drilling may still be at least two years away and will remain subject both to routine and extraordinary administrative and judicial review. . . . [T]he lease sale itself is only a preliminary . . . stage."[139]

There has been some preexploration action, including platform construction to determine if rigs can withstand ice, but "a lessee may not drill an oil well until an exploration plan has been approved and application for a permit to drill has also been approved for the proposed site."[140] The process continues and, because of the permit system, continues to be open to representatives of the Inupiat.[141]

I wonder how efficacious this representation can be. For one thing, capital investment and momentum carry operations like oil and gas development beyond a point of no return. For another, even before that point is reached there is always the great obstacle of some balancing test or other. In this case, the court said that neither the Inupiat nor their environment is "an overriding veto staying the Secretary's hand. . . ."[142] It believed that the Secretary is required to effect a balance between the public and social interests involved. Underlying the tension of such a balance, the court found "the irony that has the same group of plaintiffs urging the preservation of endangered whales so that Eskimos may subsist on those same endangered whales."[143]

The court's sense of irony is confused. The real irony is "innocence savaged and destroyed,"[144] now legitimated by the court. The Inupiat's bowhead were driven to extinction by the technology of a fishing industry alien to them; they may now be destroyed by the appetite for fuel of another alien industry's technology.

If the viability of an indigenous people is to be balanced against the existence of the oil industry and American demand for oil, the people will not win. Do not the Inupiat and their culture have a right to survive? And is this right not a veto or trump?[145] For federalism to have meaning and to survive, it cannot consign any powerless minority's survival to a balancing test. As Madison said, "in a society under the forms of which the stronger faction can readily unite and oppress the weaker, anarchy may as truly be said to reign, as in a state of nature where the weaker individual is not secured against the violence of the stronger."[146]

III

Modern international law of the sea was inaugurated by the Grotian concept of a society of nations enhanced by fellowship in diversity, with the sea and law of the sea serving as its medium.

Although the sea and the legal regime for it have tended in the meantime to promote national exploitation, a sea-forged bond of human fellowship still asserts itself. We find international deference to the freedom of the high seas beyond national jurisdiction, to the deep seabed as the common heritage of mankind, and to the practice of consensus of the Third United Nations Conference on the Law of the Sea.

Domestically we have looked upon the sea primarily as a source of wealth, and law has been employed to aid in this exploitation and apportionment. Law has been used to exclude foreign competition, to parcel out jurisdiction within coastal waters, and to protect franchises on the shelf. The tidiness of this division of dominion and the seeming efficiency of exclusion are misleading. They mask confusion.

I think there is an alternate to this apparatus and practice of law as bulwark. Our marine territory may serve as an occasion for federalism with law as its medium. Madison discovered in "a judicious modification and mixture of the federal principle"[147] the future of "a government which will protect all parties, the weaker as well as the more powerful."[148] He envisioned a political community preventing majority as well as minority tyranny and celebrating a "communion of interests and sympathy of sentiments."[149] I have suggested that the permit system is an indication that law may be a medium of this political community.

I do not mean that Madisonian federalism has been achieved through the permit system. The realization of federalism in the permit system is predicated upon challenges to agencies and invocation of judicial review. There are dangers and deficiencies. Citizen participants are dependent upon legal counsel—hired rather than elected representation—without the communal ties that form the matrix of representation in Madison's conception. And there is missing a distribution of wealth and opportunity in our society that would enable all concerned citizens to be equal participants. Also, engagement with agencies may well be an assault on the Tar Baby and constitute the sapping of political energy best applied elsewhere. For those mired in bureaus and bureaucratic processes, the politics of an authentically human community may appear exceedingly remote.

All of these things can be said along with many more elaborate counterarguments. Nevertheless I think permits as I have portrayed them do indicate how an experiment in federalism might emerge through law.

Active citizens, legislation, agency practice, and judicial review have turned permits into events of representation, stages along the way of a political enterprise. The formerly closed leasing system has been opened to public scrutiny and participation. And activities on the shelf are not the result of a one-time, once-for-all decision. We have seen decision making drawn into a serial whose installments are marked by permits. Government of marine and coastal affairs has become a rolling judgment containing secretarial approval, state- and local-government consultation, judicial review, and citizen opinion. Because the system is not self-executing, the citizenry, including minorities, may participate in and influence the course of the process. From exploration plans and environmental impact statements to drilling and rig-construction licenses, permits make for verification and political legitimation. They provide citizens with forums and entry to agencies and courts. They serve a reality in which arguments count. Arguments have to be answered and made, and the language of genuine public discourse helps to determine governmental deeds.

The missing ingredients—such as protection of people like the Inupiat—can be supplied only by an appropriate context for Madisonian permits. That will be the subject of the last chapter.

5 STATE LAW

Rigidity and permanence have been worked out of the shoreline. Nature abhors a hard edge. The coast is far less an edge than an interdependent procession of sea, beach, island, estuary, grassland, and forest. The whole is dynamic and rich in life. It is also itinerant. It rolls some each day, stirred by wind, waves, and tide. When assaulted by storm, it relocates violently overnight. Over time, the rise and fall of sea level has sent the shore steadily, massively advancing and retreating.

Georgia prides itself on being the largest state east of the Mississippi River. The state's dry land mass has been larger. In an earlier epoch it reached farther seaward. There are archeological sites, now submerged, where prehistoric humans shucked oysters by a seaside that presently lies under water 16 miles at sea. But the dry-land area has also been smaller, much smaller. Computer-enhanced satellite photographs reveal clearly a fall line cutting diagonally across the state. The fall line is the limit of the landward march of the coastline and shows that more than half the state was inundated. My youngest daughter has dug petrified sharks' teeth out of clay from an ancient sea-washed beach near Macon, now 170 miles inland. The road through the southeast Georgia plain toward today's coast unexpectedly drops down a gentle ridge lying across the otherwise flat, even soybean and pine country. Long ago that raised landform was a coastal island. It gives you a sense of the sea's former presence and the shore's wandering.

The United States has over 100,000 miles of coast, all of it migratory.[1] At our geological moment, the sea is rising—14 inches at Charleston, S.C., in fifty years—so the coast is moving inland again.[2] The gradual, natural compression from without comes at a time of centrifugal demographic pressure from within. Population expansion is greatest at the edges. The nation's seven largest cities lie in the coastal zone (counting the shores of the Great Lakes). Estimates indicate that 80 percent of the population will live within 50 miles of the coast by the year 2000.[3] Barrier islands are being urbanized at a rate twice that of the mainland.[4] Coastal urbanization is a severe test of environmental as well as spatial capacities—the developmental load that the ecosystem can tolerate, pollution levels, potable water, refuse disposal, wildlife, and aesthetics.

With the sea moving inland and urbanization pressing outward, stability along the coast is sought in law. The law purports to lay down boundaries, the most obvious of which is the shoreline. Here we encounter a coincidence of legal and natural boundaries. It is the first we have seen except for the outer limit of the continental shelf where the slope falls to the abyssal plain and national jurisdiction ends.[5] The coastline divides land from sea and private from public ownership. From the free high seas and common deep seabed, to the nationally divided 200-mile zones, to the territorial sea partitioned among the coastal states—all forms of public control—we now cross the shore to real estate.

As will become evident in what follows, I do not think that this boundary is more certain or unambiguous than any other boundary we have seen. I also do not think that in crossing it we arrive at some qualitatively different legal reality. Therefore, although ownership, division, land as partitionable commodity—the law as bulwark—are very much in evidence, I shall propose that here also are to be discerned possibilities for giving specific, operable content to law as medium.

First let me describe the system as it predominantly is. Its very technicality—and I shall only skim the surface—is itself instructive. It gives a sense of the backing and filling required to make artificial rules appear determinate, necessary, and applicable to the stuff of life. Stay with me long enough, and I shall try to convince you of the impossibility of law as bulwark on the coast and of the possibility for the alternate, law as medium.

Boundaries

STATE OWNERSHIP

State ownership of the territorial sea was discussed in the preceding chapter, and there is little to add to the subject, save for the public-trust doctrine which must be reserved for discussion until later. You will remember that the state's ownership of the sea to the 3-mile limit is subject to a variety of overriding federal interests. You will also remember that the relation between state and federal governments in that area is one of contention lacking clarity. One thing is clear: in the territorial sea as elsewhere, state law ordinarily has more bearing upon the life of the citizen than does federal law. State law tends more to the daily: matters of fishing, port business, and crime. Doctrine, regulation, and interest can vary markedly from one state to another. Virginia has the Chesapeake Bay; Alaska, the king-crab fishery; California and Florida, water-related recreation industries. Each has a different legal history, a different body of common and statutory law, and a different way of going about regulation and enforcement.

Notwithstanding the legal diversity among coastal states, there remain certain similarities. Although the state agencies may have various names and mandates, given a limited number of possible techniques for managing territorial-sea affairs and with ample interstate contact among the concerned officials, there is a certain gravitational pull toward uniformity in state practice. Also, partly under the stimulation of the federal government—the Fishery Conservation Management Act and the Coastal Zone Management Act are examples— and partly because natural circumstances invite it, there are significant instances of multistate cooperation in the government of marine affairs. For example, the coastal states are joined in regional commissions to establish fishery regulations. And such area enterprises as the Port of New York are governed by interstate authority. Moreover it is to be borne in mind that state law in the territorial sea is overlaid by federal law. The more this federal priority is exercised through statutes, the greater is the impetus to uniformity. In the absence of statutes the Constitution as interpreted by the Supreme Court also militates against the balkanization of markets and resources: a state may not reserve its marine resources for its own citizens at the expense of the citizens of other states.[6]

All of this having been said, the states do have jurisdiction over the territorial seas, and there are boundaries between the waters of one state and those of its neighbors. And the coast is a boundary between the state-owned areas and those that are privately owned.

PRIVATE PROPERTY

On the landward side of the coastline boundary, the law provides boundaries between private owners. Land is made divisible real estate.

In feudal times land served as the focal point for the obligations of a hierarchical social structure.[7] The king reigned at the top of a pyramidal system that was at the same time a method of government and a method of holding property. The king, from whom all land was ultimately held, conferred estates upon his lords, and the lords upon their vassals, and those vassals upon subordinate vassals, and so on down. Each tenant held his property (his fee or feud) in exchange for service (military or ceremonial duty, food, prayers) rendered the lord above him in the feudal pyramid.

In postfeudal times, land was the source less of political obligation than of family income. It became more a private matter and was the productive means of family support and cohesion.

American land was not tied up in either feudal holdings or postfeudal family estates in the strict sense. When the settlers came, they brought with them property law that bore traces of its ancient European history. Some traces are still evident. But the baggage with the greatest impact on land was the European style of living in an ecosystem. Its primary characteristic was bounded land and the fence.

In Native American practice, land had been managed, but not in the European manner. The indigenous peoples had a different relationship to their environment.[8] The Indian harvest of foodstuffs was the result of practices like selective burning which made the forest a productive habitat for favored wildlife species. Indians hunted, lived communally, and moved with the seasons. They sought "maximum abundance through minimal work" with the least impact on the land.[9]

The arrivals from Europe favored permanent settlements and fixed features on the landscape. Their agricultural practices divided uses of the land and called for raising crops and domestic animals together. Fences were necessary to keep the animals out of the crops. Fences "marked off, not only the map of a settlement's property rights but its economic activities and ecological relationships as well."[10] The landscape was radically altered. Indian country became bounded fields.

The newcomers, with their notions of fixity, did not perceive Indian mobility as a valid way to live with the land. Their perceptions reinforced the ideology of conquest. Because Indians did not practice European-style fixity, they were perceived to be backward, lazy, and wasteful. Their unbounded land was declared to be open for the taking. It could be expropriated by those willing to divide and develop it.[11] To the colonists, the fence was

> the most visible symbol of an "improved" landscape: when John Winthrop had denied that Indians possessed anything more than a "natural" right to property in New England, he had done so by arguing that "they inclose no Land" and had no "tame cattle to improve the land by." Fences and livestock were thus

pivotal elements in the English rationale for taking Indian lands.[12]

Rock walls were an import from Europe, the symbol of a life-style, a reinforcement of conquest ideology, and so a realization of bulwark thought and practice.

Bounded land and fences came to have an added and eventually dominant connotation: they describe a commodity. In doing so they perform as bulwark apparatus in an additional, more modern way. Early New England towns decided which agricultural activities would take place on which parcels in their territory.[13] Later the divisions and uses of land were determined by the market. When this happened, a piece of land's profitability to a speculator was more decisive than its ecological characteristics or agricultural suitability. The land of New England became an article of commerce.

The land west of the original thirteen states had a different history, but it too was expropriated from the Indians and turned into goods. The Western Territory was surveyed into squares and transferred into private hands. The fences and forts moved west, and land speculation followed. Even that Western land which remained public was generally rendered into commodities through extraction and marketing of the underlying minerals, timber sales, and leases of grazing ranges.[14]

Throughout the United States land is a commodity. Boundaries and fences now figure not so much in conquest as in ownership. The conceptual differences are not great. The bulwark is evident in the exhibition and defense of property holdings.

Property lines can be walked, staked out, and built upon. In this respect they are unlike the marine boundaries effected by law. But like lines on water, they seldom bear any relationship to the contours and limits of the earth. For example, square townships and sections were simply superimposed upon the land of the Western Territory. They are a creation of the law. They secure the real-estate system, protect economic interests in land, and aid development primarily because they can be reduced to paper, the lines and symbols of the surveyor's map as well as the words of a deed and the recording system. The paper is the heart of the land-as-commodity system. The pieces of paper can be recorded and filed as well as handed over in a transaction. They are brought out to establish ownership.

Generally, property is equated with ownership. To have a property in a piece of land is to have a form of ownership. Property lines delineate and secure the thing possessed. All kinds of lines can be drawn creating goods where none had been seen to exist before. Horizontally, land can be partitioned into ever smaller parcels. Vertically, a multistory building can be sold by the unit (condominium); the air space above may acquire salability in the form of transferable development rights; and the minerals underneath can be sold separately. In addition to these horizontal and vertical divisions of space, there are divisions of time. Lawyers can render time, too, into piece goods: time sharing provides for ownership of a property for a certain period of the year. In a dimension beyond space and time, the law also provides for multiple simultaneous marketable interests in a piece of land—such things as leases, usufructs, easements, profits à prendre, and licenses.[15] Where before there was earth, property law's distinctions produce a wealth of commodities and protect the owner's interests in them.

All of these possibilities for lines of division and their multiplication are practiced with particular zeal on the coast. However, they are not peculiar to coastal-land law. The distinctive feature of coastal law is the disappearance of the subject matter, lost to tide, wave, and wind. The stakes can be high: undeveloped coastal land in Southampton, N.Y., already commanded $200,000 an acre some years ago;[16] beachfront homes in Georgia, valued in the 1970s at $200,000 to $500,000 each, face a slide into the sea.[17] Of the coastline hurricanes from 1900 to 1979, two caused damages in excess of $2 billion each, and two others topped $1 billion each.[18]

The ownership of shifting land is sorted out by rules for adjusting property lines—the rules of accretion, erosion, avulsion, and reliction.[19] Like so much else in property law these rules are descriptions of legal outcomes. They are not descriptions of natural phenomena. Accretion is the gradual accumulation of land as a result of the deposit of soil (alluvion) from the action of wind or water. Erosion is the gradual loss of soil. Avulsion is the sudden alteration of land by storm or flood. Reliction is the recession of the sea that uncovers formerly submerged land. The basic common-law rule is that legal boundaries move with the natural boundary where the change is gradual (accretion, erosion, reliction), but that legal boundaries remain unchanged where the alteration is sudden (avulsion). There is no clear natural point at which a change ceases to be gradual (accretion) and becomes fast enough to constitute avulsion.

The shoreline has on occasion moved inland, submerging whole parcels of subdivided land, and then retreated, slowly disgorging the parcels it had swallowed. Who owns what then? The courts have answered this question by interpreting the rules to deny a return of legal ownership to the original, antediluvian owner and to award an extension of his tract to the lucky owner of the land newly made riparian.[20]

TRANSBOUNDARY INTERESTS

The boundaries are not impervious according to the received view. In a variety of ways, interests are recognized and asserted across the lines. The lines are made to give a little in order to survive.

Between Private Parties

Owners of the coast, like all property owners, can grant uses of their land to others. These are the lesser property interests that I have already mentioned: leases, easements, and the like. And groups of owners may also voluntarily limit the uses they will make of their land by entering joint private covenants. Uses of land may be limited involuntarily where they interfere with the interests of others. This is the law of nuisance. At the base of nuisance law lies one of the oldest and most universal of rules: one may not so use his own as to do damage to that of another.[21] In all of these cases, the adjustments support the maintenance of private-property lines. The boundaries yield as they must.

Between Private and Public

Nor is the division between public and private absolute. Although the coast is the boundary where state ownership ends and private property begins, it is not an unbreachable barrier. It is no more determinate than the 3-mile limit between state and federal areas. Considerable intrusion is to be observed.

Private rights may extend into the public area. Subject to qualifications imposed by the public trust doctrine, which I shall discuss later in the chapter, the state can sell parcels of publicly owned tideland to private parties.[22] And without any purchase necessary, an upland owner can "wharve out" across the public shore.[23]

There is reciprocal penetration of private property by both federal and state governments. Private property can always be taken by the government so long as due process and just compensation are provided. Privately owned land on the coast is also subject to the federal "navigational servitude." Where this servitude is successfully invoked, land is taken by the federal government without compensation. For example, a federal harbor project below Cape Kennedy interrupted littoral drift. In consequence, landowners south of the project lost their beach to erosion. One of them lost four acres. He was denied compensation because the loss was attributable to the "navigational servitude."[24]

Governmental intrusion is not always so physically direct. More often it serves only to limit landowners' choices for development, as happens when Congress enacts environmental or navigational legislation.

The statutes that bear most heavily on coastal landowners' choices are the Rivers and Harbors Act of 1899[25] and the Federal Water Pollution Control Act.[26] These statutes prohibit certain activities on land—discharges of pollutants or dredging and filling—that may have negative consequences for the marine environment. For example, some Louisiana bayou land, subject to flooding, was cleared of timber. It was to be converted to soybean farming. The federal courts, interpreting the Water Act, halted the activity. They held it to be an unpermitted discharge of dredge-and-fill material in violation of federal law.[27]

Besides federal law, there are also state statutes and local ordinances that may curtail choices about how to use privately owned coast and wetland. State law provides for zoning and land-use regulation. Where state and local governments have used this power to protect their coasts—and increasingly they have—then landowners may be limited to "natural and indigenous" uses of their wetlands, i.e., no filling and no development are permitted.[28]

OWNERSHIP

The accepted qualifications upon the legal boundary system are viewed as exceptions to an apparently stable, necessary, even natural rule. According to appearances, there is a major division between public and private parcels on fast land. The system tries to accommodate pressure from the sea by redrawing beachfront lines. There are individual winners and losers; the system is kept intact. The system tries to respond to demographic pressure from within through two types of line manipulation. One is to draw more lines, i.e., subdivide: lots on the horizontal plane (two dimensions), condominium units vertically (three dimensions), periods of time sharing (four dimensions). The other is to allow or enforce a certain amount of reciprocity across lines (covenant, nuisance law, zoning). Where the government requires a property owner to meet certain standards and obligations, this control is viewed as an intrusion gradually and grudgingly accepted. Preserved is the belief that a system of property law is firmly in place. The boundary lines it provides allow us the claim, backed by law: "this is mine, not yours." The emphasis is upon "not yours."

Ownership is inherently exclusive and monopolistic. It does not admit of mutuality and common participation. Augustine observed that in a world where people are driven by acquisitiveness "what is longed for either suffices for none, or not for all."[29] So did Romulus slay Remus as Cain slew Abel: "for he who wished to have the glory of ruling would certainly rule less if his power were shared by a living consort. In order, therefore, that the whole glory might be enjoyed by one, his consort was removed; and by this crime the empire was made larger indeed, but inferior, while otherwise it would have been less, but better."[30]

The drive to possess the glories of property brooks no consorts. As Blackstone declared, the possession of property "is that sole and despotic dominion which one man claims and exercises over the external things of the world, in total exclusion of the right of any other individual in the universe."[31] Ownership is competitive. It can be satisfied only at the expense of others and has to be maintained over against them.

In its own way, the landscape of suburban America is an icon of Blackstonian property. Suburbs are haphazard patterns of "despotic dominion" lacking any coherent center like a church, town hall, or common. There are few points of contact or interchange. Instead there is retreat into the antisocial diversion of mini-estates with backyard recreation systems. For those who can afford them, there are security systems and security guards. Mostly what suburbanites have in common is individual ownership. Property-law lines separate the owners. Zoning-law lines separate the classes.

This is law as bulwark. In operation on the coast, it is not what it appears to be. It is a Potemkin's village. The real-estate system provides at least as much contradiction and incoherence as protection.

QUESTIONS ABOUT PRIVATE PROPERTY OWNERSHIP

Private?

The legal fiction of private ownership of coastal property conceals huge government subsidies.

The barrier islands on the Atlantic and Gulf coasts have become a matter of growing public concern.[32] With this concern has come awareness of the extent to which private property is supported by governmental action and public funds. The barrier islands are not the stage for playing out the drama of private initiative in which hardy souls venture forth to carve out patches of civilization from the wilderness by dint of their own labor, skill, and risk taking. The undramatic fact is prior, continuing, and substantial federal-government presence.

A 1982 government study reported that federal subsidies for development of the islands exceeded $25,000 per acre; "in terms of replacement costs, the estimated federal subsidies are more than $53,000 for each developed acre."[33]

Another study found that in three years the federal government had committed half a billion dollars to projects that encouraged barrier-island development.[34] This sum did not include amounts expended under federal flood insurance amd disaster relief. The National Flood Insurance Program covers more than $60 billion of policies nationally and pays out more than three dollars for every dollar collected in premiums.[35] Congress finally voted to prohibit issuance of such insurance for construction on remaining undeveloped islands after 1983.[36] Ironically, the Environmental Protection Agency has been the big spender on barrier islands; it accounts for more than half the funds expended.[37] Before an island is developed, there must be access (bridges and highways); then fresh water must be supplied and wastewater treated. Then loss must be prevented (erosion control) and compensated for when it occurs (insurance). From start to finish, one or another federal agency is actively, supportively involved. Developers do not argue that the federal government should stay out of the private sector; they argue that it should not withdraw.[38]

And there is indirect as well as direct federal help. For example, the Government Accounting Office has pointed out that an individual suffering a loss not covered by insurance may be out of pocket only 5 to 20 percent of the costs thanks to a combination of tax deductions and disaster assistance.[39] And then there are tax shelters, grants-in-aid from the Economic Development Administration, and the mortgage and loan insurance programs of the Department of Housing and Urban Development.

The coastal land development industry has depended upon the federal tax dollar. What kind of private ownership is that?

Best Interest?

Barrier Inconstancy

The urbanization of the islands—aided by law and by federal subsidy—may be elaborately self-destructive. If there is doubt that private coastal property is private, there is also doubt about its permanence. Instead of serving stability, as purportedly it does, the system encourages destabilization.

Barrier islands survive by moving with rather than by holding place against the energy of wind, wave, and tide.[40] The movement of the sand is that of migration. There is no net loss of sand naturally. With a rising sea, barrier islands make a strategic retreat. They roll over and roll up the continental slope. The whole island ecosystem migrates inland. Islands tend to move out from under buildings erected upon them.

Sea walls and other artificial shore protection and erosion-control devices—frequently built along property lines—are intended to defend owned property against the sea. They are engineered to save coastal property, but they actually accelerate and spread what they seek to stop. The natural movement of the island that allows it to survive is converted into erosion in which sand is lost.

Various rigid engineering structures have various negative effects.[41]

Seawalls run parallel to the shore replacing the dunes. They are destructive in several ways. They end the exchange of sand between the dunes and the beach. The beach can no longer maintain its shape and loses the slope that dissipates the energy of waves. The wave energy, instead of spreading out over the beach, is concentrated; the sand is mined and carried away by the longshore current. The beach disappears. The water eats away the foundation of the seawall, whose seeming impenetrability disguises imminent collapse and catastrophe.

Groins extend out at right angles to the shore. They interrupt the current and catch sand as it drifts by. Sand collects on the updrift side of the groin and erodes from the downdrift side. The beach is scalloped. It also loses sand. As the deflected drift moves out and around the end of the groin, sand is lost to the longshore current.

Beach nourishment is a nonstructural manipulation of the coast. It means pumping or shipping in sand and recreating or nourishing an eroded beach. A source of unpolluted sand is necessary. The imported sand also has to have a grain size to match the existing sand or it will be quickly lost again. The nourishment of 9.3 miles at Miami

Beach cost over $60 million for the first installment.[42] Once restored, a beach continues indefinitely to require periodic infusions. Nourishment never ends.

The negative effects of protective measures at one site may spread to others. "A good example can be found in Worcester County, Maryland, where efforts to stabilize the beach in front of Ocean City by jetty construction and beach nourishment during the last 20 years reduced the supply of sediment to the undeveloped beaches to the south. The result has been rapid erosion and landward displacement of the northern end of Assateague Island National Seashore."[43] These downdrift consequences teach another lesson: there is limited success in attempting to reserve patches of undeveloped natural shore out of a manipulated system.

Human Danger

Attempts to halt the movement of barrier islands are attempts to save privately owned real estate. Often the rigid engineering structures realize property lines or are built along their lines of projection into the sea. They are products of and are meant to shore up the system. The fact that they stimulate the erosion they seek to prevent leads to a more dreadful irony. Development of the islands, which offers the lure of the good life, may be a deadly ensnarement. As I have noted, barrier islands survive by strategic retreat—yielding, rolling over, and regrouping. The concrete and steel of seawalls, houses, and high-rises deceive when their rigidity promises stability.

There has been a low level of storm activity during the past two decades. Particularly uncharacteristic has been the lull of hurricanes along the Gulf and south Atlantic coasts. This period of storm inactivity has helped to produce developmental hyperactivity. Nearly 80 percent of the people now living in island communities have never experienced a hurricane.[44]

A storm in 1900 killed 6,000 people in the barrier-island city of Galveston, Texas, and as many as 2,000 in other coastal areas.[45] Developed barrier islands have been termed death traps, with escape to the mainland cut off by high waters.[46] Along the southwest coast of Florida, there are 60,000 new residents on barrier islands an average of four or five feet above sea level. Had Hurricane Donna followed its predicted path in 1960, the storm would have driven surges fifteen to twenty-five feet above sea level on those islands.[47] It is said that Florida and other areas "have built toward major hurricane disasters which could reach catastrophic dimensions."[48]

Privacy?

In addition to its destructive and endangering effects, the drive to own pieces of barrier islands produces one other irony: the diminishing privacy of private property.

Human dignity is sustained by a sense of place. However, ownership and division are not necessary for a sense of place and may even be inimical to it. Indians did not draw lines on the earth or value it by a gold standard.[49] One may revere and draw strength from the earth and never think to own it.

On the coast, as more lines have been drawn, and more real estate has been divided and sold, and the desire to own a differentiated piece of land has been encouraged, satisfaction of some basics has become increasingly qualified. Units are smaller, high-rises taller, numbers of people greater, environmental demands more serious, erosion is faster, and danger greater. And there is less privacy. It can be argued that privacy in ownership has been sacrificed to equality. The power of this argument is compromised by two factors. One has to do with the purpose of partition. The history of enclosure is surely not one of egalitarianism. The private possession of the bounty of nature has for centuries served class distinctions and class control:[50] With some island acreage selling at $1,000 a foot and with fishing and agricultural communities being displaced to make way for resorts, acquisition of a piece of coastal realty is a contemporary privilege of wealth and a sign of status rather than a token of egalitarianism.

The other factor compromising the egalitarian argument is the type of development. The issue is one of the character of uses and not simply of numbers of people. Joseph Sax has pointed out that ski-resort entrepreneurs in remote mountain areas stimulate a bundle of demands.[51] They want large numbers of people spending money in shops, bars, restaurants, and clubs, as well as on the slopes. It is unprofitable to offer only skiing at a skiing resort. The same stimulation of multiple demands and intensive consumption is evident in barrier-island development. Profit lies in volume and distraction.

It has been observed that Ocean City, Maryland, "is designed to lull city people on vacation into thinking they haven't gone far." It "prefers groups to individuals. It gets downright nervous with people who are not part of the nonstop, slowly moving current on the Boardwalk, people always heading south towards the arcades."[52] As is true also of Atlantic City and Miami Beach, the ocean at Ocean City is just another, incidental entertainment possibility. Ocean City, Atlantic City, and Miami Beach are extremes, but the same profit-making excitation of a bundle of demands is also to be found, for example, at the "planned community" of Hilton Head Island, South Carolina. In its early stages Hilton Head was held up as a model of thoughtful, environmentally sound development. But as a government study now reports: "The attitude of the current developers appears to be one of letting market demand rather than the environment determine the capacity. A result is that condominiums are being constructed, a new four lane highway and bridge are being built to accommodate the increasing populations, and—the wastewater treatment load is exceeding the capacity of the treatment plant, valuable shellfish beds are being polluted, and the important shellfish industry is threatened."[53] That same study concludes that "the character of most developments changes as tax dollars are consumed for more highways, more parking lots, more marinas, and more lodging facilities."[54] It adds that retail sales in four Florida counties increased more than 200 percent from 1967 to 1972.

The loss of privacy in the barrier islands is caused less by egalitarianism in an expanding population than by the desire to divide and own, by a land-development industry that stimulates and feeds the desire, and by the law that makes it all possible.

If equality of coastal access were the real end sought, then it could be better satisfied in a variety of ways other than those currently in force. For example, access could be restricted by assignment on a nondiscriminatory basis. Areas like Coney Island could be set aside for those who sought ease of access and crowds while other areas could be reserved for special or more limited use. Also, particular needs could be identified and separated, a diversity of choice could be made available, and uses could be given an order of priority, with those uses peculiarly suited to the coast given highest priority. There is no compelling reason to believe that casinos, conventions, boardwalks, highways, parking lots, "honky-tonk, amusements, that kind of stuff"[55] should be thought of as singularly coastal. There is no compelling ground to believe that they should have priority of appropriation of the scarce, fragile, and vanishing space of barrier islands. There is compelling ground for alloting high priority to scientists and artists who consume little or nothing of the islands and whose works are widely shared, thereby extending the satisfaction of the coast. Equality could be achieved given the will for it.

Fresh Possibilities: Law as Medium
in the Form of Public Trust

Nothing I have said is a categorical argument against private property. But substantial doubts about the private-property system are raised by the public subsidization of barrier-island development and by that development's self-destructive tendency to aid ecological destabilization, to invite catastrophe, and to compromise privacy.

From a purely ecological standpoint, private ownership can be reconciled with the environmental limits and migratory nature of barrier islands if they are owned whole. The possessor of an entire island could ride it as it rolled. Such migrating kingdoms for the very wealthy are exactly what the Golden Isles of Georgia were until the lure of developmental profit or the burden of property taxes overthrew them. Georgia has barrier islands now because of such ownership in the past.[56]

Another ecologically compatible but more popular exercise of private ownership would be the erection of small, low-cost structures on stilts. Their demise in an advancing sea would be assumed. They would be enjoyed while they lasted and not occupied in hurricane season. Such shelters would not accommodate a large, concentrated population, but this fact does not fully explain their general absence on the coast. They are not found where it would be obvious and possible to raise them. I suspect the real reason is that they do not satisfy the demands of permanence, possessiveness, ostentation, and profit. These latter demands are associated with a particular conception and practice of property—private property as ownership promoted and defended by law as bulwark.

Other conceptions and practices of property are possible. James Madison spoke of a "larger and juster meaning of property," an illustration of which is "opinions and the free communication of them."[57] Such property requires others and is valueless if its possession is sole and despotic. It is fulfilled in exchange. How are opinions formed and of what significance are they apart from sharing?

According to this alternative, property provides place for people rather than extension of personality, and space for freedom rather than reinforcement of hierarchy. It is not an object to be reduced to possession by individuals. I have already noted that human dignity is served by a sense of place and that ownership is unnecessary and even inimical to this sense. When the legal referents are not those associated with ownership, then property may be thought of in spatial/political terms. It is the place for the formation and exchange of opinion. In his later years, Thomas Jefferson repeatedly urged that counties be divided into wards. Wards would be the next governmental step up from the basic political unit of the farm, so that the republic as a whole would consist of republics from "the great national one down through all its subordinations, until it ends in the administration of every man's farm by himself."[58] Land would not be divided into the hedonic miniestates of suburbs with their civic apostasy. We would not have units of ownership but units of government, "elementary republics" or spaces within and from which citizens would be competent to participate in the "government of affairs."[59]

Property may be said to be space for persons and freedom.[60] On the Jeffersonian model, opinion begins on the farm, is exchanged in the ward, and is refined through graded, representative bodies. In contemporary terms, the house or apartment may be thought of as something other than a bedroom, pleasure garden, or fortress allowing its commander "to look any man in the eye and tell him to go to hell."[61] It may be said to be a place for gathering independence of thought to be shared and so invested in politics.

Within an alternative conception and practice of property, even boundaries and fences could have a positive, communal, if secondary, function.[62] Instead of marking the extent of ownership, they might be an opportunity for exchange—for bringing people together the way Christo's *Running Fence* did. But then, like Christo's *Running Fence*, they would have to be understood as temporary and for the purpose of drawing people together rather than dividing them.

Robert Frost's poem "Mending Wall"[63] contains a possibility for the drawing power of a fence. "Good fences make good neighbors," the unquestioning neighbor in the poem keeps repeating, the old conquest ideology dumbly asserting itself. Frost in the poem shows that it is bad fences that make good neighbors. It is when the rocks have rolled out of place that the fence brings the neighbors together. Each gathers up the rocks on his side, some "nearly balls" so that there is "just another kind of outdoor game, / One on a side." For Frost, mending wall is a neighborly exchange and therefore an end in itself. The exercise is not for him a means to something else, as though the wall had some other, independent reason for being, some walling in and walling out to do.

However, the neighbor, "Bringing a stone grasped firmly by the top / In each hand, like an old-stone savage armed," approaches the task from a different world; he is intent on being not a neighbor or being a neighbor only in spite of himself. "He moves in darkness, as it seems to me, / Not of woods only and the shade of trees." He is adamant, resisting the invitation to make the wall a neighborly mending connection. But, then, he and those New England fences have behind them an old history of division and conquest, and of property lines keeping individual owners apart. It is hard to be a neighbor in a world of despotic dominion. On the other hand, there are alternatives.

My present purpose will be served if I simply note that property may be dissociated from ownership, dominion, and exclusion. One of its functions may be to provide privacy, the privacy necessary to politics. But ownership is not at all necessary for privacy. Thoreau enjoyed property in the human, personal sense at Walden Pond where he was a temporary squatter. Privacy may be found at the coast on public barrier islands. In fact, privacy may be more freely available on public land. Privacy and intensity of delight in the coast, as contrasted to entertainment and intensity of consumption, are satisfied by wildlife refuges, sanctuaries, and state and national parks.

What is essential for privacy is not ownership but selection. Private property and its uses are determined by the market (more or less). Who determines the uses of public property? Privacy, richness of personal experience, and room for being human in are not coincident with private ownership and may be incidents of public property. But what will determine their location and availability? Who makes decisions about diverse uses, and how? Where is there to be the possibility for solitude and where for masses of people? When is a setting to be preserved and when developed? Which will be the places reserved for people to study natural ecosystems and which to enjoy a day of sandwiches, beer, and volleyball? This is not a matter for the market. It is a question about the government of affairs.

This is similar to the question which animated the United Nations Conference on the Law of the Sea and was answered by negotiation, consensus, and conciliation. It is also like the question precipitated by outer-continental-shelf development that may find an answer in the public discourse generated through the permit system. How do we commit the coast so that the spirit of popularity is preserved at the same time that diversity and minorities are nourished?

PUBLIC TRUST

The most striking feature of coastal law is the public trust. Most coastal land above high tide is owned by private parties. Some is owned by state or federal government, typically for parks and wildlife refuges. But everywhere the foreshore—the tidelands or wetsand area—is impressed with a trust for the benefit of all citizens. This public trust is a possibility for saying what law as medium might mean on the coast.

The public trust doctrine can be narrowly stated in terms of the received concepts of boundaries and ownership: the state owns the tidelands up to the boundary line established by high tide but owns them subject to a trust obligation to maintain them for the public uses of navigation, fishing, and commerce. The state may grant small parcels of public trust land to private parties for publicly beneficial purposes like oyster culture and wharves. Grantees of such parcels may own them subject to the public's continuing rights of usage.

In the oft-cited case of *Illinois Central R. Co. v. Illinois,* the Supreme Court observed that states hold title to the beds underlying navigable and tide waters and that this "title is held in trust for the people of the state, that they may enjoy the navigation of the waters, carry on commerce over them, and have liberty of fishing therein, freed from the obstruction or interference of private parties."[64] The Court said that a state may not abdicate its responsibility over these lands and the waters above them. It said that a state might grant small parcels of submerged land to private parties to be used for public purposes but that Illinois had overreached the mark. It had granted a 1,000-acre tract of harbor. The tract was to be put to publicly beneficial uses by the grantee, but so large a grant exceeded what was permissible under the public trust.

The public nature of the coast is anciently established in jurisprudence. The origins of modern American public trust are usually traced to Roman law and to Magna Carta. According to the Institutes of Justinian, by "the law of nature these things are common to mankind—the air, running water, the sea, and consequently the shores of the sea. Any person is at liberty to place on (the sea-shore) a cottage, to which he may retreat, or to dry his nets there, and haul them from the sea; for the shores may be said to be the property of no man."[65] Just as one inhaled the common air, so might one use the shore for a shelter or fishing. And like exhaled air, once the use of the shore by an individual was concluded that portion again became common. The shore could be described as *res publica,* public property.

A nation within whose borders a public thing was found might permit its use but was obliged to prevent its injury.

In England, public trust is traced to spare language in Magna Carta. Its implications were subsequently expanded in statutes and common-law decisions. It came to stand for the legal proposition that the sovereign owned but could not grant tideland and that the people enjoyed the rights of navigation, fishing, and commerce.[66]

In the United States it is said that the powers and responsibilities of the sovereign—including the public trust—devolved upon the people and the states following the Revolution. The public trust emerged in cases in the early nineteenth century and became, by the end of the century, "a viable means for judicial allocation of valuable resources."[67]

Professor Joseph Sax reawakened interest in the public trust in 1970 when he wrote about it as the most comprehensive legal approach to resource management. He thought it might be a broad and unifying doctrine to replace the pastiche of environmental claims which had been argued in citizens suits.[68] Even before Professor Sax wrote (and increasingly since), the public trust idea was being liberated from its originally narrow restrictions. The trust responsibility is no longer confined to the beds of navigable waters. And it is no longer an obligation that attaches only to state-owned property.

The first expansion of the public trust doctrine was the broadening of its protection to include a wider diversity of uses. Recreation, esthetics, and environmental protection were added to embrace areas beyond tidelands: lakes, streams, and public lands. And it has been argued that the public trust ought to include all air, water, and land resources.[69] Last, the public trust has been made an affirmative obligation of the state whether or not the state owns the subject in question—in-place water uses, for example.[70]

In addition to this expansion of the public trust doctrine specifically, there are developing concepts which function like public trust. They may properly be identified as examples of the broader application of public trust even though they do not employ the trust terminology.[71] These functional public trust cases include the protection of certain riparian rights, public uses, vital areas, and the navigation servitude.[72]

The public trust has grown from a limitation upon the prerogatives of the sovereign's ownership of tidelands to a more comprehensive statement of citizen rights and governmental responsibilities bearing upon natural resources. Symbolic of this blossoming is the National Environmental Policy Act's declaration that the government must so act that the nation may "fulfill the responsibilities of each generation as trustee of the environment for succeeding generations."[73]

The public trust as a juridical doctrine provides that certain public uses are to be protected. It does not assign these uses any order of priority, does not establish any means for determining their priority, and does not indicate how a conflict between permissible uses might be justly resolved. The flowering of public trust as a comprehensive statement of resource rights and responsibilities comes to little, therefore, unless there is a satisfactory elaboration of the way it functions. How does it operate?

The decisive issue is who decides about uses, how, and to which ends. The critical service that could be performed by public trust law is to channel resource use into appropriately political forums.

Public trust doctrine is a device employed by the courts. Citizens gain nothing if the courts use the trust doctrine to rescue resource decisions from the bureaucratic labyrinth only to trap them in the courts. There is little to choose between a judge's and a bureaucrat's conception of the public good for which the trust is to be managed. In the courts, such decisions are classically subjected to a balancing test. In the balancing test, a court appears dispassionately to weigh conflicting interests or uses against each other on the scales of reason. What is reasonable and what constitutes a reasonable balance are left to the court to determine. For the citizen, the promising judicial moves associated as public trust are not those which put interests on the scales of a balancing test. The promising moves are those which drive resource decisions into the open and make provision for carrying them forward by an appropriate politics.

The methods by which courts can execute this political maneuver in public trust law are various. Let me present enough of the material to illustrate.

When he recalled the public trust to public attention, Joseph Sax observed:

> It is virtually unheard of for a court to rule directly that a policy is illegal because it is unwise; the courts are both too sophisticated and too restrained to adopt such a procedure. Rather, they may effectively overrule a questionable policy decision by requiring that the appropriate agency provide further justification; alternatively, the courts may, in effect, remand the matter

for additional consideration in the political sphere, thus manip-
ulating the political burdens either to aid underrepresented and
politically weak interests or to give final authority over the matter to a more adequately representative body.[74]

Using the public trust doctrine, courts have manipulated the mechan-
ics of decision making in Sax's sense in the following ways: An agency's decision to lease an unspoiled forest for an elaborate ski development was held a violation of public trust. The court said the
agency's action had no precise legislative directive.[75] Where precise
legislative action had been taken but would result in the complete
destruction of a resource, it, too, was struck down (legislative authorization for a private developer to drain a lake was ruled invalid).[76]
And a governmental body of limited jurisdiction (and therefore not
fully representative of all involved) was prevented from converting a
general resource to specific, preemptive use (a local government had
attempted to designate a navigable stream for power generation).[77]
  In these cases courts halted agency or legislative actions affecting a
resource on the ground that they were violations of public trust. The
proposed actions were not absolutely prohibited. Rather, the issue
was punted back to the agency or legislature, giving the opponents
and the public a chance to defeat it in the political arena. (Such re-
mands by the courts generally do mean that the measures will be
killed. It is difficult for them to survive a second look in the open.)
  The political, dialogic thrust of public trust cases is illustrated by
the aftermath of *Wilbour v. Gallagher.*[78] In that case, the Washington
Supreme Court upheld an injunction that stopped the filling of a lake
bed. The decision questioned the general practice of allowing navigable waters to be filled. It suggested that the disposition of such
resources ought to be a thoughtful, open decision. It said that a planning, zoning, and permit process allowing public participation ought
to be available for such decisions. The legislature answered with a
shoreline-management act, complete with a permit requirement, em-
bodying the court's suggestion.[79]
  In brief, when a court is skeptical of government conduct reallocat-
ing a resource to restricted private or consuming purposes, it can be
led by public trust doctrine to a variety of remedies. The effect of
these remedies is to make resource decisions visible and to create the
possibility for public involvement. That is why Joseph Sax called the
public trust doctrine in the hands of the courts "an instrument for
democratization."[80]
  You will remember that Madison thought "democratization"—he

would not have used the word—was only one of the purposes served by the federal republic. He believed government was to be not only visible and majoritarian but also inclusive of the powerless few and solicitous of their rights. He saw that older examples of democracy failed on just this count. He thought the greatest challenge lay in protecting the few against the tyranny of the many.

Joseph Sax thinks that majority tyranny is not the problem that arises in natural-resource litigation. He says the problem is one of a "diffuse majority" subjected to the will of a concerted minority.[81] Accordingly, he thinks that the protection effected by public trust differs from the minority-rights protections of the Bill of Rights. The courts are called upon only "to promote equality of political power for a disorganized and diffuse majority by remanding appropriate cases to the legislature after public opinion has been aroused."[82]

Not all public trust cases are obvious instances of minority-majority conflict, but close examination shows them to be such according to Sax. He gives the example of a hypothetical dispute between those who want to use parkland for a highway and those who want to preserve the park. The sides are not clearly a minority and a majority. Nevertheless, one will have power—representation, influence, and access—denied to the other. "In such cases," Sax concludes, "all that is asked of courts is that they try to even the political and administrative postures of the adversaries."[83]

If public trust law is to be the medium of a Madisonian federalism, then it has to be more than the democratizing instrument described by Sax. To be such a medium public trust law must do what Sax says it does, i.e., protect a diffuse majority against a willful, well-financed, well-connected minority and its despoliation of a natural resource. And it must also give the contestants an equality of posture in the governmental process. These are necessary, but they are not sufficient. Public trust must be more to be the medium of a Madisonian community. To serve as a possibility for the medium I am looking for, it must protect minorities, and it must protect them in ways other than by simply giving them equality of administrative posture.

It may be that the "diffuse majorities" described by Sax as the beneficiaries of the public trust are often in fact minorities.[84] I am not sure. On the coast, there are instances of what I can describe only as the powerless few: those who cherish privacy at the shore, who wish to study or merely to see the natural ecosystem, who simply want to preserve some of the coast, or who want to save their fishing and farming communities from the massive land-development industry.

It may also be that all a minority needs is equality in the process of decision making. I am not sure about this either. If it means that minority parties must be willing and able financially to hire legal representation, then it seems to me insufficient. It also seems insufficient to me if the administrative process is only a way of absorbing dissent. Powerless minorities and their rights are to be nourished quite apart from their willingness and ability to engage in administrative, judicial, or legislative battles. There is no citizen duty to fight. There is a governmental duty to protect rights. Equalizing handicaps for a fair fight does not appear to be a complete fulfillment of that duty.

All is not lost. It is possible that public trust law does or could be made to supply additional protection of powerless minorities. This possibility is suggested by public trust concern for future generations. Preservation of a resource for the future is a recurrent motif of public trust law. Let me develop the point.

Roman jurisprudence held that the shore belongs to the people in the sense that "it belongs to them to see that none of the uses of the shore are lost by the act of individuals."[85] This emphasis upon preservation was repeated in the Illinois case when the Supreme Court said that American public trust law "requires the government of the state to preserve" the trust subject. And in current public trust law it is said that certain public lands are withdrawn from disposal or development to be set aside for future generations. According to the Bureau of Land Management, "the public land's greatest potential may likely be a wealth of yet to be discovered opportunities, as well as acknowledgment of historical, cultural and scientific values, or even isolation and outdoor recreation. The very existence of these lands, held in trust for all people, may be their greatest value."[86]

I do not want to make too much of this often-expressed concern for the future and for the preservation of future options—"no significant deterioration of public rights in public resources."[87] It is prompted by complex forces. For example, it may be the product of romantic, even religious, regard for nature. It may be the product of skepticism about present governmental and business choices, a skepticism heightened by experience with the hazards of nuclear power plants, toxic wastes, and asbestos. It may be the product of a calculation that a resource will be more profitable if held for future exploitation. Or it may be the product of a pride in leaving things better (or no worse) for one's children and grandchildren who ought to be able to enjoy the national assets.

There are these explanations and others. I want to focus on one: talk of preservation for the future may be the way the powerless are protected. This is so in two possible ways.

State Law

First, succeeding generations have no voice in present deliberations. They may be regarded as a kind of present, voiceless minority.
They would be deprived of their right to make decisions about the
public trust by a coalition of the living who consumed a nonrenew-
able resource. Perhaps we preserve the trust not for the sake of preservation but for the sake of those yet to be born.

Second, public trust reference to the future may be a way of talking
about the present. In 1980, the Council on Environmental Quality
and Department of State submitted to the President *The Global 2000
Report*. This document projects into the future the conditions that will
result if contemporary policies, practices, and trends continue unchanged. It is a way of constructing a hypothetical future to serve as
a mirror in which to examine the reflected present. The report tells
us nothing about life in the year 2000 and does not claim to. It does
tell us something about life in the 1980s—the hunger, decimation of
species, and resource depletion we are generating.

Public trust law's talk about the future has a similar function. It
tests our present as the present is imaged and enlarged in the mirror
of a projected future. We see better what we are now doing—and to
whom—when we project the effects of trust-resource plans upon
succeeding generations.

To take away a barrier island's capacity for strategic retreat dooms
it forever and leaves the mainland it defends unprotected. To deprive
seekers of privacy and students of nature of undeveloped stretches
of coast or to deprive fishermen of their locale and livelihood destroys
possibilities for all time for all who would have succeeded them. Self-
inflicted injury—our impoverishment of our defenses, diversity, and
choice—is exposed in an added dimension. The consequences of our
acts become clearer. Our victims, who might otherwise be over-
looked, are brought to light because they are seen to stand in the
shoes of a future succession.

Or so it may be.

PUBLIC TRUST: COAST

In its original context, i.e., the shore, the public trust provides a political means for governing uses.

The public trust reduces the scope of private property. It does so
by not allowing private ownership to reach beyond the high tide and
by tempering the use that can be made above this line. Activities on
private property that have impacts below the high-tide line may re-

quire permits and public hearings. Trust law may also extend public uses, such as the right of passage, across the private upland.

The public trust reduces the scope of state discretion. If unencumbered choice is denied to the owners of private property, then the government is also denied license for unrestricted discretion. Not even a democratically elected legislature may freely dispose of trust resources. The range of options is channeled by the responsibility of the trustee, a higher responsibility than accountability to one's constituents.

The public trust enlarges the potential of popular participation and minority rights. Governmental actions regarding the coast—or irresponsible inaction—have frequently not involved citizens or have reached points of no return before citizens could become involved or before rights of minor parties could be considered. Public trust, that is to say, has frequently been inoperative. Moreover, when it is engaged, the public trust contains no fail-safe device to prevent courts from interpreting it again, as they have in the past, to be synonymous with urbanization and economic growth.[88] Nevertheless the public trust's reduction of private dominion and state discretion can yield a corresponding increase in involvement of citizens and in minority protection. The remedial measures which realize the public trust— the various judicial manipulations of governmental process along with responsive legislative and administrative change—may be a medium in which to realize a coastal reality that is both popular in spirit and supportive of powerless minorities.

Conclusion

Private ownership of property and the real-estate system are ill adapted to the coast. The conceptual categories of real-estate law along with rigid engineering devices and an intensely consuming land-development industry are too rigid for the migrating shore. The law as bulwark is poor defense for the ownership of shifting littoral sands.

Property does not have to be owned and defended in order to be personal. After all, property law is basically a statement of the relations between persons with respect to things. It is not static of necessity. On the coast it cannot afford to be. It must roll with and like the barrier islands. I think the public trust may be a means for elaborating the relations between persons with respect to the shore in such a way as to be the medium of an authentically human community.

State Law

This community is not brought into existence by law, although, as is true of any medium, the law does have an affective influence upon it. If public trust law may be a medium of Madisonian-like political reality, how are we to understand or achieve this community? If law makes choice available, to what end is that choice to be exercised? This line of questioning brings me to the last chapter.

6

LAW IN THE

PEACEABLE KINGDOM

Conceptual metaphors live not alone but in clusters that share family resemblances.[1] In this chapter I shall indicate the principal features of a cluster where law as medium may be said to belong. More than the rounding out of my experiment requires that I do so. I believe the dominant metaphor for law is to be at least supplemented or, better, replaced. This is not a surgically precise operation to be performed on a single metaphor in isolation. It requires posing an alternate to the whole complex of metaphors of which law as bulwark is a member.

I

In chapter 1 of this book, I made use of Hilary Putnam's saying that the mind and the world jointly make up the mind and the world. There is no objective foundation. I suggested that the absence of a foundation established conditions for our taking responsibility for ourselves and our world. In chapter 2, I proposed that the self-conscious identification and control of our conceptual metaphors for law are ways to take responsibility for it. Since chapter 2, I have been sifting the law of the sea and coast for specific possibilities for law as a medium as an alternate to law as bulwark.

In the dominant metaphor law figures as a defensive works holding back chaos, a device for restraining and dividing, a system of rules and boundaries safeguarding property, a protection of production. I pointed to sequelae of this metaphor in the law of the sea and coast. International law encloses vast marine zones for exclusive national exploitation. United States law divides state from national waters, subdividing the former between the states and the latter between developers of lease tracts. State law separates public tidelines from private upland and plats the private into parcels whose seaward limits are often set in the concrete of erosion-control structures. The law purports to divide and defend.

Law in The Peaceable Kingdom

We have seen that the dominant conceptual metaphor does indeed dominate the law of the sea and coast. I now call your attention to the signs that it does not rule alone. It occurs together with a more or less consistent pattern of metaphors for society, politics, and nature indicative of a reigning family. Law is done not for the sake of law alone but for other things or in conjunction with them. Ways of thinking about law fit in with ways of thinking about these other things.

In arguing for seas enclosed by law, John Selden had other things in mind. For him the sea was territory, and English seas—that jewel for the national treasury and national pride—were an object to be secured against enemies. When President Truman issued his proclamations, he was using law as a protective device to exclude competitor nations. He saw these interests threatened. The world had just been at war. Law as a defensive works was called to the national service.

At the United Nations Conference on the Law of the Sea what finally carried the day was the hegemony of the metaphors of the sea as commodity in tandem with law as enclosing device. Once there was tacit agreement that the sea was goods and law could divide them, all that remained to be done was the negotiation of distribution. I do not mean that negotiation was simple, only that there was no need to negotiate a clash of conceptual metaphors for the two principal subjects, sea and law. Once all sides accepted the premise that it was meaningful to talk about the sea as "territorial sea" or as "exclusive economic zone," then it was evident that they shared a conceptual metaphor for the sea and a compatible one for the law. They thus shared agreement about what they were arguing over and about the terms of argument. They could get on with their disagreements about who should get what without having to establish the appropriateness of thinking that there was a what, that it could be gotten, and that law was an instrument for its getting.

Similarly the states of the United States accept that the continental shelf is a divisible resource and, relatedly, that law establishes the division. The dispute is about staking claims. Last, individual purchasers of pieces of coast fittingly turn to the metes and bounds and stable courthouse files of real-estate law for securing their investment and safeguarding marketability.

Law as bulwark is found in association with related metaphors that together make up a constellation, or mythology, or world view, or ideology, or conceptual way of experiencing life, or, as I have chosen to say, a family of metaphors. The metaphors kin to law as bulwark tend to the individualistic and competitive: life as struggle, society as contract, politics as battlefield or marketplace, and nature as resource. Within this constellation humans are by nature individuals with conflicting self-interests. They seek achievement through a struggle in which each tries to master himself, his fellows, and his world. Fulfillment lies in competitive success. Wealth distinguishes winners from losers. Because individuals (nations, corporations) pursue their own interests and because resources are limited, the war of each against all is always near at hand. It is avoided by temporary armistices of contending wills. Lasting justice is at best an ideal. Law settles for stability. It defends holdings allowing them to be exhibited and increased. Man is alien individual, nature is resource, and law is bulwark.

I name this family of metaphors—its current domestic branch anyway—Fortress America. This image from the days of Herbert Hoover has returned to public discourse and policy. James Watt, the former Secretary of the Interior, is among those who have participated in its revival.

For Secretary Watt, Fortress America and its implications for the continental shelf were explicit, direct, and plain. In describing the Watt plan for oil and gas leasing, an official spokesman for the Secretary once explained to a congressional committee that the plan would stimulate "an inventory of America's offshore energy resources, estimated to be over one-half of the nation's total untapped oil wealth."[2] It would also "provide new jobs, reduce our dependency on foreign sources of oil, enhance our national security and provide significant revenues for the federal treasury—while fully protecting environmental values."[3] According to one report, the spokesman "emphasized the 'Fortress America' approach" as follows:

> For America to be strong in the long run, we must have abundant supplies of energy . . . in the short term, America's greatest hope for reducing our dependency on foreign sources is the Outer Continental Shelf. The President has made a primary issue [of] the need for changing the management of our natural resources in order to reduce the vulnerability of America caused by those sometimes unstable and unfriendly countries which supply us.[4]

In other words: There is a war or contest in which we must prove ourselves (strength for the long run). There are distressing signs of weakness (dependence on untrustworthy outsiders). We can arm ourselves and train for the battle by turning nature to account. We

Law in The Peaceable Kingdom

will not know how great is our potential wealth and will have no training exercises in independence unless we drill. Not to drill is irresponsible. Law stimulates exploration and production by establishing the continental shelf as a field for competition offering profits and their security.

There is one other driving component in James Watt's family of metaphors: the "Second Coming." I suspect that it is one of the more influential metaphors in the Fortress America constellation. We must prove ourselves in the field with the resources supplied by nature because of an unending and escalating conflict leading to the return of Jesus. According to Watt, his responsibility as Secretary of the Interior was "to follow the Scriptures which call upon us to occupy the land until Jesus returns"; he added: "I do not know how many future generations we can count on before the Lord returns."[5] Jesus is absentee commander of the fortress. His return to settle accounts and conduct Armageddon is imminent.

Watt's approach to leasing the continental shelf is bound up with an interrelated cluster of metaphors for society, politics, nature, law, and religion. Together they compose a version of Fortress America. His views are representative of a significant pattern in American culture.[6] We would be wrong simply (or scornfully) to dismiss James Watt's family of metaphors. We must pose an alternate to it. There is urgency in the task and not because Jesus might come back and catch us.

II

I have proposed law as medium—law as connecting rather than disconnecting, enhancing a flow of dialogue, containing the dynamics of life in common. I have gone to the jurisprudence of the sea and coast to discover what law so conceived might mean.

At the beginning, Grotius argued for the freedom of the seas that he thought concordant with the trade winds and human society appointed by the economy of God. In modern times, at the third United Nations Conference on the Law of the Sea, consensus shaped the parliamentary language for a diverse community of nations. In federal law, the permit system potentially expresses the interactions of Madisonian federalism by enabling a dialogue of citizens engaged in governing marine affairs. And in state law, the public trust keeps going a conversation with words that work on the worlds of coastal property and coastal administration. Public trust law breaks down the divide between private property and public jurisdiction through a process that allows for a diversity of citizen opinion and a diversity of coastal opportunities.

Like the dominant metaphor, law as medium is to be located in a family cluster. Its allied metaphors tend to the vital and pacific. In this cluster nature is gift and occasion for a gift cycle, a sharing of the advantages of time and earth. Politics is the action of forming, exchanging, and distilling opinion—the action of a body politic. And law is then a medium of solidarity.

The name for this constellation of metaphors, the alternate to Fortress America, is: The Peaceable Kingdom. A recurrent theme for American primitive artists, the image comes from Isaiah:

> The wolf shall dwell with the lamb,
> and the leopard shall lie down with the kid,
> and the calf and the lion and the fatling together,
> and a little child shall lead them.
>
> . . . .
>
> They shall not hurt or destroy
> in all my holy mountain;
> for the earth shall be full of the knowledge of the Lord
> as the waters cover the sea.[7]

Perhaps the best-known icon of The Peaceable Kingdom is one of Edward Hicks's many paintings of it. To one side of the canvas we see William Penn under an elm covenanting with Indians. To the other side are stylized figures from Isaiah 11: leopards, lions, fatlings, forest, and children together—all staring out at us, their eyes wide and a little startled. The Hicks painting is logically, historically, and zoologically incongruous, but it works. All of the elements are there: politics, the natural world, law in the form of a treaty relating disparate peoples. The harmony of beasts with each other and with humans is esthetically linked to the politics of the treaty, not as cause and effect but as companion parts of a whole.

Woody Allen says: "When the lion and the calf lie down together, the calf doesn't get much sleep."[8] He reminds me that the choice of The Peaceable Kingdom is not unassailable. I do not worry so much about its naïveté as about its employment of the idea of kingdom. "Kingdom" may borrow too much from the leading cluster's notion of domination, ownership, and hierarchy. Also the use of "peace" may have the connotation of stasis for many people in the same way

Law in The Peaceable Kingdom

that "climax forest" is thought of as a static ideal. Any real forest is always growing, changing, and developing. And peace, as I understand it, is dynamic. Hicks's painting certainly achieves a dynamic quality with its play of dimensions and radically different elements. If law is medium, the dialogue it generates and conducts may well be robust. The connection it provides may necessitate breaking down barriers. For example, in order for appropriate conversation to be implemented between whites and blacks in the South, *Brown v. Board of Education*[9] and its aftermath required the disassembling of the wall of apartheid. I suppose that the intervention of a permit system opening up the oil and gas leasing system to the public seemed to oilmen to be an upsetting intrusion by outside agitators. There are times when law as a medium of solidarity will precipitate conflict with the obstructions to community. Also it is to be expected that putting an alternate to the dominant metaphor will appear as an act of insurgency. Because I do not think peace is to be equated with the absence of conflict, I do not find certain forms of destabilization necessarily inconsistent with The Peaceable Kingdom.

There may be more suitable or acceptable images than The Peaceable Kingdom—Turtle Island,[10] for example, or Mother Earth.[11] I choose Peaceable Kingdom because I am drawn to its content and because of the American as well as biblical tradition that lies behind it. I also favor the contrast it affords to Fortress America.[12]

No contrast is more dramatic than that between the theological components central to both of these metaphor clusters: the apocalyptic Jesus of James Watt's Fortress America and the little child of Isaiah's and Hicks's Peaceable Kingdom. The one is an image of power, the other of powerlessness. In order to clarify the difference that this distinction makes, I shall have to address some theological issues.

The first reader of these materials (in an earlier version) objected to what follows. When she picked up a book on law, she said, she did not want or expect theology.

My response then and now is: if not theology, what? I mean this: I am trying to state an alternate way to think about and do law. Law is not a discrete phenomenon. I must think about and do law in context. I have said that we conceive law metaphorically. I have then observed that a conceptual metaphor for law exists in a cluster of metaphors— for life, politics, society, etc.—bearing family resemblances. The intellectual and social environment of law includes a theological constituent.

You may well disagree with my way of doing theology or believe that any way of doing theology is irrelevant. I shall not be banging on a recruiting drum seeking to enlist you in a theological army. Nothing could be more alien to my experiment or alienating to you.

My purpose is to describe the context of law. I find theology a constitutive element in that context. As a matter of personal history, my engagement in legal studies followed from my doing theology, and theology continues to be the matrix of my secular jurisprudence. But this book is not an autobiography or the mapping of my patterns of thought. It is a statement about conceptualizing and realizing law.

The dominant metaphor cluster with its nationalism and exploitation politics and obdurate law is driven by religious images, as witness James Watt. I shall explore a critical theological alternate. Experience has taught me that there is large potential for misunderstanding of theological categories. The acceptance of theology as a legitimate academic discipline has atrophied; and, worse, we have suffered a general loss of familiarity with the biblical tradition as a source for serious political-social-religious critique. However, as Northrop Frye recognizes, the Bible, "whatever we may think we believe about it," keeps exerting pressure upon our culture and imagination: "It insistently raises the question: Why does this huge, sprawling, tactless book sit there inscrutably in the middle of our cultural heritage like the great Boyg or sphinx in *Peer Gynt,* frustrating all our efforts to walk around it?"[13] I shall not attempt to walk around the great Boyg.

In the process of taking seriously the Bible's relevance to legal imagination and legal practice, I shall try to be as clear as possible about my own use and understanding of theological argument. (Where particular terms in the text seem to require it, further explanation for my usage will be included in the notes.) I seek clarification for my own sake as well as yours; I want to see what I think.

There is also this hope: perhaps my experiment—especially if you take exception to my or any theology—will prove occasion for you to undertake an experiment of your own. What performs for you the role that I claim for theology? What is this component of yours, and how does it function in the whole? You will have a family of metaphors, and the family will include an equivalent to theology. Is it equally provocative, motivating, and generative of meaning? Are its terms of discourse equally free of domination by the reigning institutions? How else talk about these things? We live at a time of access to a rich plurality of stories of origin and destiny. Properly done, theology is the repetition in other words of the biblical story. Which are the stories and which the metaphors that shape, make sense of, and inspire your existence? How express them for others, including law-

yers and judges? If not the biblical stories and a Peaceable Kingdom—if not theology—what?

DIETRICH BONHOEFFER AND A THEOLOGY OF THE NATURAL

In elaborating the theology of the alternate family of metaphors, I
shall be following clues left by Dietrich Bonhoeffer. Bonhoeffer had
begun to work out an important restatement of critical theological
questions when his life was cut short by the Nazis. Because his late
thought has to be collected from the scraps of paper permitted him
by his jailers, much remains cryptic. But much can be read from his
life and death.[14]

One of Bonhoeffer's new departures was his nonreligious[15] theology of the natural. Before Bonhoeffer, the category of the natural had
become lost to Protestant thinking. The natural had been understood
as the antithesis to grace. Instead of contrasting the natural to the
unnatural, Protestants contrasted both of them to the Word. Bonhoeffer would not follow this path. Nor would he proceed in the reverse direction by attempting to find analogies or vestiges of the divine in nature, so-called natural theology.[16] Instead he set a wholly
new course first indicated by Karl Barth.[17]

We catch a glimpse of Bonhoeffer's thinking from a letter he wrote
to his parents from prison. (He was a member of the resistance movement, a conspirator against Hitler, and he was seized by the Ge-
stapo.) He commented on the pleasure he took from his walks in the
prison yard with its nesting tomtits, a small anthill, and bees in the
lime trees. Prison life, his treatment by the Nazis, and frequent, fearful Allied bombing raids had sharpened his perception of the quiet,
open life of animals and plants. It gave relief from the soullessness of
wartime prison. But Bonhoeffer was aware that the prisoner "may
react too strongly to anything sentimental that affects him personally."[18] And when this happens he should "call himself to order with
a cold shower of common sense and humour, to avoid losing his
sense of proportion." He added: "I believe it is just here that Christianity, rightly understood, can help particularly."[19] Tomtits, ants, and
bees—like turtles or modern American wildernesses—have a place
but an unsentimental one. What is that place, and how does Christianity help us keep a sense of proportion about it?

According to Bonhoeffer, the natural is penultimate, the thing before the last. The ultimate—"Christianity rightly understood"—both
gives nature its meaning and limits it. Nature is preparation but has
its own time and place, paradoxically receiving from the ultimate its

autonomy.[20] The natural is preserved "as a penultimate which re-quires to be taken seriously in its own way, and yet not to be taken seriously, a penultimate which has become the outer covering of the ultimate."[21]

1.

Because nature is penultimate, it cannot rule over us in any form, including the form of ultimate natural law.

Natural law is a way of talking about the science of ethics. It is reflection upon human behavior and human law according to the higher law accessible to reason.[22] Natural law has a long, complex history. In the course of that history, it has linked the moral direction for human action with the recurrent patterns or necessities perceived in the natural world. It is *natural* law. This linkage may make it a "grotesque pun on the word 'law.'"[23] However, while the metaphorical connections still have strength, there are senses in which the link has been broken.

On the one hand, the hold of nature upon human action is now investigated, free of connection to traditional natural-law categories, under such rubrics as Social Darwinism, sociobiology, social physics, etc. In these investigations nature is thought of as the physical source of influence upon or the programming of human behavior (e.g., universal patterns of behavior encoded in the genetic information of DNA.) Good instruction is to be found in these undertakings. They teach us new terms and modes for taking the physical world seriously. They may claim to do more. They may claim to give an explanation of causes (e.g., evolutionary or genetic determinism) and of ends (e.g., preservation of the status quo, survival).[24] In this event, they are claiming that physical processes, forces, and goals are to be taken not only seriously but with ultimate seriousness. However, if nature is penultimate, it cannot be ultimately determinative of human life and behavior.

On the other hand, natural law is now carried forward by the study of what reason (either self-discovered or divinely implanted) shows to be required of humans. Connections to the processes and forces of the physical world do not figure directly; "nature" stands for rationality or divine reason. In this form, as the science of ethics, natural law concerns the question and relevance of justice. It has performed an especially important, beneficial role in the protection of citizens' rights in the United States. At critical junctures, natural-law arguments for rational behavior have prevailed over willful behavior, and higher law has prevailed over positive law.

Law in The Peaceable Kingdom

Even so, the strength of natural law is also its weakness, for natural law has also provided arguments in justification of the unequal treatment of blacks and of women. And, sometimes with religious claims, it has endorsed obedience to the state.[25] Natural law seeks to overcome desire with reason, arbitrariness with law. However, it makes normative claims for reason which reason cannot bear. We do not agree about what is reasonable. Natural law appeals to standards, but there are no universally accepted standards. The equivocal content of natural law is exposed when social, political, and economic fragmentation break up consensus about fundamentals. There is no unequivocal answer to the question: What is good? Reason is not normative and cannot control the will. So in the United States, the tyranny of the majority is supposed to be constrained by judicial review, and the tyranny of the judiciary is supposed to be constrained by the rationally principled rule of law. But the principles and the law must be neutral and empty; they have no power to constrain.[26] Claims for the ultimacy of reason are in no better case than those for physical processes and forces. If nature is penultimate, it is not ultimate.

2.

On the other hand, because it is penultimate and for the sake of the ultimate, nature must be respected. Nature is not a means only. James Watt and Karl Marx both conceive of nature as raw material for production. However, if nature is end as well as means, i.e., penultimate, then its exploitation is foreclosed.[27]

Christian emphasis upon the priority of humans in the natural order has been identified as the inspiration for environmental degradation in modern America. In a famous article, Lynn White, Jr., argued that environmental destruction would not abate "until we reject the Christian axiom that nature has no reason for existence save to serve man."[28] In place of the "orthodox Christian arrogance toward nature," White wanted to depose "man from his monarchy over creation" and to establish "a democracy of all God's creatures."[29]

A theology of the natural that attributes penultimacy to nature envisions harmony with the creatures rather than a democracy with them. Within the whole formed by humans and their world, humans are to rule. In the biblical story, humans subdue the earth.[30] However, "subdue" does not mean "exploit." The climactic high point of the creation story is the Sabbath (Gen. 1:1–3), God's rest with His creation. The fulfillment of creation lies in recreation, i.e., in enjoyment rather than in exploitation. The breathtaking humanistic affirmations of the biblical story—like those of Psalm 8 and Hebrews 2—are not uttered at the expense of nature. The biblical celebration of human life follows always from glorification of God, never from denigration of nature. The vision of Isaiah which gives us the image of The Peaceable Kingdom is surely typical: nature takes an honored place. Included with human social elements are natural ones. Included with equity for the poor is harmony with the creatures.

Nature is honored in The Peaceable Kingdom, however, because priorities are settled. Equity for the poor precedes harmony for wolf and lamb. Ecological crises are resolved after and because the primary human crises are resolved. A revitalized, romantic animism cannot resolve, even if it recognizes, the underlying human dilemma. Worse, the search for a "spiritual autonomy of all parts of nature"[31] may divert us from the demands of justice presented by the human dilemma.

3.

The notion of penultimacy encourages us to think of nature in political-theological[32] terms. Bonhoeffer put it this way: "the natural is that which after the Fall, is directed towards the coming of Christ."[33] There is an infinite qualitative distinction between this formula of Bonhoeffer's and the superficially similar belief of James Watt that we are supposed to occupy the land until Jesus returns.

In Bonhoeffer's terms, the coming of Christ toward which the natural is directed is an immediate political reality designated by the phrase, kingdom of God. "With respect to its origin," Bonhoeffer once wrote, the natural world "is called creation, with respect to its goal it is called the 'kingdom of God.'"[34] This goal is near at hand, but not in James Watt's sense. The penultimate always verges toward the ultimate. In fact we know what is penultimate only from the ultimate, which is immediately present. The kingdom of God, or the presence of God, occurs and is always about to occur at the center. It is always at hand in the specific, present form of the neighbor. To be directed toward the coming of Christ is to be directed by the neighbor. Natural life is an expectant political life, one lived in a nexus of responsibility for others and with others.[35]

We take nature seriously when we take the neighbor with ultimate seriousness. We must have regard for physical processes and forces, reason, the creatures. Nature counts. But the neighbor guides. Our relation to nature is natural when it is determined by a relation of responsibility to our neighbor. What is good for the neighbor is good for the natural world. (The converse is not necessarily true.) For example, as Hicks's Peaceable Kingdom shows, white Americans' appropriate relation to the natural environment depends upon their appropriate political relation with Indian nations. In Hicks's iconography, children, forest, and beasts form a community because whites and Indians share a just treaty. (Correspondingly, whites will trash the environment to the same degree that they savage Indians.) The world, like ourselves, belongs to our neighbor. We are sovereign over and in the world as we are servant to the neighbor.

LAW IN CONTEXT AND THE EVENTS OF FAITH

Natural life so understood may well be episodic and will certainly be diverse. The neighbors to be served are specific people with specific needs. Responses to them will be different and may also be complex since all of us exist in this world in institutional, ecological, esthetic, economic, social nests that have to be taken into account. Appropriate responsive action to the needs of the neighbor may vary from supplication to protest, from preserving turtles and memories of Ibos to artistic and scientific studies of the coast, from participation in liberation movements to advocacy of the cause of just one person, to the kind of old-style menial office labor my eldest daughter discovered is still necessary to a new order of presidential campaigning. Dietrich Bonhoeffer's responses included the solidarity with members of the resistance that led to his arrest and death.

1.

A life for others—a natural and therefore political life—may be one of complex episodes, but it will not be one of romantic enthusiasm. It has structure and discipline. And it requires taking responsibility seriously, which, as Bonhoeffer observed, "cannot happen without power. Power enters the service of responsibility."[36]

Among other nonromantic options, a life for others may also include practicing, making, and participating in law. Law will then be natural law—i.e., penultimate, directed toward the coming of Christ—because it will become the medium for the citizen's and the lawyer's being for others.

I sought to find out how law might be such a medium by consulting the law of the sea and coast. My experiment yielded specimens: free seas for a bond of human fellowship, international negotiation in the form of arguments and consensus, a permit system serving Madisonian federalism, public trust giving voice and sustenance to the powerless. These are examples or types and not models. They are limited by their conceptual, structural orientation. Many other examples, especially of specific practice of law, remain to be turned up. Even so, my specimens from the law of the sea and coast indicate how law may be said to be a medium.

Citing my examples now in this way gives a more complete way to talk about them. If you think back over those chapters on the law of the sea and coast in light of my subsequent comments about a family cluster of metaphors, you will find a recurrent problem has been resolved.

Grotius argued for free seas as the medium of international reciprocity, but you will remember that freedom of navigation was later used as a tool of imperialism. And when the sea itself became an object of desire, free seas were argued as supporting the liberty of all to exploit. International law of the sea as a matter of argumentation evolved at the United Nations conference in the form of consensus, an intricate method of persuasion allowing many nations with disparate interests to act. Nevertheless, I could find nothing in argument itself—nothing in conversation as such—that equips its participants or enlarges the circle to include those left out. One person or nation must believe the other deserves equal dignity before dialogue can begin. Otherwise, we have instances like that of the Dutch using the freedom of the seas to sail to Java, not thinking to engage the natives in a dialogue of equals.

Or, to take an example from domestic law, I pointed out how the federal permit system in Alaska may salvage little or nothing for the Inupiat. They and their culture face destruction. The permit system has no capacity in and of itself to enable effective participation for those whose economic, social, or physical circumstances make them outsiders.

The same is true of public trust law at the state level. Public trust law may, at its best, ensure equality of posture in state administrative proceedings. But this is not the nurturing of powerless minorities necessary to Madisonian federalism.

In each of these instances, law as medium seemed faulty or not equal to the task. Taken by itself law as medium can mean or be used for oppression, or prove inadequate for the expression of human community. In isolation, law as medium leaves us with prior questions: How and why engage in dialogue? Where does it lead? Why see another as conversational partner rather than as enemy or slave? Why grant equal dignity? What is the source of willingness to negotiate meaning? If law is to be anything other than a bulwark, what transforms the fear, self-protectiveness, and love of power that the bulwark serves?

Law in The Peaceable Kingdom

My talk of a cluster of metaphors lets us see that an alternate conceptual metaphor for law not only belongs with a particular family but also depends upon its family connections for its vitality and fullness of expression.[37] Without that family, law as medium can undergo a metamorphosis into its opposite. Within the family, its integrity is maintained. Law is a medium of solidarity where there is a community needing a medium for its mutuality—and where, as I have described the conceptual constellation, politics is an activity of a body with diverse members, nature is a gift (the penultimate to a transcendent communal reality), and authentic humanity is being for others. It arises out of and is directed toward a community of reconciliation. Law is fitly a medium in and for a Peaceable Kingdom.

Given reconciliation and an authentic community, law as medium even in the form of litigation is appropriate. Lawsuits—those expensive, dreadful engines of animosity—are prime candidates for banishment from a Peaceable Kingdom. Nevertheless, that sometime lawyer John Calvin said litigation is a good and pure gift of God.[38] Lawsuits not only may but must arise from affection. Calvin thought enmity should disqualify any litigant, notwithstanding the justice of the cause, for "no lawsuit can ever be carried on in a proper manner by any man, who does not feel as much benevolence and affection towards his adversary, as if the business in dispute had already been settled and terminated by an amicable adjustment."[39] This is hard for us to understand. Is not enmity—i.e., conflict, controversy, and adverse parties—a necessary condition rather than a disqualification for litigation? What sense does it make to litigate from love? What could Calvin have been talking about?

Given reconciliation, there is a place for litigation. A lawsuit is a medium of affection when it is initiated as if the matter in dispute had been totally conceded to the other side.[40] Such lawsuits are not a form of war.

Courtrooms do not have to be conceived as settings for battle. We have lapsed into the habit of thinking about any kind of argument in battle-metaphor terms: "His criticisms were right on target"; "I demolished his argument"; "He shot down all of my arguments."[41] We are especially given to perceiving legal arguments as martial exercises. Litigation, we say, substitutes a war of words for trial by combat and vendetta. Because we think about and engage in them this way, lawsuits are, next to death and disease, most to be avoided by sensible people. You have to be driven to litigate by extremes of hurt, bitterness, greed, or political oppression.

However, there is another way to conceive and engage in litigation. Start with the idea of argument. A person who argues with you may not be assaulting you. You could understand that a person arguing with you is giving you her time in a joint effort at mutual understanding.[42] That way, argument is a form of cooperation. Argument might be thought of theatrically, along the lines of a dance, for example. The participants would then be taking part in a joint enterprise whose purpose is a performance that works. Litigation may then be conceived the same way. Courtrooms are theaters.[43] A lawsuit is a theatrical event where legal argument is devoted to achieving an affecting, just performance. In a performing, theatrical—as opposed to martial—setting, the advocate may thus view herself as engaged in a joint enterprise with the other advocate with whom she is making common cause. The action becomes dialogue rather than diapolemics. And the outcome is something other than victory for one party and defeat for the other. The success of a play or piece of music can be measured, it has been suggested, "by its ability to elicit connectedness."[44] This is a good measure also for the judicial process as I am talking about it. Litigation works when it elicits connectedness rather than the disconnectedness associated with battle.

For example, the standard outcome of battle-metaphor criminal cases is a jail sentence, i.e., disconnectedness. I know of criminal cases, however, where the outcome is a sentence of restitution imposed upon the convicted party. The wrongdoer, instead of being sent to jail, is reconnected to the victim and to the community. Colin Turnbull reports that African tribunals strive for reconciliation and effect restitution even in murder cases. He observed that the standard for the Bira courts in Zaire is the distribution of blame so that communal ties are reaffirmed:

> Thus, one of the first steps is to establish the positive attributes of the "accused" as a good father, a good son, a good brother, a good friend, a good farmer, and so forth. To this end the entire community is expected to testify. Any "badness" that is left over, and which became manifest in the anti-social act, is thus fractional and is by equally diligent enquiry apportioned among those who however indirectly or unconsciously contributed to the manifestation of that latent badness: the wife who burned his breakfast that morning, the friend who refused to repay a debt, the child who laughed at him when he tripped and fell, the fact that his best piece of cloth was caught by the

current and swept away while being washed. . . . [T]he Bira say it is more important publicly to reaffirm an ideal for all to benefit, than to harm a weak and foolish individual.[45]

Such criminal litigation as occasion for the reaffirmation and strengthening of communal ties can take place where reciprocal human obligations are recognized.

To take an example from the civil side, Richard Abel has noted that tort litigation presently makes pain into a commodity.[46] Money damages are substituted for suffering. Large awards stimulate envy instead of compassion for victims and justify the desire to have nothing further to do with them. Money is even substituted for love in the expanding tort remedies for injury to relationships. Abel proposes reversing tort-law priorities to reflect human priorities so that safety would come before compensation: "surely we think first about the safety of those we love and not about whether they will be compensated if they are injured."[47] He also advocates doing away with compensation for nonpecuniary loss. We should respond "to misfortune with personal care rather than by relegating the victim to the scrap heap of welfare and custodial institutions."[48] Freeing tort litigation of the necessity to adjudicate damages, fault, and cause would also free victims from dependence upon predatory personal-injury lawyers. Litigation would then be occasion for the administration of care, a reaffirmation of the mutual responsibilities of personal concern within the community.

The point is that, given reconciliation, law as medium, even in the form of the lawsuit, has fruitful integrity. Given the context and will for it, litigation is a gift expressing affection. As I say, however, law as medium must have its conceptual and ethical cognates in The Peaceable Kingdom. An alternate conceptual metaphor for law cannot be worked out in an intellectual or ethical vacuum. It has integrity and vitality only within a larger, sustaining alternate to the whole.

The question, then, is how such an alternate to the whole is to be put forward. If law is a medium only in a Peaceable Kingdom, how do we precipitate that larger pattern of thinking and acting? How advance the transfiguration of the way politics, nature, society, law—life itself—are experienced?

This is not a question of strategy. "Strategy" is a military term and belongs to Fortress America. If a Peaceable Kingdom is our purpose we do not have a strategy. We are not assaulting the citadel and do not seek merely a change of command. Instead of a strategy, we have a praxis, i.e., an affective way of living—for others. I must try to say how we come to such a life. How does The Peaceable Kingdom happen?

2.

Dietrich Bonhoeffer was not exceptional. He was not, that is, a saintly or heroic cut above the rest of us. It would be a serious misreading to conclude that he was sustained in extraordinary circumstances by the strength of uncommon personal qualities. The explanation of how he was upheld and led lies in an "arcane discipline."[49] In essence, this discipline is simply the biblical story.

Any story can help us make sense of our lives.[50] Narrative—very close to metaphor—"'grasps together' and integrates into one whole and complete story multiple and scattered events."[51] It thereby allows us to "re-configure our confused, unformed, and at the limit mute temporal experience."[52] But narrative does not necessarily sustain us "in the trust and openness, the caring and responsiveness, that make for humanness."[53] For that we need a saving story. Bonhoeffer recognized in the biblical story the saving story that transfigured as well as reconfigured his experience. His incognito life in the Resistance Movement and the arcane discipline were mutually interpretive.[54]

The discipline is arcane in part because silence is needed to protect "the world from violation by religion."[55] The biblical story does not license claims to solutions for insoluble problems. These are left to religion, religious people, and the deus ex machina.[56] Silence is called for on those occasions—far more frequent than might be supposed—when there is no answer and nothing to say. Silence is appropriate on other occasions for reasons of tact. For example, in the midst of a bombing raid, a fellow prisoner was lying on the floor exclaiming "O God, O God!" Bonhoeffer offered no religious comfort: "all I did was to look at my watch and say, 'It won't last more than ten minutes now.' . . . I felt that it was wrong to force religion down his throat just then."[57]

Another, related reason for silence is identification with others. In the face of the Allied advance and the confusion of the closing days of the war, Bonhoeffer was hastily moved, along with other prisoners, from one camp to another. He was thrown together with a Russian, Kokorin, the nephew of Molotov. On a Sunday in April 1945, the day before he would be executed, Bonhoeffer, a Lutheran pastor, was asked by another prisoner to conduct a worship service in the school which served as a temporary jail. Reportedly he did not wish to do so. The majority of his comrades were Catholic, and the young

Kokorin was an atheist. Bonhoeffer had exchanged addresses with Kokorin and "didn't want to ambush him with a Church service."[58] Identification with his fellows instructed silence.

In addition to regard for others, there is an entirely different reason that the arcane discipline is arcane. Secrecy is necessary for the preservation of the story. The mysteries of the faith must be safeguarded. The danger here is that protective secrecy will erect a barrier and create a privilege from which others are excluded. Bonhoeffer did not in his writing resolve this problem. However, as his friend and biographer Eberhard Bethge suggests, in the arcane discipline "Christ takes everyone who really encounters him by the shoulder and turns him round to face his [neighbors] and the world."[59] The story is preserved behind the barrier of the arcanum exactly and paradoxically to do away with all barriers. "In other words, the 'ultimate' is praised with the initiates gathered together, so that in the 'penultimate' . . . there can be a share in godlessness. Christ prays a cultic psalm and dies a profane death."[60] Bonhoeffer identified with others because his own identity was preserved and nourished by the central, secret discipline of faith.

This center was not subject to outward propagation or demonstration in Bonhoeffer's day; nor is it now.[61] There is still mystery in the middle: The Peaceable Kingdom occurs where the Word of the biblical story intersects the world.

AFTERWORD

Nature does not usually exhibit death. Death is more typically unexposed, secret. You can walk deep into the woods all over the United States and find plenty of plant-life decay but hardly any sign of fauna mortality. You have to guess at the magnitude of death among the animals from the numbers you see dead on the road.

The coast is an altogether different scene. There at the land's margin nature reveals death casually. Death is exposed and always on display: turtle carcasses at the Atlantic shore and sea-lion parts at the Pacific; everywhere the drying remains of shellfish, fish, waterfowl, and too often, tragic whales.

There is an accepted way of talking about both the coast and death that makes them out as hard and fast limits. I do not believe it necessary to talk about them this way—about the coast as a boundary and about death as the end. Bonhoeffer thought that religious talk about human weakness and human boundaries is a way of exploiting them so as to reserve some space for a God, a God at the outer limits beyond what we understand and can do.

Instead of human boundaries and a God on the further side of them, Bonhoeffer directs us to the center and to a God who "is beyond in the midst of life."[1] This is not to carve out a retreat in the center rather than at the edges. Priestly, privileged sanctuary is done away with. Therefore our relation to God cannot be a religious relationship to a highest, most powerful, supreme being. In fact, God lets us know that we must live as those who manage their lives without him; before God, we "live in the world without the working hypothesis of God."[2]

Human freedom is complete. To live as if there were no God is to live also as if there were no God substitutes, no idols: "not orders, not laws and peremptory dogmas."[3] With no external, nonhistorical authority or foundation, we are fully free. Accordingly, we are fully responsible, for there is no objective repository for our transferred responsibility.

By living in Nazi Germany, Dietrich Bonhoeffer lived at the edge of civilization during the most profound darkness of the human spirit in modern times. Because of the arcane discipline of faith with its consequent attachments of responsibility to others and to the world around, he was not lost.

The chaos that was Nazi Germany erupted in war. But chaos also expressed itself in the law-and-order of Fortress Germany. Bonhoeffer was surrounded by war *and* by prison walls. Both meant death. At that time, order was clearly a form of chaos. We know well enough that order is not truly opposed to chaos.

Freedom is the opposite of chaos. According to the biblical story, and by it, we are made free to be persons for others so that giving them our lives—dying—becomes our living. This is not at all morbid and is certainly not saintly, exalted, or exceptional. It is simply and ordinarily to find the neighbor transcendent.[4] We are freed for that binding to others which locates and holds us no matter the dissolution of ordering boundaries or an order of oppressing boundaries.

Barth urged that we quit thinking of limitation as derogatory or as a curse or affliction. He said that "the limitation which comes from God . . . is not a negation but the most positive affirmation. Limitation as decreed by God means circumscription, definition, and therefore determination. Only the void is undefined and therefore unlimited."[5]

I think the determining limit God gives us is the neighbor. This limit is also the transcendent. With this limit we are set free. There is no other necessary or natural circumscription. We have no need for false limits or their false transcending. We have no need for law as bulwark against chaos. There is no threat of chaos. There is the story and therefore The Peaceable Kingdom and therefore the neighbor. And there is law made a medium of our life together, containing some the joint life we jointly make up.

I hope you invent your own, better way to talk about these things and do them. It will be better if you and law are made more responsive to your neighbor, those victimized by the system as it now is.

NOTES

INDEX

NOTES

CHAPTER 1

1. *See* R. JONES, PHYSICS AS METAPHOR 228–29 (1982).

2. 16 U.S.C. § 1131 (1982).

3. R. NASH, WILDERNESS AND THE AMERICAN MIND xiii (3d ed. 1982).

4. *Id.*

5. H. PUTNAM, REASON, TRUTH AND HISTORY xi (1981).

6. R. RORTY, PHILOSOPHY AND THE MIRROR OF NATURE 12 (1979).

7. On euphemism and the passive voice in World War I, see P. FUSSELL, THE GREAT WAR AND MODERN MEMORY (1975).

8. F. KERMODE, THE GENESIS OF SECRECY 13 (1979). I have taken the episode from Kermode's account.

9. J. WEIZENBAUM, COMPUTER POWER AND HUMAN REASON 189, *quoted in* D. HOFSTADTER, GÖDEL, ESCHER, BACH: AN ETERNAL GOLDEN BRAID 600 (1979).

10. A. DILLARD, PILGRIM AT TINKER CREEK 19 (1975).

11. *Id.* at 20.

12. I have relied upon L. HYDE, THE GIFT: IMAGINATION AND THE EROTIC LIFE OF PROPERTY (1979).

13. Hyde says "the gift must always move." *Id.* at 4. Boundaries, stop points, and limits are characteristics of a commodity in a market economy. *Id.* at 23. A commodity can cross the line between independent spheres "without any change in its nature: moreover, its exchange will often establish a boundary where none existed before." *Id.* at 61. In contrast, the "gift moves in a circle, and two people do not make much of a circle." *Id.* at 16.

14. *Id.* at 22.

15. K. MARX, GRUNDRISSE, *in* THE PORTABLE KARL MARX 375, 380 (Kamenka ed. 1983).

16. HYDE, *supra* note 12, at xiv.

17. J. WHITE, WHEN WORDS LOSE THEIR MEANING 278 (1984).

18. I shall return to the question of the nature of boundaries in the last chapter.

19. On the way in which dialogue can constitute and reconstitute a universe of meaning, *see* WHITE, *supra* note 17.

The gift cycle is inherently oriented and guided. As Hyde points out, "The gift moves toward the empty place. As it turns in its circle it turns toward him who has been empty-handed the longest, and if someone appears elsewhere whose need is greater it leaves its old channel and moves toward him. Our generosity may leave us empty, but our emptiness then pulls gently at the whole until the thing in motion returns to replenish us." HYDE, *supra* note 12, at 23. He goes on to observe: "Just as gifts are linked to the death that moves toward new life, so, for those who believe in transformation, ideologies of market exchange have become associated with the death that goes nowhere." *Id.* at 45. In the last chapter of the present book, I shall have more to say about death that moves toward new life.

20. Marbury v. Madison, 5 U.S. (1 Cranch) 137, 163 (1803) (Marshall, C. J.).

141

21. W. Stringfellow, An Ethic for Christians & Other Aliens in a Strange Land 84 (1973).
22. Id. at 86.
23. Id. at 85–87.
24. K. Barth, The Epistle to the Romans 436 (E. Hoskyns trans. 1933).
25. Powell, Constitutional Metaphors, New Republic, Feb. 11, 1925, at 314.
26. Id. at 314–15.
27. W. Auden, The Collected Poetry of W. H. Auden 74–76 (1945).
28. J. Calvin, Institutes of the Christian Religion 48 (Allen trans. 1949).
29. P. Ricoeur, The Symbolism of Evil 348 (1967).

CHAPTER 2

1. Njal's Saga 159 (M. Magnusson & H. Palsson trans. 1960).
2. G. Lakoff & M. Johnson, Metaphors We Live By (1980).
3. On concealment in communication, see also F. Kermode's The Genesis of Secrecy (1979).
4. R. Rorty, Philosophy and the Mirror of Nature 377 (1979).
5. The leading work and the one that set me thinking about many of these things is James Boyd White's The Legal Imagination (1973). I gained new respect for Lon Fuller's little volume Legal Fictions (1967) upon rereading it. The concluding essay in Fuller's book is an account of Vaihinger's Die Philosophie des Als Ob. Fuller describes Vaihinger's view that fictions "taint" all our thinking. Vaihinger's precept for the proper self-conscious use of fiction in our thinking was: "The fiction must drop out of the final reckoning." Id. at 117. We speak of corporations as persons. This is to introduce a fiction. We make the necessary correction by dropping out those attributes of "person" legally inappropriate to the corporation. According to Vaihinger, much of our thinking is the process of opposing mistakes which are mutually compensatory. The failure to drop the fiction from the final reckoning—hypostatization—is described by Fuller as "the isolation of one step in a reasoning process out of its compensatory context." Id. at 119. (In Chapter 6 I shall be talking about the context of conceptual metaphors for law. I view the context as supportive rather than as compensatory. I do not view metaphors as signs of weakness or error needing compensation. I do not believe that metaphors "taint" our thinking. They are the way we think, and they enrich our thinking.) The notion of dropping the fiction out of the final reckoning is curious. It is as though Vaihinger was unable to come to terms ultimately with his observation that metaphors "taint" all our thinking. Fuller concludes that Vaihinger "never fully realized what he had proved." Id. at 124. (Compare Thomas Kuhn's account of Priestley's never recognizing the oxygen he had "discovered." T. Kuhn, The Nature of Scientific Revolutions 53–60 (2d ed. 1970). Fuller recognizes but does not develop Vaihinger's discovery.

It is to be noted that Fuller uses the words "fiction" and "metaphor" interchangeably. A distinction between them is drawn by Pierre Olivier. Olivier defines a legal fiction as "an assumption of fact deliberately lawfully and irrebuttably made contrary to the facts proven or probable in a particular case, with the object of bringing a particular legal rule into operation or explaining a legal rule, the assumption being permitted by law or employed in legal science." P. Olivier, Legal Fictions in Practice and Legal Science 81 (1975). He then includes among the "institutions" not to be regarded as legal fictions: "Metaphors and symbolic expressions which endeavor to describe legal institutions or concepts but which do not require a false actual assumption, e.g. prescription 'runs.'" *Id.* I do not buy this distinction. Olivier's understanding of a false assumption is too qualified and contrived.

I accept Edward Lueders's proposal that a "metaphor is a deliberate lie which contains the truth, not as, but in solution. . . . The metaphor deals simultaneously with the things in themselves and in their union, demanding that we assemble even as we dissemble, that we pursue unity through a willing duplicity with 'the facts.'" Lueders, *The Need for an Essential Metaphor: The Lie We Can Believe* (unpublished); *see also id.,* THE CLAM LAKE PAPERS (1977).

The fullest treatment of the subject is Paul Ricoeur's THE RULE OF METAPHOR (1981). One of Ricoeur's central themes is "that metaphor is the rhetorical process by which discourse unleashes the power that certain fictions have to redescribe reality." *Id.* at 7.

The artist Robert Irwin resists metaphor. It is said that, with his canvases, "he has been trying to approach that presence which would not be metaphorical. Irwin sees presence and metaphor as polar opposites. Presence requires presence, whereas metaphor allows—indeed, requires—absence, evasion. A recent incident further illustrates this point. A few months ago, Irwin addressed, at their invitation, a convention of psychologists meeting in Los Angeles. Following his presentation, one psychologist came up to him and asked whether he'd be willing to submit to a Rorschach test. Available, as usual, Irwin agreed, and they made a date for the following afternoon at Irwin's place. When the psychologist arrived, she offered him the first of the inkblots and asked him to describe what he saw. 'Well,' Irwin replied, 'that's a black shape— not terribly interesting actually. Symmetrical . . . ' But what did the shape remind him of? 'Nothing. Just that: it's a black shape.' No associations whatsoever? 'Lady,' Irwin endeavored to explain, 'I've spent twenty years trying to hone my perceptions so that when I see that card, I see that card.'" Weschler, *Profiles: Taking Art to Point Zero (Robert Irwin),* THE NEW YORKER, Mar. 15, 1982, p. 52, at 99–100.

Whatever the case may be with Rorschach tests, seeing in the things of this world the figures of another, i.e., making metaphors, is humanly necessary. M. M. Liberman describes the making of similitudes as "a necessary act of desperation, an altogether human defense against abysmal meaninglessness, insofar as poetry reflects the visible world seen as finite. A visible world, so seen, pitifully needs poetry as poetry needs metaphor. Neither is needed—one might say they are impossible—where the visible world is seen as its own poem: a world, that is, without end." Liberman, *The End of Metaphor,* THE GEORGIA REVIEW, Winter 1984, at 749, 751.

6. *See* Horwitz, *The Doctrine of Objective Causation, in* THE POLITICS OF LAW 201 (Kairys ed. 1982).

7. *See* Tushnet, *Corporations and Free Speech, in id.* at 253.

8. *See* M. BALL, THE PROMISE OF AMERICAN LAW 48–52 (1981).

9. *See* WHITE, *supra* note 5, at xxxiii, 807.

10. McCulloch v. Maryland, 17 U.S. (4 Whet.) 316, 431, 426–27 (1819) (Marshall, C. J.).

11. James Madison, in an address to the first Congress on June 8, 1789, referred to the federal courts as "an impenetrable bulwark against every assumption of power in the Legislative or Executive . . ." 1 ANNALS OF CONG. 439 (1834). Lord Denning in 1981 described freedom of the press as "one of the great bulwarks of liberty." Schering Chemicals v. Falkman, (1981) 2 All E. R. 321, 330.

12. The conceptual system of law as the ramparts of civilization is at least partially reinforced by a metonymy, the identification of or reference to law by the early means of its recordation and communication: the two tablets of stone which Moses bore to the

Israelites, for example, or the stele, an eight-foot diorite shaft, on which the Code of Hammurabi was inscribed. The jurisprudence of the past has attributes of a quarry.

13. MacLeish, *Apologia,* 85 HARV. L. REV. 1505, 1508 (1972).

14. *Id.* at 1509–10.

15. A colleague, Dorinda Dallmeyer, recently sought to rescue the metaphor for me by pointing out that corals build reefs along and not in opposition to ocean currents so that their effect is more channeling than opposing.

16. Chambers v. Florida, 309 U.S. 241 (1940).

17. 347 U.S. 483 (1954) (Brown I); 349 U.S. 294 (1955) (Brown II).

18. The sense of refuge for aliens in association with law is found in Aeschylus's THE EUMENIDES.

19. *See* COCHRANE, CHRISTIANITY AND CLASSICAL CULTURE 354–55 (1944).

20. The law cuts the hydrologic cycle into discrete segments, each of which is treated differently: rain, diffuse surface waters, rivers (both navigable and nonnavigable), lakes (both navigable and nonnavigable), percolating groundwater, subterranean pools, and oceans. The contradictory results of this foolish exercise establish by negative example the need to treat water as a dynamic, ecological whole.

21. According to Grant Gilmore, before they put the image aside in the eighteenth century, "[l]awyers continued to think of themselves, as they were thought of by others, as being plumbers or repairmen." G. GILMORE, THE AGES OF AMERICAN LAW 3 (1977).

22. Poetry also aids human relationships by saving and transfiguring the language. At the moment poets seem to be read primarily by other poets, and this unfortunate divorce from a larger public entails—at least on the surface—a frustrating separation from power. This separation also enables poets to preserve a language that can bear human freight. So the withdrawal ultimately serves communion.

23. RORTY, *supra* note 4, at 378.

24. Eugenio Montale celebrates what he refers to as "the second life of art," i.e., its circulation through conscience and memory, the "entire flowing back into the very life from which art took its first nourishment." Montale, *The Second Life of Art,* THE NEW YORK REVIEW OF BOOKS, April 16, 1981, at 19 (Galassi trans.).

25. For a summary of Gadamer's notion of the horizon, see Richard Bernstein's SCIENCE, HERMENEUTICS, AND PRAXIS 143–44 (1983).

26. LAKOFF & JOHNSON, *supra* note 2, at 231.

27. Amos 5:24.

28. OPEN SECRET: VERSIONS OF RUMI, frontispiece (J. Mayne & C. Barks trans. 1984).

29. *Id.,* Introduction, at xiv.

30. A well-known referent for "medium" is a spiritualist who serves as a conduit for messages from the dead to the living. For some people, consulting a lawyer may be very like consulting a medium, although the paraphernalia are generally not the same. The real problem of the image for me is the unilateral character of the movement. Do spiritualists ever carry messages from the living to the dead?

This one-way movement is also characteristic of the mass media, especially television, and is one of the several reasons I shrink from fastening law to the mass media. To the degree that law is a conduit for messages to the masses from the ruling commercial and political powers, it is like other mass media but distinctly unlike what I mean by law as medium, as I hope will become clear.

31. 6 OXFORD ENGLISH DICTIONARY (L–M) 299 (1961).

32. LAKOFF & JOHNSON, *supra* note 2, at 143.

33. GILMORE, *supra* note 21, at 111.

34. Northrop Frye says that "[w]e see by means of light and air: if we could see air we could see nothing else, and would be living in the dense fog that is one of the roots of the word 'vanity.'" N. FRYE, THE GREAT CODE 124 (1982). Exactly as it is a bulwark, we see law. To the degree that we see it, we cannot see by means of it.

35. ST. ANSELM, PROSLOGIUM: MONOLOGIUM: AN APPENDIX IN BEHALF OF THE FOOL BY GAUNILON; AND CUR DEUS HOMO (S. Deane trans. 1958).

36. K. BARTH, ANSELM: FIDES QUARENS INTELLECTUM 70 (I. Robertson trans. 1960).

CHAPTER 3

1. My decision to exclude admiralty law is a stylistic one based on the amount of material I can manage. By including "public" law and omitting "private" law of the sea, I do not mean to imply that there is any necessary or natural distinction between a private and a public sphere of law. Critical Legal Studies scholars have made us properly sensitive to the falsity of such a distinction. For example, women have long been consigned to a "private" sphere where the protection of law was not accessible. In the case of the sea, it would be wrong to think of a difference in essence between public and private law. The shipping industry and its regulation have never been wholly separable from government and public law. Gilmore and Black pass on the report, for example, that "when the Egyptian fleets sailed to trade in the 'land of Punt,' it was the Pharaoh that sent them there." G. GILMORE & C. BLACK, THE LAW OF ADMIRALTY 959 (1975).

The most authoritative summary of the law of the sea is also the most recent and most readable: L. SOHN & K. GUSTAFSON, THE LAW OF THE SEA IN A NUTSHELL (1984). I recommend this volume for any reader needing a handy reference work on the subject.

See generally, e.g., E. BORGESE, ed., PACEM IN MARIBUS (1972); S. BROWN, N. CORNELL, L. FABIAN, E. WEIS, REGIMES FOR THE OCEAN, OUTER SPACE AND WEATHER (1977); J. COLOMBOS, THE INTERNATIONAL LAW OF THE SEA (6th ed. 1967); W. FRIEDMANN, THE FUTURE OF THE OCEANS (1971); GALEY, MARINE ENVIRONMENTAL AFFAIRS BIBLIOGRAPHY (Law of the Sea Institute Special Publication No. 6, February 1977); R. KEOHANE & J. NYE, POWER AND INTERDEPENDENCE (1977); H. KNIGHT, THE LAW OF THE SEA (1975); P. JESSUP, THE LAW OF TERRITORIAL WATERS AND MARITIME JURISDICTION (1927); M. McDOUGAL & W. BURKE, THE PUBLIC ORDER OF THE OCEANS: A CONTEMPORARY INTERNATIONAL LAW OF THE SEA (1962); WOODROW WILSON INTERNATIONAL CENTER FOR SCHOLARS, OCEAN AFFAIRS BIBLIOGRAPHY (Oceans Series 302, 1971); M. WHITEMAN, DIGEST OF INTERNATIONAL LAW (1965); E. WENK, THE POLITICS OF THE OCEAN (1972); B. WESTON, R. FALK, A. D'AMATO, INTERNATIONAL LAW AND WORLD ORDER 956–58 (1980). For a book and bibliography which emphasize economic analysis, see R. ECKART, THE ENCLOSURE OF OCEAN RESOURCES (1979). In addition, there are several law reviews and annual law-review symposia which are devoted to marine and coastal issues.

2. P. JESSUP, supra note 1, at 3–4, n. 3.

3. See Chapter 5 infra note 65.

4. Fulton refers to a "less selfish explanation" than monopoly for appropriating seas in the Middle Ages: "In the state of wild anarchy which prevailed after the break-up of the Roman empire, pirates swarmed along every coast where booty might be had. Scandinavian rovers infested the Baltic, the North Sea and the Channel; Saracens and Greeks preyed upon the commerce of the Mediterranean; everywhere the navigation of trading vessels was exposed to constant peril from the attack of freebooters. The sea

was then common in the sense of being universally open to depradation." T. FULTON, THE SOVEREIGNTY OF THE SEA 5 (1911).

5. F. DAVENPORT, EUROPEAN TREATIES BEARING ON THE HISTORY OF THE UNITED STATES AND ITS DEPENDENCIES TO 1648, at 56–63, 71–83 (papal bulls); 86–100 (Treaty of Tordecillas) (1967).

6. Fulton notes that Queen Elizabeth, upon complaints from the Spanish concerning Drake's exploits, maintained that the Pope's division could not bind her and that "the use of the sea and air is common to all; neither can any title to the ocean belong to any people or private man, forasmuch as neither nature nor regard of the public use permitteth any possession thereof." Fulton, *supra* note 4, at 107. There was earlier English precedent at least for freedom of fishing, in the treaty Intercursus Magnus of 1496. See *id.* at 72.

It must be added that, before Grotius, two Spaniards had written in opposition to a closed, appropriable sea. They were Francis Alphonso de Castro and Ferdinand Vasquez. See FULTON, *supra* note 4, at 341.

7. H. GROTIUS, THE FREEDOM OF THE SEAS 28 (Magoffin trans. 1916). See also *id.* 7–9 *passim;* DE JURE BELLI AC PACIS, bk. 2, ch. 2, pts. xiii–xiv, at 199–201; pt. iii, at 190–91; bk. 2, ch. 3. pt. x, at 211 (Kelsey trans. 1925).

8. The last sentence of Selden's MARE CLAUSUM reads: "And without question it is true, according to the collection of testimonies before alleged, that the very shores or ports of the neighbor-princes beyond-sea, are bounds of the sea-territorie of the British empire to the southward and eastward; but that in the open and vast ocean of the North and West, they are to be placed at the utmost extent of those most spacious seas, which are possessed by the English, Scots, and Irish." J. SELDEN, OF THE DOMINION, OR, OWNERSHIP OF THE SEA, 459 (Nedham trans. 1652; reprint 1972). Fulton notes how claims to the "British Sea" were placed at greater or lesser distances and made with greater or lesser bellicosity in concert with domestic political fortunes. See FULTON, *supra* note 4, at 11, 15, 20.

9. J. SELDEN, *supra* note 8, at 123–26.

10. *Id.,* at 141.

11. *Id.*

12. *Id.,* author's preface, unpaginated.

13. See FULTON, *supra* note 4, at 18.

14. J. BOROUGHS, THE SOVEREIGNTY OF THE BRITISH SEAS, PROVED BY RECORDS, HISTORY AND THE MUNICIPALL LAWES OF THIS KINGDOME, *quoted in* Fulton, *supra* note 4, at 365.

15. FULTON, *supra* note 4, at 413.

16. P. MEADOWS, OBSERVATIONS CONCERNING THE DOMINION AND SOVEREIGNTY OF THE SEAS: BEING AN ABSTRACT OF THE MARINE AFFAIRS OF ENGLAND, *quoted in* FULTON, *supra* note 4, at 524.

17. By the time he published *De Jure Belli ac Pacis* in 1625, Grotius was persuaded that bays and straits were subject to acquisition. H. GROTIUS, *supra* note 7, bk. 2, ch. 3, pts. viii–xiv, at 209–15. He was also of the opinion that sovereignty might be acquired over areas of the sea beyond "through the instrumentality of persons if, for example, a fleet, which is an army afloat, is stationed at some point of the sea; by means of territory, in so far as those who sail over the parts of the sea along the coast may be constrained from the land no less than if they should be upon the land itself." *Id.* bk. 2, ch. 3, pt. xiii, at 214. A tax might be laid on such passage, therefore, but only to the extent that it was fair and fairly related to the merchandise, as it would be, for example, if it were collected in order to defray the cost of protection. *Id.* pt. xiv, at 214–15; bk. 2, ch. 2, pt.

xiv, at 200. It may be that this constitutes a change, maybe a partial reversal, in view after the writing of *Mare Liberum*. However, sovereignty over coastal waters is expressly mentioned in *Mare Liberum*, GROTIUS, *supra* note 7, at 43, and the argument of the book is pointedly directed not at the questions of an "inner sea" or gulf or strait but at the outrage of Portuguese claims to the "whole expanse" of "outer sea" beyond what is visible from shore. *Id.* at 37.

18. *See* FULTON, *supra* note 4, at 556; JESSUP, *supra* note 2, at 5–6.

19. 1 WAIT'S STATE PAPERS, 195–96 (1817); MOORE, 1 INTERNATIONAL LAW DIGEST 702–3 (1906). The equation of the cannon-shot rule with the 3-mile limit was made before artillery had a range that great. *See* S. SWARTZTRAUBER, THE THREE-MILE LIMIT OF TERRITORIAL SEAS 23–35 (1972); Kent, *Historical Origins of the Three-Mile Limit*, 48 AM. J. INT'L L. 537 (1954); Walker, *Territorial Waters: The Cannon Shot Rule*, 22 BRIT. Y.B. INT'L L. 210 (1954). Other standards of measurement included the line of sight and the marine league. *See* S. SWARTZTRAUBER, *supra*, at 36–50.

20. *See, e.g.*, 1 OPPENHEIM, INTERNATIONAL LAW 584–86 (H. Lauterpacht 8th ed. 1958); J. COLOMBOS, *supra* note 1, at 49–51.

21. It is a reprint issued by Arno Press, a New York Times company.

22. K. MARX, *The British Rule in India*, in THE PORTABLE KARL MARX 329, 330 (E. Kamenka ed. 1983).

23. Wertenbaker, *A Reporter at Large: Law of the Sea Conference—Part 2*, THE NEW YORKER, August 8, 1983, at 56.

24. For accounts of the events discussed in the text, see F. DE PAUW, GROTIUS AND THE LAW OF THE SEA 14–22, 43–75 (Arthern trans. 1965); Scott, *Introductory Note* to GROTIUS, ON THE FREEDOM OF THE SEAS, *supra* note 7, at ix–xxii.

25. "International law may, despite its pretensions, have a damaging net impact. Its invocation may disguise the extent to which the war system serves the imperial needs of the powerful, rather than the community needs of order, restraint, and guidance. . . ." R. FALK, THE ROLE OF LAW IN WORLD SOCIETY: PRESENT CRISIS AND FUTURE PROSPECTS, IN WORLD ORDER AND HUMAN DIGNITY (Reisman & West eds. 1976) *quoted in* WESTON, FALK & D'AMATO, *supra* note 1, at 1162, 1164.

26. D. WALCOTT, THE STAR-APPLE KINGDOM 53 (1979).

27. Presidential Proclamation 2667, 3 C.F.R. 67 (1943–48 Comp.), *reprinted in* 59 Stat. 884 (1945). *See generally, e.g.*, 4 WHITEMAN, *supra* note 1, at 740–931; Hollick, *U.S. Oceans Policy: The Truman Proclamations*, 17 VA. J. INT'L L. 23 (1976).

28. Presidential Proclamation 2667, *supra* note 27.

29. "The character as high seas of the waters above the continental shelf and the right to their free and unimpeded navigation are in no way thus affected." *Id.*

30. White House Press Release, Sept. 28, 1945, 13 DEP'T ST. BULL. 484 (1945).

31. Annual Report of the Secretary of the Interior, Fiscal Year Ended June 30, 1945, at ix–x, *quoted in* 4 WHITEMAN, *supra* note 1, at 760. The proclamation was later "ratified" by the Outer Continental Shelf Lands Act, 43 U.S.C. §§1331–1343 (1982).

32. Presidential Proclamation 2668, 3 C.F.R. 68 (1943–48 Comp.), *reprinted in* 59 Stat. 885 (1945). *See generally, e.g.*, 4 WHITEMAN, *supra* note 1, at 945–62; Allen, *Fishery Proclamation of 1945*, 45 AM. J. INT'L L. 177 (1951).

33. Presidential Proclamation 2668, 10 Fed. Reg. 12304, *reprinted in* 59 Stat. 885 (1945).

34. Fishery limits were not created in implementation of the proclamation on fishing. The Bartlett Act of 1964 prohibited foreign vessels from taking the sedentary living resources of the continental shelf out to a depth of 200 meters. Pub. L. No. 88–308, 78 Stat. 194 (repealed 1976). In 1966 a 12-mile fishery zone was created. Act of October 14, 1966 Pub. L. No. 89–658, 80 Stat. 908 (repealed 1976). And in 1976 Congress extended

148

Notes to Pages 47–48

the fishery-conservation zone out to 200 miles. Fishery Conservation and Management Act of 1976, tit. 1, §101, Pub. L. No. 94–265, 90 Stat. 336 (codified at 16 U.S.C. §1811 (1982). Conservation of continental-shelf fisheries is continued under the Fishery Conservation and Management Act of 1976, 16 U.S.C. §1812 (1982).

35. *See* L. JUDA, OCEAN SPACE RIGHTS: DEVELOPING U.S. POLICY 11–21 (1975); Watt, *First Steps in the Enclosure of the Oceans: The Origins of Truman's Proclamation on the Resources on the Continental Shelf, 28 Sept. 1945,* MARINE POLICY, July 1979, at 211.

36. *See* 51 U.S. Naval War College, INTERNATIONAL LAW SITUATIONS AND DOCUMENTS 1956, at 265 (1957); K. HJERTONSSON, THE NEW LAW OF THE SEA: INFLUENCE OF THE LATIN AMERICAN STATES ON RECENT DEVELOPMENTS OF THE LAW OF THE SEA 20–24 (1973).

The American delegation to the Santiago negotiations in 1955 argued that the Truman proclamation on conservation was not intended to serve as a unilateral assertion of exclusive jurisdiction, but was preliminary to future *bilateral* agreements, and was thus not a precedent for the declarations of Peru, Chile, and Ecuador. 33 DEP'T ST. BULL. 1025.

37. *See* G.A. Res. 1307, 13 U.N. GAOR Supp. (No. 18) at 54, U.N. Doc. A/L 253 (1958); Dean, *The Second Geneva Conference on the Law of the Sea: The Fight for Freedom of the Seas,* 54 AM. J. INT'L L. 751 (1960).

38. Convention on the Territorial Sea and Contiguous Zone, done April 29, 1958, 15 U.S.T. 1606, T.I.A.S. No. 5639, 516 U.N.T.S. 205 (effective Sept. 10, 1964). Although the breadth of the territorial sea is not specified, this convention established the sovereign rights of nations to belts of adjacent waters and the airspace above along with the soil beneath; the baseline from which it could be measured; and the right of innocent passage.

The convention also provided for "contiguous zones." Article 24 provides in part:

"(1) In a zone of the high seas contiguous to its territorial sea, the coastal State may exercise the control necessary to:
  (a) Prevent infringement of its customs, fiscal, immigration or sanitary regulations within its territory or territorial sea;
  (b) Punish infringement of the above regulations committed within its territory or territorial sea.
"(2) The contiguous zone may not extend beyond twelve miles from the baseline from which the breadth of the territorial sea is measured." *Id.*

The idea of a contiguous zone gives legal expression to the long-standing practice of nations in the exercise of extraterritorial jurisdiction for some purposes. The term "contiguous zone" came into official use with the Hague Conference of 1930, a conference convened under the auspices of the League of Nations to codify the law of the sea. *See generally,* SWARTZTRAUBER, *supra* note 19, at 132–40.

39. Convention on the High Seas, done April 29, 1958, 13 U.S.T. 2312, T.I.A.S. No. 5200, 450 U.N.T.S. 82 (effective Sept. 30, 1962).

40. Convention on Fishing and Conservation of the Living Resources of the High Seas, done April 29, 1958, 17 U.S.T. 138, T.I.A.S. No. 5969, 559 U.N.T.S. 285 (effective March 20, 1966). High-seas fishing is typically regulated by agreements.

41. Convention on the Continental Shelf, done April 29, 1958, 15 U.S.T. 471, T.I.A.S. No. 5578, 499 U.N.T.S. 311 (effective June 10, 1964). The convention provides for coastal national sovereignty over the continental shelf for the purpose of exploring it and exploiting its resources, but this sovereignty over the bed does not affect the legal status of the superjacent waters.

42. Convention on the High Seas, *supra* note 39.

43. *Id.* art. 2.

44. Convention on the Territorial Sea, *supra* note 38. Articles 3 and 4 provide for the baseline from which a territorial sea may be measured. All that Article 6 specifies for the seaward distance of the territorial sea is "the line every point of which is at a distance from the nearest point of the baseline equal to the breadth of the territorial sea." *Id.*

45. 1951 I.C.J. 116 (*Norwegian Fisheries* Case).

46. Convention on Fishing and Conservation of the Living Resources of the High Seas, *supra* note 40, arts. 4, 6.

47. Convention on the Continental Shelf, *supra* note 41, art. 1.

48. *See, e.g.*, Oda, INTERNATIONAL CONTROL OF SEA RESOURCES 167 (1963). *See also* Brown, *The Outer Limit of the Continental Shelf*, 1968 JURID. REV. 111 (1968).

49. Convention on the Continental Shelf, *supra* note 41, art. 6.

50. In 1966 a continental-shelf boundary dispute broke out between West Germany on one side and Holland and Denmark on the other concerning division of the North Sea Continental Shelf. Because of the configuration of her coast, West Germany would have a relatively small share of the shelf if equidistance were to be the rule. She had not ratified the Geneva Convention, and the International Court of Justice, in a 1969 decision, found both that the convention did not control the question and that the equidistance principle was not a matter of customary law. [1964] I.C.J. 3. The court did accept the Truman-initiated, Geneva-confirmed concept of the continental shelf; the shelf is a "natural prolongation" of a nation's land. However, the court decided that division of it was to be effected in accordance with equitable principles. Factors to be taken into account include configuration of the coasts, geologic structure and resources of the shelf, and a reasonable degree of proportionality between shelf portion and coastline length.

In a more recent dispute resolved by a court of arbitration in 1977, the continental-shelf boundary between the United Kingdom and France was fixed in the English Channel and Atlantic Ocean. The United Kingdom of Great Britain and Northern Ireland and the French Republic, Delimitation of the Continental Shelf, Court of Arbitration Decision of 30 June 1977; and Interpretation of the Decision of June 1977, Decision of 14 March 1978. The conflict primarily involved the Channel Islands, the Crown fiefdoms adjacent to the French coast. The Continental Shelf Convention was in force, and equidistance was agreed as the guiding method, with limited French exceptions. The result of the court of arbitration's decision was to recognize the islands as enclaves on the French shelf. The continental shelf of the United Kingdom was not to reach over and connect with that of the islands, which were given 12-mile zones to the north and northwest leaving territorial-sea boundaries to the east, between the islands and France, to be determined by agreement. An equidistant boundary was found in the Channel. The westward projection of that boundary down into the Atlantic out beyond the confines of the Channel then followed an equidistance-special circumstances rule, i.e., the westernmost of the islands were given half effect in drawing the line so that they pulled the equidistant boundary and skewed it in their direction to the advantage of the United Kingdom.

51. 1974 I.C.J. 1.

52. 2 WEEKLY COMP. PRES. DOC. 930–31 (1966).

53. *Note verbale* from the Permanent Mission of Malta to the United Nations Secretary-General, dated August 17, 1967, circulated as U.N. Doc. A/6695 (1967).

54. *Id.; see generally,* Knight, *The Draft United Nations Convention on the International*

Notes to Pages 50–51

Seabed Area: Background, Description and Some Preliminary Thoughts, 8 SAN DIEGO L. REV. 459, 477–79 (1971); L. SOHN, THE UNITED NATIONS AND THE OCEANS, CURRENT ISSUES IN THE LAW OF THE SEA 23 (Report to the Commission to Study the Organization of Peace, 1973).

55. G.A. Res. 2467 A, 23 U.N. GAOR Supp. (No. 18) at 15.

56. Declaration of Principles Governing the Sea-Bed and the Ocean Floor, and the Subsoil Thereof, beyond the Limits of National Jurisdiction. G.A. Res. 2749, 25 U.N. GAOR Supp. (No. 28).

57. G.A. Res. 2750 C, 25 U.N. GAOR Supp. (No. 28).

58. For a sampling of accounts, see, e.g., Mink, Foreword to Law of the Sea X, 15 SAN DIEGO L. REV. 357 (1978); Charney, Law of the Sea: Breaking the Deadlock, 55 FOREIGN AFFAIRS 598 (1977); Darman, The Law of the Sea: Rethinking U.S. Interests, 56 FOREIGN AFFAIRS 373 (1978); Law of the Sea X, 15 SAN DIEGO L. REV. 357 (1978); Law of the Sea IX, 14 SAN DIEGO L. REV. 507 (1977); Law of the Sea VIII, 13 SAN DIEGO L. REV. 483 (1976); Swing, Who Will Own the Oceans? 54 FOREIGN AFFAIRS 527 (1976).

59. United Nations Convention on the Law of the Sea, done at Montego Bay, Dec. 10, 1982, 21 I.L.M. 1261 (1982); U.N. Pub. E. 83 V. 5 (1983).

60. The only nations joining the United States in voting against the treaty were Israel, Turkey, and Venezuela. All three might well have been willing to allow the treaty to pass by consensus.

61. U.N. Convention on the Law of the Sea, supra note 59, art. 3.

62. Id. art. 57.

63. Id. art. 76.

64. Id. art. 87.

65. Id. art. 156.

66. See U.S. DEP'T OF STATE, NATIONAL CLAIMS TO MARITIME JURISDICTION (Limits in the Seas, No. 36, 3d rev. 1975); 3 INT'L LEGAL MATERIALS 926 (1964) (China); McDOUGAL & BURKE, supra note 1, at 1180 (1962) (Russia).

67. In the notes first laying claim to a 3-mile zone, Jefferson was careful to qualify it as "for the present," reserving the ultimate extent for future deliberation. See note 14, supra. Moreover, John Quincy Adams reported that, as president, Jefferson had informally maintained that "the neutrality of our territory should extend to the Gulf Stream, which was a natural boundary. . . ." 1 J. Q. ADAMS, MEMOIRS OF JOHN QUINCY ADAMS 375–76 (C. F. Adams ed. 1874). James Madison also thought a neutrality zone might be as wide as the Gulf Stream. 1 KENT, COMMENTARIES ON AMERICAN LAW 31 (11th ed. 1967). A limit for fisheries was set at three miles in the Convention of 1818 between Great Britain and the United States. Convention Respecting Fisheries, Boundary, and the Restoration of Slaves, October 20, 1818, United States-United Kingdom, 8 Stat. 248, T.S. 112. More recently, however, the United States has extended fishery jurisdiction first to twelve and then to two hundred miles. See note 34, supra. At the beginning of World War II, the American republics issued the Declaration of Panama establishing a security zone which reached several hundred miles into the Atlantic and Pacific. 1 DEP'T ST. BULL. 331 (1939). See 7 HACKWORTH, DIGEST OF INTERNATIONAL LAW 702 (1943). Following the war, the United States created Air Defense Identification Zones whereby incoming aircraft receive clearance and make position reports when they are within two hours' cruising distance of the coast. 15 Fed. Reg. 9319 (1950). See Note, Air Defense Identification Zones, 4 N.Y.L.F. 365 (1958).

68. Act of March 2, 1799, ch. 22, §§27, 54; 1 Stat. 627, 668. In 1935 jurisdiction was set at sixty-two miles. Anti-Smuggling Act of 1935, Pub. L. No. 74–238, 49 Stat. 517 (codified at 19 U.S.C. §§1701–1711 (1982)). With the passage of the eighteenth amend-

ment and the resulting concern over liquor smuggling along the coasts, Congress provided for the enforcement of prohibition legislation also to the four-league mark. Tariff
Act of 1922, Pub. L. No. 67–318, 42 Stat. 858. Subsequent negotiations with Great Britain produced the "Liquor Treaty" of 1924 which provided for the boarding, search, and
seizure of offending vessels at a distance no greater than the suspected vessel could
travel in one hour, a variable limit which might range from one to twenty or thirty
miles depending upon vessel speed. Convention on Smuggling of Intoxicating Liquors,
Jan. 23, 1924, United States-United Kingdom, 42 Stat. 1761, T.S. 685. For accounts of
earlier willingness of the U.S. to expand territorial-sea limits, see Dean, *The Geneva
Conference on the Law of the Sea: What Was Accomplished*, 52 Am. J. Int'l L. 607 (1958);
Dean, *supra* note 37, at 751.

69. Carlisle, *The Three-Mile Limit: Obsolete Concept?* 93 U.S. Naval Inst. Proc. 24
(1967). *See* Hedman, *The U.S. Position on the Breadth of the Territorial Sea: National Security
and Beyond, in* Some Current Sea Law Problems 14, 17 (Wurfel ed. 1975).

70. Brown, *Maritime Zones: A Survey of Claims, in* 3 New Directions in the Law of
the Sea 157, 165 (R. Churchill, K. Simmonds, J. Welch, eds. 1973); U.S. Dep't of State,
Sovereignty of the Sea 22–27 (Geographic Bull. No. 3, 1969); D. Logue & R. Sweeney,
Economics and the Law of the Sea Negotiations 20 (A.E.I. Original Paper 6, 1977).

71. U.N. Convention on the Law of the Sea, *supra* note 59, art. 38.

72. Convention on the Territorial Sea and Contiguous Zone, *supra* note 38, art. 14.

73. The court held that states in time of peace have a right to send their warships
through straits used for international navigation between two parts of the high seas
without the previous authorization of a coastal state, provided that the passage is innocent. 1949 I.C.J. 4, 28, *reprinted in* 43 Am. J. Int'l L. 558, 576 (1949). *See generally, e.g.,*
Note, *Passage through International Straits: Free or Innocent? The Interests at Stake*, 11 San
Diego L. Rev. 815 (1974).

74. Convention on the Territorial Sea and Contiguous Zone, *supra* note 38, art. 14.

75. *Id.* para. 6.

76. Convention on the Law of the Sea, *supra* note 59, arts. 17, 45.

77. *Id.* art. 37.

78. *Id.* art. 38, para. 2.

79. *Id.* art. 76.

80. *See, e.g.*, Hedberg, *Relations of Political Boundaries of the Ocean Floor to the Continental Margin*, 17 Va. J. Int'l L. 57 (1976). It would seem to be clear that national sovereignty is not to be extended to the bed of the high-seas area.

81. Convention on the Law of the Sea, *supra* note 59, art. 57.

82. *Id.* art. 58, 56(2).

83. In 1976 Congress enacted the Fishery Conservation and Management Act, 16
U.S.C. §§1801–1882 (1982), which created a fishery-conservation zone with a seaward
limit of 200 miles. 16 U.S.C. §1811 (1982). Within this zone fisheries are to be conserved
and managed to "prevent overfishing while achieving, on a continuing basis, the optimum yield from each fishery." 16 U.S.C. §1851 (a) (1) (1982). Foreign fishing in the
zone may be conducted pursuant to international fishery agreements. 16 U.S.C.
§§1821–1824 (1982). The total allowable level of foreign fishing is "that portion of the
optimum yield of such fishery which will not be harvested by vessels of the United
States. . . ." 16 U.S.C. §1821(d)(1982).

There may be some discrepancy between the UNCLOS text and the F.C.M.A. regarding management of anadromous species. The F.C.M.A. provides for the United
States to exercise "exclusive fishery management authority" over "[a]ll anadromous
species throughout the migratory range of each such species beyond the fishery con-

servation zone; except that such management authority shall not extend to such species during the time they are found within any foreign nation's territorial sea or fishery conservation zone. . . ." 16 U.S.C. §1812(2).(1982). Article 66 of the UNCLOS text provides:

"(1) States in whose rivers anadromous stocks originate shall have the primary interest in and responsibility for such stocks.

"(2) The State of origin of anadromous stocks shall ensure their conservation by the establishment of appropriate regulatory measures for fishing in all waters landwards of the outer limits of its exclusive economic zone and for fishing provided for in paragraph 3 (6). The State of origin may, after consultations with other States. . . . fishing these stocks, establish total allowable catches for stocks originating in its rivers.

"(3)(a) *Fisheries for anadromous stocks shall be conducted only in the waters landwards of the outer limits of exclusive economic zones, . . . Enforcement of regulations regarding anadromous stocks beyond the exclusive economic zone shall be by agreement between the State of origin and the other States concerned.*" (Emphasis added.)

On the international implications of the F.C.M.A., *see* Note, *International Ramifications of the Fisheries Conservation and Management Act of 1976,* 7 GA. J. INT'L & COMP. L. 133 (1977). On the provisions for anadromous species, *see* ALASKA POSITION ON INTERNATIONAL FISHERIES MANAGEMENT WITH SPECIAL REFERENCE TO THE REVISED SINGLE NEGOTIATING TEXT OF THE UNITED NATIONS CONFERENCE ON THE LAW OF THE SEA 51–55 (1977). For discussion of the conflict between F.C.M.A. and the Law of the Sea Convention, *see* Jacobson and Cameron, *Potential Conflicts between a Future Law of the Sea Treaty and the Fishery Conservation and Management Act of 1976,* 52 WASH. L. REV. 451 (1977).

84. The 1977 amendments to the Federal Water Pollution Control Act, for example, extended certain of that Act's oil and hazardous spill provisions from the 12- to the 200-mile limit. Act of Dec. 27, 1977, Pub. L. No. 95–217 §58(a)–(c), 91 Stat. 1593.

Then the Environmental Protection Agency announced its intention of extending regulations under the Clean Air Act to activities related to exploitation of the resources of the continental shelf. Notice of Final Determination of Applicability of the Clean Air Act to Exxon Corporation's Platform Hondo, 43 Fed. Reg. 16393 (1978).

The 1978 amendments to the Outer Continental Shelf Lands Act also spawned considerable debate over the desirability and proper scope of federal or state environmental regulation on the continental shelf. *See, e.g.,* [1978] 8 ENV'T REP. (BNA) 54, 323, 799, 1465.

85. "Offshore islands and other man-made coastal installations are proving to be very much in demand, if not necessary, in urbanized coastal areas. There have been a vast variety of such structures and installations proposed for continental shelf areas, including airports, floating cities and hotels." Krueger, *An Evaluation of United States Oceans Policy,* 17 McGILL L.J. 603, 668, n. 219 (1970). "The UNCLOS provisions are the first time that such structures have been clearly authorized under international law when used for purposes other than the exploitation of seabed resources." Krueger, *An Overview of Changes Occurring in the Law of the Sea—Implications for Federal-State Relations,* 10 NAT. RESOURCES J. 225, 233 (1977).

86. *See generally* U.S. DEP'T OF THE INTERIOR, OCEAN MINING ADMINISTRATION, OCEAN MINING: AN ECONOMIC EVALUATION (1976); U.S. Congress, Senate Subcommittee on Public Lands and Resources of the Committee on Energy and Natural Resources and the Committee on Commerce, Science and Transportation, *Joint Hearings on Mining of the Deep Seabed,* (Publication No. 95–78, 1978); R. FRANK, DEEP SEA MINING AND THE ENVIRONMENT (1976).

87. One of the arguments in favor of unilateral licensing of deep-seabed mining by the United States was that American strategic interests required protection against cartelization of the subject minerals. *See generally* Discovery II, Fall 1977, at 1, 3 United Methodist Joint Law of the Sea Project; House debates on H.R. 3350, 124 CONG. REC. H 7341 (daily ed. July 26, 1978). In opposition it was pointed out that there was no danger of cartelization of these minerals. *See generally* Raymond, *Seabed Minerals and the U.S. Economy: A Second Look,* 123 CONG. REC. 3, 733 (daily ed. Feb. 10, 1977).

88. *See Deep Seabed Mineral Resources Act,* S. REP. No. 96–307, 96th Cong., 1st Sess., August 9, 1979.

89. Convention on the Law of the Sea, *supra* note 59, art. 156.

90. *Id.* art. 158.

91. *Id.* Annex 6.

92. *Id.* arts. 159–60.

93. *Id.* art. 162.

94. *Id.* art. 161.

95. *Id.* arts. 163–65.

96. *Id.* art. 166.

97. *Id.* art. 170.

98. *Id.* art. 153.

99. *Id.* arts. 140, 150–51.

100. *Id.* art. 140.

101. *Id.* Annex 6, art. 2.

102. *Id.* Annex 6, art. 15.

103. *Id.* arts. 186–91; Annex 6, arts. 14, 36–41.

104. On the New International Economic Order generally, *see* Programme of Action on the Establishment of a New International Economic Order, 16 May 1974, U.N.G.A. Res. 3202 (S-VI), 6 (Special) U.N. GAOR Supp. (No. 1) at 5, U.N. Doc. A/9559 (1974); Charter of Economic Rights and Duties of States, Dec. 12, 1974, U.N.G.A. Res. 3281 (XXIX) 29 U.N. GAOR Supp. (No. 31) at 50, U.N. Doc. A/9631 (1975). On the Group of 77 and the relationship of the NIEO to the law of the sea, *see, e.g.,* Borgese, *The New International Economic Order and the Law of the Sea,* 14 SAN DIEGO L. REV. 584 (1977); *id., A Constitution for the Oceans: Comments and Suggestions Regarding Part XI of the Informal Composite Negotiating Text,* 15 SAN DIEGO L. REV. 365 (1978); Juda, *UNCLOS III and the New International Economic Order,* 7 OCEAN DEV. & INT'L L. 221 (1979); Symposium, *Influence and Innovation in the Law of the Sea: Latin American and Africa,* 7 OCEAN DEV. & INT'L L. 1 (1979). *See also,* THE LAW OF THE SEA: NEEDS AND INTERESTS OF DEVELOPING NATIONS (Proceedings of the Seventh Annual Conference of the Law of the Sea Institute, L. Alexander ed., 1973); R. ANAND, LEGAL REGIME OF THE SEA-BED AND THE DEVELOPING COUNTRIES (1975).

105. Convention on the Law of the Sea, *supra* note 59, Annex 3, art. 5.

106. *Id.* arts. 150–51; Annex 3, arts. 6–7.

107. *Id.* Annex 3, art. 13.

108. *Id.* art. 155.

109. Arts. 314, 161 (7) (d), 159. Amendment of the convention with respect to matters other than seabed activities could be effected through simpler procedures, one of which involves convening a conference for the purpose. *Id.* art. 312. For an expedited procedure, *see* art. 313.

110. Convention on the Law of the Sea, *supra* note 59, art. 159.

111. *Id.* art. 161.

112. *See, id.* Annex 3, art. 13 (1) (b). Changes in the financial system of production

charges and share of net proceeds were responsive, if only in a limited way, to the argument that the financial burdens were too great to attract miners.

113. Pub. L. No. 96–282, 96th Cong., June 28, 1980.

114. See Gorove, *The Concept of "Common Heritage of Mankind": A Political, Moral or Legal Innovation*, 9 SAN DIEGO L. REV. 390 (1972).

The Charter of the United Nations provides that the General Assembly may discuss subjects within the scope of the Charter and may make recommendations to its members. U.N. CHARTER, art. 10, 59 Stat. 1031, T.S. No. 993. It also provides that studies and recommendations may be made for the purpose of encouraging the development of international law and its codification. With respect to internal matters of the organization, General Assembly decisions may be binding on members but resolutions generally are not. *See, e.g.*, R. HIGGINS, THE DEVELOPMENT OF INTERNATIONAL LAW THROUGH THE POLITICAL ORGANS OF THE UNITED NATIONS (1963); O. ASAMOAH, THE LEGAL SIGNIFICANCE OF THE DECLARATIONS OF THE GENERAL ASSEMBLY OF THE UNITED NATIONS (1966); Johnson, *The Effect of Resolutions of the General Assembly of the United Nations*, 32 BRIT. Y.B. INT'L L. 97 (1956).

In the course of debate concerning the General Assembly resolution designating the seabed as the common heritage of mankind, John Stevenson, then legal adviser to the U.S. State Department, said that "concepts such as the 'common heritage of mankind' were for the time being without any specific legal content. . . ." A/AC.138/SC.1/SR.13. Subsequently, Stevenson stated that the concept "will be elaborated in the internationally agreed regime to be established." Statement by Honorable John R. Stevenson, before the First committee of the United Nations on Agenda Item 25 (a), Dec. 15, 1970. *See also*, R. DUPUY, THE LAW OF THE SEA 39 (1974).

115. *See*, Goldie, *A General International Law Doctrine for Seabed Regimes*, 7 INT'L LAW. 796, 809–10 (1973); Ely, *The Laws Governing Exploitation of the Minerals beneath the Sea*, in Marine Technology Society, EXPLORING THE OCEAN 373 (1966). *See generally*, 1 OPPEN-HEIM, *supra* note 20, at 628. *See also*, L. HENKIN, LAW FOR THE SEA'S MINERAL RESOURCES (1967); Burton, *Freedom of the Seas: International Law Applicable to Deep Seabed Mining Claims*, 29 STAN. L. REV. 1135, 1169–80 (1977).

116. Grotius, Letter of 1637, *quoted in* PAUW, *supra* note 24, at 75–76.

117. *See, e.g.*, A. PARDO, THE COMMON HERITAGE: SELECTED PAPERS ON OCEANS AND WORLD ORDER, 1967–1974 (1975); Granoff, Not to Put the Sea to Bed, unpublished essay (1978).

118. Convention on the Law of the Sea, *supra* note 59, art. 125. Article 3 of the 1958 Convention on the High Seas, *supra* note 43, provided: "In order to enjoy the freedom of the seas on equal terms with coastal States, States having no sea coast should have free access to the sea."

119. Convention on the Law of the Sea, *supra* note 59, arts. 61–62, 69–70.

120. *Id.* art. 82.

121. *Id.* art. 266.

122. Convention on Fishing and Conservation of the Living Resources of the High Seas, *supra* note 40, arts. 1, 2, 4, 9, 6–7. On the question of fisheries and their regulation, *see generally*, for example, CHRISTY & SCOTT, THE COMMON WEALTH IN OCEAN FISHERIES (1965); A KOERS, INTERNATIONAL REGULATION OF MARINE FISHERIES (1973); Department of Fisheries, Food and Agriculture Organization of the United Nations, Report on Regulatory Fishery Bodies, FAO Circular No. 138 (1972); Chapman, *The Theory and Practice of International Fishery Development-Management*, 3 PACEM IN MARIBUS 137 (1971).

123. See, e.g., Mirvahabi, Significant Fishery Management Issues in the Law of the Sea Conference: Illusions and Realities, 15 SAN DIEGO L. REV. 493 (1978).

124. Convention on the Law of the Sea, supra note 59, arts. 56, 57, 61.

125. For example, the 1980 catch of cod in Iceland exceeded 400,000 metric tons. Marine biologists had recommended a maximum of 300,000 tons while the government's Ministry of Fisheries had thought 360,000 should be the maximum. The Cod Take Heads beyond 400,000 Tons, NEWS FROM ICELAND, No. 59, Dec. 1980, at 1, col. 1.

The following is also to be borne in mind: "The International Commission on Whaling has become the epitome of ineffectiveness in international cooperation aimed at conservation, or the rational management, of high seas fisheries. Its failure provided the arguments for those who would divide up the ocean into national sectors, but it must be noted that Chile's 200-mile territorial sea claim was supported in great part from its desire to avoid regulations established by the International Whaling Commission. Since IWC regulations applied only to the high seas, and all of Chile's whaling occurred within 200 miles, this measure solved that problem. It must also be noted [that] Peru after enforcing its 200-mile limit against other whaling countries killed migratory sperm whales passing through its 'territorial sea' with sufficient effort to overfish them by its own activity." Chapman, supra note 122, at 150 (citation omitted).

For economic analysis favoring enclosure of fisheries, see R. Eckert, The Enclosure of Ocean Resources 116–53 (1979) and sources cited therein.

126. See J. SCHNEIDER, WORLD PUBLIC ORDER OF THE ENVIRONMENT: TOWARDS AN INTERNATIONAL ECOLOGICAL LAW AND ORGANIZATION 108–12 (1979).

127. Convention on the Law of the Sea, supra note 59, arts. 62, 69.

128. Id. art. 61.

129. Id. art. 63; Annex 1.

130. Id. art. 66.

131. Id. arts. 65, 120. Recently the protection of whales has received unexpected support. See Trade in Most Whale Products Is Outlawed, N.Y. Times, Saturday, Mar. 7, 1981, at 3, col. 4 (trade in oil, meat and bone of the sperm, sei, and fin whales, virtually the only species still commercially hunted, added to Appendix 1 of the Convention on International Trade in Endangered Specie of Wild Fauna and Flora which lists plants and animals banned from international commerce). Subsequently the International Whaling Commission voted a ban on hunting sperm whales. Conservationists Gain a Victory in Hunting Ban on Sperm Whales, N.Y. Times, July 27, 1981, at 3, col. 1.

132. See, e.g., Our Oceans Are Dying, N.Y. Times, Nov. 14, 1971, at 13, col. 3. On the general question of marine pollution, see MARINE POLLUTION (R. Johnston ed. 1976); IDENTIFICATION AND CONTROL OF POLLUTANTS OF BROAD INTERNATIONAL SIGNIFICANCE 77–93, United Nations Conference on the Human Environment, U.N. Doc. A/Conf.48/8(1972); OCEAN DUMPING: A NATIONAL POLICY, (Report to the President by the Council on Environmental Quality, 1970); ENVIRONMENTAL QUALITY—1972, at 85–91 (Third Annual Report of the Council on Environmental Quality, 1972); ENVIRONMENTAL QUALITY—1980, at 15–27 (Eleventh Annual Report of the Council on Environmental Quality, 1980); SCIENCE AND ENVIRONMENT 49–53 (1 Panel Reports of the Commission on Marine Science, Engineering and Resources, 1969).

The general principle of conservation has taken shape in different legal forms: nuisance, abus de droit, good neighborship, abstention. It was recognized or discussed in the decision of the Trail Smelter Arbitral Tribunal, reported Mar. 11, 1941, 3 U.N.R.I.A.A. 1905, 35 AM. J. INT'L L. 684 (1941); The Corfu Channel Case, 1949 I.C.J. 4; and in the Lac Lanoux decision, French-Spanish Arbitral Tribunal, reported Nov. 16, 1957, 53 AM. J. INT'L L. 156 (1959). See 1 OPPENHEIM, supra note 20, at 346–47.

Treaties and other documents intended to bear on the subject include:

—1958 Geneva Convention on the High Seas, arts. 24 ("Every State shall draw up regulations to prevent pollution of the seas from the dumping of hazardous waste. . . .").

—1958 Geneva Convention on the Continental Shelf, art. 5 ("The coastal State is obliged to undertake, in the safety zones, all appropriate measures for the protection of the living resources of the sea from harmful agents.")

—1954 International Convention for the Prevention of Pollution of the Sea by Oil (amended 1962 and 1969) (prohibits international discharge of oil into the sea; prosecution for violation left to discretion of flag nation; no compensation provision).

—1957 International Convention relating to the Limitation of the Liability of Owners of Seagoing Ships (limits shipowner liability to $7 million).

—1962 Convention on the Liability of Operators of Nuclear Ships (strict liability; $100 million limit).

—1963 Treaty Banning Nuclear Weapon Tests in the Atmosphere, in Outer Space and under Water (banning of explosions in environment outside nation).

—1969 International Convention relating to Intervention on the High Seas in Cases of Oil Pollution Casualties (nations have right to intervene on high seas to protect coasts from oil spills).

—1969 International Convention on Civil Liability for Oil Pollution Damage (strict liability for damage in coastal nation's territory; $14 million limit).

—1971 International Convention on the Establishment of an International Fund for Compensation for Oil Pollution Damage (relieves shipowners from additional financial burden under 1969 Convention; adds compensation to victims; $30 million limit).

—1972 Oslo Convention for the Prevention of Marine Pollution by Dumping from Ships and Aircraft (prevents or regulates dumping in North Sea/North Atlantic).

—1972 Declaration of the United Nations Conference on the Human Environment, Principle 7 ("States shall take all possible steps to prevent pollution of the seas by substances that are liable to create hazards to human health, to harm living resources and marine life, to damage amenities or to interfere with other legitimate uses of the sea."); Principle 21 ("States have . . . the sovereign right to exploit their own resources pursuant to their own environmental policies, and the responsibility to ensure that activities within their jurisdiction or control do not cause damage to the environment of other States or areas beyond the limits of national jurisdiction."); Principle 22 ("States shall co-operate to develop further the international law regarding liability and compensation for the victims of pollution and other environmental damage caused by activities within the jurisdiction or control of such States to areas beyond their jurisdiction.")

—1972 London Convention on the Prevention of Marine Pollution by Dumping of Wastes and Other Matter (nations agree to ban dumping; to be done through national authority).

—1973 International Convention for the Prevention of Pollution from Ships (standards for vessel discharge of oil and hazardous substances; rules for design and construction of vessels carrying same; standards for handling ship-generated sewage).

—1976 Barcelona Convention (covering Mediterranean); 1978 Final Act, United Nations Conference of Plenipotentiaries of the Coastal States of the Mediterranean Region for the Protection of the Mediterranean Sea against Pollution from Land-based Sources; for recent Mediterranean development *see Mediterranean Nations Approve Plan to Clean Up the Sea,* N.Y. Times, Wednesday, Mar. 11, 1981, at 3, col. 1.

See generally, e.g., Who Protects the Oceans? Environment and the Development of the Law of the Sea (Hargrove ed. 1975); International Environmental Law (Teclaff & Utton eds. 1974); Bleicher, *An Overview of International Environmental Regulation,* 2 Ecology L.Q. 1, 35–43 (1972); Hillman, Towards an Environmentally Sound Law of the Sea, (Report of the International Institute for Environment and Development, 1974); Henkin, *Arctic Anti-Pollution: Does Canada Make—or Break—International Law,* 65 Am. J. Int'l. L. 131 (1971); Schachter & Serwer, *Marine Pollution Problems and Remedies,* 65 Am. J. Int'l. L. 84 (1971); *see also* Schneider, *supra* note 126; Weston, Falk, D'Amato, *supra* note 1, at 958 (bibliography).

133. Convention on the Law of the Sea, *supra* note 59, arts. 192–237.

134. *Id.* art. 194.

135. *Id.* arts. 217–20.

136. *Id.* art. 221. The flag nation may preempt proceedings except where there has been a major casualty. *Id.* art. 228.

137. *Id.* art. 193.

138. *See, e.g.,* Alexander, *The Reaganites, Misadventure at Sea,* Fortune, Aug. 23, 1982, at 129.

139. Wertenbaker, *supra* note 23, at 56.

140. Lakoff & Johnson, Metaphors We Live By 231–32 (1980).

141. *Id.* at 146.

142. *See, e.g.,* F. Y. Chaim, Consultation and Consensus in the Security Council, UNITAR (1971); Jenks, *Unanimity, the Veto, Weighted Voting, Special and Simple Majorities and Consensus as Modes of Decision in International Organizations, in* Cambridge Essays in International Law, Essays in Honor of Lord McNair 48 (1965); Sohn, *United Nations Decision Making: Confrontation or Consensus?* 15 Harv. Int'l L.J. 438 (1974); *id., Voting Procedures in United Nations Conferences for the Codification of International Law,* 69 Am. J. Int'l. L. 310 (1975).

143. On the subject of these instruments generally, *see* Lauterpacht, *Gentlemen's Agreements, in* International Law and Economic Order 381 (Flume et al. eds. 1977).

144. The statement was approved by the U.N. General Assembly on November 16, 1973, and then adopted by the conference along with the rules of procedure at Caracas on June 27, 1974. *See,* Sohn, *Voting Procedures in United Nations Conferences for the Codification of International Law,* 69 Am. J. Int'l. L. 310 (1975); Stevenson & Oxman, *The Third United Nations Conference on the Law of the Sea: The 1974 Caracas Session,* 69 Am. J. Int'l. L. 1, 3–5 (1975); Vignes, *Will the Third Conference on the Law of the Sea Work according to the Consensus Rule?* 69 Am. J. Int'l. L. 119 (1975).

145. Third U.N. Conference on the Law of the Sea, Rules of Procedure, Appendix, UN Doc. A/CONF.62/30/Rev.2 (1976): Oxman, *The Third United Nations Conference on the Law of the Sea: The Seventh Session* (1978), 73 Am. J. Int'l. L. 1, 2–3 (1979) (vote on resolution confirming president's continuation in office).

146. Rules of Procedure, *supra* note 145, rules 34, 37.

147. *Id.* arts. 161 (7), 159 (6).

148. *Id.* Annex 6. *See generally, e.g.,* Adede, *Settlement of Disputes Arising under the Law of the Sea Convention,* 69 Am. J. Int'l. L. 788 (1975); *id., Law of the Sea—The Integration of the System of Settlement of Disputes under the Draft Convention as a Whole,* 75 Am. J. Int'l. L. 84 (1978); Sohn, *Settlement of Disputes Arising out of the Law of the Sea,* 12 San Diego L. Rev. 495 (1975); *id., Settlement of Fisheries Disputes in the Exclusive Economic Zone,* 73 Am. J. Int'l. L. 89 (1979).

149. *See* Sohn, *The Role of Conciliation in International Disputes,* Fine Print, May 1, 1981, at 3. *See generally,* L. Sohn and K. Gustafson, *supra* note 1, at 238–46.

150. Convention on the Law of the Sea, *supra* note 59, pt. 15, arts. 297–98.
151. *Id.* Annex 5, art. 7(1).
152. *Id.* art. 7(2).
153. Sohn, *supra* note 144, at 353.
154. *See* Sohn & Burke, Discussion, *in* THE UNITED STATES WITHOUT THE LAW OF THE SEA TREATY: OPPORTUNITIES AND COSTS 138–39 (Juda ed. 1983).
155. Convention on the Law of the Sea, *supra* note 59, art. 161 (8) (e).
156. *Id.*
157. Consensus is mandated for the Council in one other instance, this one having to do with experts.

The use of experts has posed interesting questions for international law, particularly in the context of environmental controls. *See, e.g.,* Contini & Sand, *Methods to Expedite Environment Protection: International Ecostandards,* 66 AM. J. INT'L. L. 37 (1972); Schachter & Serwer, *Marine Pollution Problems and Remedies,* 65 AM. J. INT'L. L. 84 (1971). The new treaty provides for drawing on experts in several circumstances. *See,* Convention on the Law of the Sea, *supra* note 59, art. 61 (2). In one, coastal nations are to take scientific evidence into account in protecting the fisheries within their zones. In the other, scientists are to play a role in determining the limits of the continental shelf. The treaty says that a nation's continental shelf may extend to the "outer edge of the continental margin." *Id.* art. 76 (1). This limit is both important and not obvious. *See id.* art. 76 (4). Accordingly, the text provides for the use of experts to determine the outer limit of the continental shelf where the margin falls outside 200 miles. The coastal nation is to mark the limits of its shelf "on the basis of" recommendations made by a commission of geologists, geophysicists or hydrographers. *Id.* Annex 2, art. 2.

By far the most interesting use of experts is that linking them to consensus in mining the deep seabed. Experts are to review work plans for deep-seabed mining. The work plans are submitted to the commission of legal and technical experts by parties wishing to take nodules from the common-heritage area. The commission then makes its recommendation for approval or disapproval of the proposal to the Council. Whether a contract is then entered depends upon consensus: if the experts recommend approval, the plan can be disapproved by the Council only if there is a consensus against. *Id.* art. 162(j). If the experts recommend disapproval, the Council can approve the plan by a three-fourths majority vote in favor of it. This use of consensus gives heavy weight to the judgment of the experts. The assumption is that a contract which satisfies the technicalities in the (presumably objective) judgment of the experts should proceed unless there is considerable opposition. The burden shifts to the opponents, who have to muster a consensus. This provision seeks to allay the fears of prospective miners who might think that their plans of work would be subject to disapproval on nontechnical, political grounds. It is of particular interest because of the way it gives priority to expert judgment but keeps this judgment within the ultimately political context allowed by consensus.

158. D'Amato, *On Consensus,* 8 CAN. Y.B. INT'L L. 104, 111 (1970).

In his book *Sharing the World's Resources,* Oscar Schachter discusses standards for the equitable sharing of resources, especially the standard for distribution according to need, and the ways in which they have been given practical effect. He presents a possibility for understanding the appropriation of ocean resources as a response to demands for equity and wider sharing. This possibility might mean that even the division of the seas could be construed in alignment with the kind of human solidarity and commonality I am pursuing. Schachter points out that recognition of equity and distributive justice among nations is attributable "not to a sudden spread of altruism, but to a widely felt necessity on the part of governmental elites to respond to tensions and grievances which threaten the equilibrium and stability of the international order." Sharing the World's Resources 16 (1977). *See id.* at 143–44.

Schachter's seems to me a more complete reading than that of Louis Henkin, who believes that what has emerged from the U.N. conference has been "at bottom . . . the result of 'political vectors,'" drawn elsewhere than at the conference. L. Henkin, How Nations Behave 215 (1979). The law of the sea, he says, will reflect "egoistic nationalist forces of coastal states," on the one hand, and, on the other, the fallout from a struggle between the third world, hard driving its New International Economic Order, and wealthy developed nations favored by the established system. *Id.* at 226–27.

Note should also be taken of the illuminating study by Keohane and Nye, *Power and Interdependence,* in which the law of the sea is demonstrated as a paradigmatic reflection of growing international interdependence. I have made passing mention of interdependence in this chapter but have tried to avoid using it as a synonym for the reality I seek to describe as "solidarity," or "commonality." Keohane and Nye point out that an order of interdependence does not necessarily imply an order of greater equity and justice since interdependence can lead to the exploitation by the powerful of the weaker who are dependent upon them. Where solidarity is recognized, then exploitation will not follow. *See* Chapter 6 *infra.*

It is also incumbent upon me to acknowledge indebtedness and to pay tribute to the seminal work of Myres McDougal and William Burke, The Public Order of the Oceans (1964). McDougal views international law as a policy-oriented, political process of authoritative decision. He has successfully focused attention on the horizontal process of interaction among nations by which they implement and clarify their common interest. This common interest, it was argued by McDougal and Burke, would seem inescapably to lie in "an accommodation of exclusive and inclusive claim which will produce the largest total output of community values at the least cost." The Public Order of the Oceans 52. The inherited old order of the oceans, they thought, had successfully accommodated the inclusive interests of all states and the exclusive interests of coastal nations so that it did not simply balance competing interests but also clarified and secured common interests. In the course of an eloquent plea, they proposed that "[c]onsidering all our contemporary ignorance and interdependence, the most rational course for the general community, and for particular states genuinely concerned for their long-term interests, would appear to be to abide by the wisdom of Grotius, as confirmed by experience and as promising the greatest common gains for all mankind." *Id.* at 563. Following the pattern established by Grotius who, years subsequent to *Mare Liberum,* wondered whether there would be any limit to territorial claims to marine areas, Professor McDougal later stated: "With strong preferences for the protection of common and rejection of special interests and for a balancing in favor of inclusive rather than exclusive interests, I confess that I may appear . . . a pleader for lost causes." McDougal, *The Law of the High Seas in Time of Peace,* 25 Naval War C. Rev. No. 3, at 35, 36 (1973). He went on to prophesy about the UNCLOS that "given the arrogant contemporary perspectives of nationalism and misperceptions of common interest, disaster may impend." *Id.* at 44.

My own approach is to be distinguished from that of McDougal and Burke in several fundamental respects. For one thing, I think the accommodation of claims is not an adequate substitute for the negotiation of meaning. I also think that interest, even common interest, is not an adequate alternative to solidarity. Perhaps my chief difference from them, however, is simply that they wrote when, not so long ago, it could still be said that the immensity of the oceans allowed nations to "seek their own ends

Notes to Pages 63–66

by freely chosen strategies, largely without reference to the choices made by others." THE PUBLIC ORDER OF THE OCEANS, *supra*, at 25. They noted that, with the growing complexity of techniques of ocean exploitation, "strategies will need to be projected in more organizations devoted to this special purpose. Inchoate efforts in this direction are now being made chiefly through the United Nations' specialized agencies." *Id.* Although I write less than two decades later, it has become a different epoch, and the U.N. conference, in my view, the dominating issue. I also find more cause for hope in it than did McDougal writing in 1973. Like Sancho Panza, I would urge him: "Don't die, Don Quixote, don't die!" If the conference has legitimated the division of most of the ocean, who is to say that this will have been too great a price for the performance it has given us of solidarity in the medium of law.

But Coleman Barks has a further sobering thought. He sent the following note:

"One possible weakness, or unfairness, of law as medium—fluid argument-shifting consensus might be: that those with the best language come out with more power— those with the most command of the most sensitive instrument (English) might plead their biases and blindnesses more than they should. I worry about the Belizians, and the Hopi, who might take a huge grand symbol into a room where slosh and counter-slosh is having its way." I share this worry now that Barks has introduced it.

CHAPTER 4

1. *See* chapter 3 *supra*, notes 66–69 and accompanying text; Ball, THE LAW OF THE SEA: FEDERAL-STATE RELATIONSHIPS (Dean Rusk Center Monograph No. 1, 1980). It will be remembered that Thomas Jefferson was the first to make official claims to a 3-mile sea. He did so in 1793. The year following Jefferson's claim Congress enacted a statute providing for federal-district-court jurisdiction of certain cases "within a marine league of the coast. . . ." Act of June 5, 1774, ch. 50, 1 Stat. 381. (A nautical mile is a measurement of arc on the surface of the earth and equals one minute of latitude or one-sixteenth of a degree. A nautical mile is about 1.15 statute miles; a marine league is three nautical miles.) Then in an early circuit-court case, Justice Story remarked that, as a matter of established international law, every nation had exclusive jurisdiction over adjacent waters for a marine league. The Brig Ann, 1 F. Cas. 926, 926 (C.C. Mass. 1812) (No. 397). *See also* Church v. Hubbart, 6 U.S. (2 Cranch) 187, 234 (1804); Commonwealth v. Manchester, 152 Mass. 230, 240 (1890), *aff'd sub. nom.* Manchester v. Massachusetts, 139 U.S. 240, 258 (1891); Cunard S.S. Co. v. Mellon, 262 U.S. 100, 122 (1923). Later, during the Civil War, Secretary of State Seward argued, in opposition to Spanish insistence upon a 6-mile limit off Cuba, that a 3-mile limit was generally recognized by nations. *See* 1 MOORE, INTERNATIONAL LAW DIGEST 706–13 (1906).

2. According to one federal court, "[t]he line between territorial waters and the high seas is not like the boundary between us and a foreign power. There must be, it seems to me, a certain width of debatable waters adjacent to our coasts. . . ." The Grace and Ruby, 283 F. 475, 478 (D. Mass. 1922). They had been debatable from the start. *See* chapter 3, note 67, *supra*.

3. Policy of the United States with respect to the Natural Resources of the Subsoil and Sea Bed of the Continental Shelf, Proclamation No. 2667, 3 C.F.R. 67 (1943–48 Comp.), *reprinted in* 59 Stat. 884 (1945); Policy of the United States with respect to Coastal Fisheries in Certain Areas of the High Seas, Proclamation No. 2668, 3 C.F.R. 68 (1943–48 Comp.), *reprinted in* 59 Stat. 885 (1945). *See generally* 4 WHITEMAN, INTER-

National Law 740–931, 945–62 (1965); Hollick, *U.S. Oceans Policy: The Truman Procla-mations*, 17 Va. J. Int'l L. 23 (1976); Allen, *Fishery Proclamation of 1945*, 45 Am. J. Int'l L. 177 (1951).

The proclamations were accompanied by a press release explaining that the declared policy "does not touch upon the questions of Federal versus State Control." White House Press Release, Sept. 28, 1945, 13 Dep't St. Bull. 484. The statement was not incidental. It had been the subject of explicit attention. *See* Dep't of State, 2 Foreign Rel. 1481 n.45 (1945) (memorandum from Sec. of Interior Ickes to Pres. Roosevelt); *id.* at 1503 (memorandum from Sec. of Interior Ickes to Pres. Truman); *id.* at 1506, 1509 n.50 (memorandum from Eugene Dooman to Assistant Sec. of State Acheson); (mem-orandum from Sec. of Interior Fortas to Sec. of State Acheson).

4. United States v. California, 332 U.S. 19 (1947). *See* United States v. Louisiana, 339 U.S. 699 (1950); United States v. Texas, 339 U.S. 707 (1950). In United States v. Maine, 420 U.S. 515 (1975), the Court observed that, in the Submerged Lands Act, "Congress transferred to the States the rights to the seabed underlying the marginal sea; however, this transfer was in no wise inconsistent with paramount national power but was merely an exercise of that authority." *Id.* at 515, 524.

5. *Id.* at 35–36.

6. Submerged Lands Act of 1953, 43 U.S.C. §§ 1301–1303, 1311–1315 (1982). Section 1312, after providing for the 3-mile boundary, added: "Nothing in this section is to be construed as questioning or in any manner prejudicing the existence of any State's seaward boundary beyond three geographical miles if it was so provided by its consti-tution or laws prior to or at the time such State became a member of the Union, or if it had been heretofore approved by Congress." The Supreme Court held that, for the domestic purposes of the Submerged Lands Act, Texas and Florida are entitled to a territorial sea of three leagues along the Gulf of Mexico. United States v. Louisiana, 363 U.S. 1 (1960); United States v. Florida, 363 U.S. 121 (1960). Texas is entitled to a 3-league boundary because of historical claims recognized upon its admission to the Union in 1845. United States v. Louisiana, 363 U.S. 1, 36–65 (1960). Florida was found entitled to a 3-league boundary in the Gulf by virtue of Article 1 of Florida's Constitution of 1868, approved by Congress upon the state's readmission during the Reconstruction. United States v. Florida, 363 U.S. 121 (1960). One of the problems in the measurement of the territorial sea is that of establishing the shoreward baseline from which the sea-ward extent is to be measured. The 1958 Geneva Convention on the Territorial Sea and Contiguous Zone, done April 29, 1958, 15 U.S.T. 1606, T.I.A.S. No. 5639, 516 U.N.T.S. 205 (effective September 10, 1964) provides that "the normal baseline for measuring the breadth of the territorial sea is the low-water line along the coast. . . ." *Id.* art. 3. Where, however, the coastline is deeply indented, the convention provides for "the method of straight baselines joining appropriate points. . . ." *Id.* art 4(1). Such base-lines "must not depart to any appreciable extent from the general direction of the coast, and the sea areas lying within the lines must be sufficiently closely linked to the land domain to be subject to the regime of internal waters." *Id.* art 4 (2). "Waters on the landward side of the baseline of the territorial sea form part of the internal waters of the State." *Id.* Art 5 (1).

The Submerged Lands Act defines "coast line" as "the line of ordinary low‚water along that portion of the coast which is in direct contact with the open sea and the line marking the seaward limit of inland waters. . . ." 43 U.S.C. §1301(c). The question of what constitutes inland waters was addressed in United States v. California, 381 U.S. 139 (1965). There the Court adopted the provisions of the Geneva Convention for the purposes of the Submerged Lands Act. *Id.* at 165. It did not, however, apply the straight-baseline form of measurement permitted by the convention since the federal government had not employed it. *Id.* at 167–69.

The U.N. Law of the Sea Convention follows the Geneva Convention with respect to normal baselines and straight baselines. Arts. 5 and 7. With respect to the latter, it adds: "[w]here because of the presence of a delta and other natural conditions the coastline is highly unstable, the appropriate points may be selected along the furthest seaward extent of the low-water line and, notwithstanding subsequent regression of the low-water line, such baselines shall remain effective until changed by the coastal State. . . ." *Id.* art. 7 (2).

The drawing of baselines and the determination of inland waters further requires the identification of bays. The Geneva Convention defines a bay as "a well-marked indentation whose penetration is in such proportion to the width of its mouth as to contain landlocked waters and constitute more than a mere curvature of the coast. An indentation shall not, however, be regarded as a bay unless its area is as large as, or larger than, that of the semicircle whose diameter is a line drawn across the mouth of that indentation." *Id.* art. 7 (2). It then adds that, where a natural entrance to a bay is no more than 24 miles wide, "a closing line may be drawn . . . and the waters enclosed thereby shall be considered as internal waters." *Id.* art. 7 (4). Where the entrance is greater than 24 miles in width, a 24-mile line is to be drawn within the bay to mark internal waters. *Id.* art. 7 (5). However, none of these provisions applies to "historic" bays. *Id.* art. 7(6). *Accord,* Law of the Sea Convention, art. 10 (6).

In United States v. Alaska, 422 U.S. 184 (1975), the Supreme Court was called upon to decide whether Cook Inlet was a historic bay. The Court found that the history of Cook Inlet lacked the significant factors required for determination of historic bay status: (1) exercise of authority over the area by the claiming nation; (2) continuity in the exercise of such authority; and (3) acquiescence in the exercise of such authority by other nations. *Id.* at 189.

7. Offshore exploitive policies parallel these governing the nation's dry land. *See* Chapter 5, note 14.

8. The historical importance of outer-continental-shelf (OCS) activities was noted in a recent decision: "Exploitation of OCS resources under the 1953 [Outer Continental Shelf Lands] Act proceeded at first at a relatively slow pace, with development activity concentrated off the coastal states bordering the Gulf of Mexico and in one small area off southern California in the Santa Barbara Channel. During this period, OCS activities were localized in impact and received little national scrutiny.

"Two major events, however, changed all that and moved OCS development into the forefront of the national consciousness. The first was the blowout of an OCS drilling project in the Santa Barbara Channel of January 28, 1969, resulting in the 'largest oil spill in U.S. history,' and high-lighting the environmental dangers associated with OCS exploitation. The second was the Arab oil embargo of 1973, which dramatically underscored the nation's dependence on foreign sources of oil. In response to the latter, President Nixon directed on January 23, 1974, that 10 million acres of the OCS be leased in 1975. This announcement was significant not only because it proposed leasing an amount of territory in one year almost equal to that which had been leased since the OCS program began in the early 1950's, but also because it envisioned moving into previously undeveloped or 'frontier' areas off the Atlantic and Pacific coasts and off Alaska.

"The announcement crystallized growing concern over the impact of OCS activities and the adequacy of the 1953 Act. . . ."

"These pressures led to the introduction of legislation in 1974 to over-haul the 1953 Act, and culminated four years later in the passage of the Outer Continental Shelf Lands Act Amendments of 1978. The 1978 Amendments were intended to provide a comprehensive framework for the 'expeditious and orderly development [of the OCS], subject to environmental safeguards, in a manner which is consistent with the maintenance of competition and other national needs.'" California v. Watt, 16 Env't Rep. Cas. (BNA) 1561, 1563–64 (D.C. Cir. 1981)(citations omitted).

Such exploitive policies continue. Justice O'Connor noted that "[the]he 'basic purpose' of the 1978 Amendments [to the OCSLA] was to 'promote the swift, orderly and efficient exploitation of our almost untapped domestic oil and gas resources in the Outer Continental Shelf. . . .'" Watt v. Energy Action Educational Foundation, 454 U.S. 151, 154, n. 2 (1981). For explanations of the 1978 amendments, see Jones, Mead, & Sorenson, *The Outer Continental Shelf Lands Act Amendments of 1978,* 19 NAT. RE-SOURCES J. 885 (1979); Krueger & Singer, *An Analysis of the Outer Continental Shelf Lands Act Amendments of 1978,* 19 NAT. RESOURCES J. 909 (1979).

9. U.S. Dep't of the Interior, U.S. Geol. Survey, Conservation Division, OUTER CON-TINENTAL SHELF STATISTICS, OIL, GAS, SULPHUR, SALT, LEASING, DRILLING, PRODUC-TION, INCOME, 1980 at 87 (1981). These funds were generally deposited into the federal treasury as miscellaneous receipts and were not shared with the states. *See* 43 U.S.C. §§ 1337 (m), 1338 (1982). The Land and Water Conservation Fund Act of 1965, 16 U.S.C. §§ 460L-4 to 460 L-11 (1982), provides that, to the extent appropriations are not suffi-cient to bring the created fund to the authorized annual level, "an amount sufficient to cover the remainder thereof shall be credited to the fund from revenues due and pay-able to the United States for deposit in the Treasury as miscellaneous receipts under the Outer Continental Shelf Lands Act. . . ." *Id.* at 460 L-5(c) (2). This fund serves the purpose of providing outdoor-recreation resources by making funds available for ac-quisition of federal lands, and also for federal assistance to the states for their outdoor-recreation sites. *Id.* § 460 L-4.

This practice is at odds with the allocation of revenue received from mineral leasing of federal lands within state borders; half of these revenues are shared with the states. 30 U.S.C. § 191 (1982). An exception is made for Alaska, which receives a 90 percent share. *Id.* The present formula provides that the state within which the mining occurs shall receive 50 percent of the revenues; the reclamation fund created by the Reclama-tion Act of 1902, 43 U.S.C. § 391, receives 40 percent; and the U.S. Treasury receives the remaining 10 percent as miscellaneous receipts.

10. Coastal Zone Management Act, 16 U.S.C. §§ 1451, 1454–1456c (1982) (coastal zone management plan aid). *See generally, e. g.,* ENVIRONMENTAL QUALITY (Tenth An-nual Report of the Council on Environmental Quality) 498–512 (1979); Hildreth, *The Operation of the Coastal Zone Management Act as Amended,* 10 NAT. RESOURCES LAW. 211 (1977). The Act also includes Coastal Energy Impact Program payments. 16 U.S.C. § 1456a (1982). Then, too, there are the Offshore Oil Pollution Fund, 43 U.S.C. §§ 1811–24 (1982); and a Fisherman's Contingency Fund, 43 U.S.C. §§ 1841–1847 (1982).

Compensation and sharing are not entirely separable. The 50 percent division of revenues from federal lands located within states seems to be predicated upon both, as does the CEIP scheme. A state's share of Mineral Leasing Act funds is to be ex-pended giving priority "to those subdivisions of the State socially or economically im-pacted by the development of minerals leased" under the Act. 30 U.S.C. § 191 (1982). There seems to be a closer relationship between CEIP payments and costs to the coastal states both in the formula by which the funds are paid and the limitations on purposes for which they may be spent. *See generally* LIBRARY OF CONGRESS, CONGRESSIONAL RE-

Notes to Page 68

SEARCH SERVICE, EFFECTS OF OFFSHORE OIL AND NATURAL GAS DEVELOPMENT ON THE COASTAL ZONE 249–57 (1976).

One of the reasons for failing to separate compensation and sharing is the uncertainty inherent in each. It is factually and theoretically easier to combine them. Thus, on the one hand, if payments are viewed as compensation, then the losses sought to be covered are not always easy to identify or quantify. On the other hand, if payments are viewed as sharing, then it is difficult to justify sharing with only the coastal states so long as the outer continental shelf is considered to be a national resource.

One of the formulae for distribution of revenues from outer-continental-shelf development submitted to Congress in 1975 sought to take account of both compensation and sharing. It would have split revenues 50/25/25 as between, respectively, the federal government, the adjacent coastal states, and the several states other than such adjacent states. S. 130, 91st Cong., 1st Sess., *reprinted in Outer Continental Shelf Lands Act Amendments and Coastal Zone Management Act Amendments: Hearings before the Joint Senate Comm. on Int. and Insular Aff. and Commerce*, 94th Cong., 1st Sess., pt. 1 at 305 (1975).

The Senate passed amendments to the OCSLA in 1975. These included a measure which would have provided $100 million per year for three years out of leasing revenues to adjacent coastal states allowing outer-continental-shelf-lands oil to be brought ashore. A House version did not include the grant program. The conference committee version followed that of the House in omitting the $100 million provision. The House voted to recommit the bill. The Senate approved S. 521, 94th Cong., 1st Sess., 121 CONG. REC. S. 14,362 (daily ed. July 30, 1975), and one year later the House approved H.R. 6218, 94th Cong., 2d Sess., 122 CONG. REC. H8021 (daily ed. July 30, 1976). The bill reported by the conference committee was recommitted to the conference and thus killed. 122 CONG. REC. H11,340 (daily ed. Sept. 28, 1976).

It was reported during consideration of the 1975 OCSLA amendments that the "Texas Input-Output Model" had determined that the net cost to state and local government in excess of benefits of development of outer-continental-shelf lands amounted to $62.1 million per year. *Outer Continental Shelf Lands Act Amendments and Coastal Zone Management Act Amendments: Joint Hearings before the Senate Committees on Interior and Insular Affairs and Commerce*, 94th Cong., 1st Sess., pt. 1, at 1329, 1338–39 (1975) (Statement of A. R. Schwartz).

On the subject of the joining of the two notions of compensation and sharing, *see Outer Continental Shelf Lands Act Amendments, Hearings on H.R. 1614 before the House Ad Hoc Comm. on Outer Continental Shelf*, 95th Cong., 1st Sess., pt. 1 at 430–31, 179–83, pt. 2 at 1183–87, 1580–82, 1588–89 (1977).

See generally Coastal Zone Management Act Amendments of 1976, S. REP. No. 277, 94th Cong., 2d Sess. 11–19 (1976), *reprinted in* [1976] U.S. CODE CONG. & AD. NEWS 1768. *Outer Continental Shelf Lands Act Amendments of 1977: Hearings on S.9 before the Senate Comm. on Energy and Natural Resources*, 95th Cong., 1st Sess. 557–59 (1977).

The idea of outer-continental-shelf revenue sharing continues to draw support.

11. 420 U.S. 515 (1975).

12. *See id.*, interpreting United States v. California, 332 U.S. 19 (1947), *supra* note 4. For the Court's most recent, technical clarification, see United States v. Maine, 452 U.S. 429 (1981).

13. 420 U.S. 515, 522.

14. 43 U.S.C. § 1333(a)(2) (82) provides: "the civil and criminal laws of each adjacent State . . . are declared to be the law of the United States for that portion of the subsoil and seabed of the outer Continental Shelf, and artificial islands and fixed structures

erected thereon, which would be within the area of the State if its boundaries were extended seaward to the outer margin of the outer Continental Shelf. . . ."

15. Rodrigue v. Aetna Casualty & Surety Co., 395 U.S. 352 (1969).

16. *Id.* at 357. The shelf is comparable in this respect to federally owned lands within a state. *Id.* at 365. *See also* Gulf Offshore Co. v. Mobil Oil Corp., 453 U.S. 473 (1981).

17. Maryland v. Louisiana, 451, U.S. 725, 729 n. 1 (1981).

18. State v. Bundrant, 546 P.2d 530 (Alaska 1976), *appeal dismissed*, 429 U.S. 806 (1976). Extraterritorial enforcement of the act was limited to citizens of Alaska or noncitizens with a sufficient "nexus" with the state. *Id.* at 556. In *Bundrant*, the majority opinion expressed the view of only one justice; a second justice wrote a separate concurring opinion, while one justice dissented and two did not participate. The *Bundrant* principles were subsequently adopted in a four-to-one decision in State v. Sieminski, 556 P.2d 929, 934 (Alaska 1976). *Bundrant* was reaffirmed by F/V American Eagle v. Alaska, 620 P.2d 657 (Alaska 1980), *appeal dismissed*, 50 U.S.L.W. 35301 (U.S. Jan. 12, 1982).

For a different result, see Hjelle v. Brooks, 377 F. Supp. 430 (D. Alaska 1974), where a preliminary injunction was granted allowing out-of-state fishermen to take king crab during the remainder of the 1973 season. However, there was no trial on the merits. *See also* People v. Weeren, 26 Cal. 3d 654, 163 Cal. Rptr. 255, 607 P.2d 1279 (1980).

One commentator believes that the Fishery Conservation and Management Act of 1976 (FCMA), 16 U.S.C. §§ 1801–1882 (1982), has abrogated Alaska's extraterritorial authority over the king-crab fishery. Curtis, *Alaska's Regulation of King Crab on the Outer Continental Shelf* 6 U.C.L.A.-Alaska L. Rev. 375, 407 (1977). This belief is not necessarily correct because the FMCA may only have placed the extraterritorial exercise of jurisdiction upon a different footing. Ostensibly, 16 U.S.C. § 1856(a) (1982) allows the extraterritorial regulation of vessels registered under the laws of the state and of fishing engaged in by "registered" vessels. The Alaska statute attacked in *Bundrant* might well be upheld under the FMCA. Thus, while the facts concerning the matter are not clear with respect to the other defendants in that case, Bundrant himself, a resident of Washington, was fishing with a vessel which was "registered" in Alaska. 546 P.2d at 534–35.

19. Portland Pipe Line Corp. v. Environmental Improvement Commission, 307 A.2d 1 (Me. 1973), *appeal dismissed*, 414 U.S. 1035 (1973).

20. The U.S. retained authority "for the purposes of navigation or flood control or the production of power" and "all its navigational servitude for the constitutional purposes of commerce, navigation, national defense, and international affairs. . . ." 43 U.S.C. §§ 1311(d), 1314(a) (1982). The extent of federal interest reserved in submerged lands was put in issue in the Fifth Circuit case of Zabel v. Tabb, 430 F.2d 199 (5th Cir. 1970), *cert. denied* 401 U.S. 410 (1971), which established the power of the U.S. Army Corps of Engineers to deny, for ecological reasons, permits for dredging and filling in navigable waters within the area ceded to the states. Landholders had argued that the Submerged Lands Act was an abandonment by Congress of its power to regulate tidelands property unless navigation, flood control, or hydroelectric power were specifically involved. The court disagreed. Congress expressly reserved rights with respect to these three specified purposes, but other language in the act "makes it clear that Congress intended to and did retain all its constitutional powers over commerce and did not relinquish certain portions of the power by specifically reserving others." *Id.* at 206. National interests continue in the bed of the coastal states' territorial seas.

21. Douglas v. Seacoast Products, Inc., 431 U.S. 265 (1977).

22. The Court said: "The Submerged Lands Act does give the States 'title,' 'ownership,' and 'the right and power to manage, administer, lease, develop, and use' the

lands beneath the oceans and natural resources in the waters within state territorial jurisdiction. . . . But when Congress made this grant . . . it expressly retained for the United States 'all constitutional powers of regulation and control' over these lands and waters 'for purposes of commerce, navigation, national defense, and international affairs.' . . . Since the grant of the fisheries license is made pursuant to the commerce power . . . the Submerged Lands Act did not alter its preemptive effect." *Id.* at 283–84.

23. Article III, section 2 of the Constitution provides that the "judicial Power shall extend to . . . all Cases of admiralty and maritime Jurisdiction. . . ." This section, distinct from the grant to Congress of power to control and improve the navigable waters under the commerce clause, speaks only of the judicial and not the legislative branch. However, it has been construed as conferring a parallel, like power upon the Congress. *See, e.g.,* Panama R.R. v. Johnson. 264 U.S. 375(1924); *in re* Garrett, 141 U.S. 1, 12–14 (1890); Note, *From Judicial Grant to Legislative Power, The Admiralty Clause in the Nineteenth Century,* 67 HARV. L. REV. 1214 (1954). *Compare* Southern Pacific Co. v. Jensen, 244 U.S. 205 (1917), *with* Knickerbocker Ice Co. v. Stewart, 253 U.S. 149 (1920). *See also* G. GILMORE & C. BLACK, THE LAW OF ADMIRALTY 47, 48 (2d ed. 1975). In Askew v. American Waterways Operators, Inc., 411 U.S. 325 (1973), the Court limited its earlier decision so as not to oust a state's law from all admiralty claims, at least where the issue was shoreside injuries caused by oil pollution from ships plying the state's waters. Nevertheless, national admiralty law remains preeminent in the territorial sea.

A similar affirmation of the primacy of national interest in surface activity in state-"owned" waters—but with allowance for some state regulation—was given in Ray v. Atlantic Richfield Co., 435 U.S. 151 (1978). The case focused on the State of Washington's Tanker Law, which regulated the design, size, and movement of oil tankers in state waters in Puget Sound. The law was struck down in its entirety by a lower federal court on the ground that it was preempted by federal law, in particular by the Ports and Waterways Safety Act in 1972. 33 U.S.C. §§ 1221–1232 (1982). The Supreme Court found that certain portions of the Washington law could stand, but did agree that much of the Washington statute was preempted by federal law: it intruded impermissibly upon paramount national needs and concerns in state waters. 435 U.S. 151, 168 (1975).

24. United States v. California, 332 U.S. 19, 35–36 (1947).

25. This test can be traced to Cooley v. Board of Wardens, 53 U.S. (12 How.) 229 (1851). In *Cooley,* the Court established an identity of exclusive federal concern with situations where "a single uniform rule" or "one uniform system" is required. It then identified state control with situations where "diversity," or "different systems of regulation, drawn from local knowledge and experience," are requisite. As that test has been more recently defined and employed, the Court has found that when Congress has not acted "the familiar test is that of uniformity versus locality; if a case falls within an area in commerce thought to demand a uniform national rule, state action is struck down. If the activity is one of predominately local interest, state action is sustained. More accurately, that question is whether the state interest is outweighed by a national interest in the unhampered operation of interstate commerce." California v. Zook, 336 U.S. 725, 728 (1979).

26. 435 U.S. 151 (1978).

27. *Id.* at 177.

28. *Id.*

29. THE FEDERALIST No. 46, at 315 (J. Cooke ed. 1961) (Madison). For recent study of and comment upon the aspects of Madison I emphasize hereinafter, see G. WILLS, EXPLAINING AMERICA: THE FEDERALIST (1981); Tushnet, *Deviant Science,* 59 TEX. L. REV. 815 (1981).

30. THE FEDERALIST No. 46, *supra* note 29, at 315–16.

31. THE FEDERALIST No. 52, *supra* note 29, at 353 (Madison).

32. *Id.* at 351.

33. *Id.*

34. THE FEDERALIST No. 10, *supra* note 29, at 61 (Madison).

35. THE FEDERALIST No. 47, *supra* note 29, at 327 (Madison)(quoting the New Hampshire constitution).

36. THE FEDERALIST No. 55, *supra* note 29, at 374 (Madison).

37. Tushnet, *supra* note 29, at 824–25.

38. *See infra* Chapter 5, text at notes 62–63.

39. 16 U.S.C. §§ 1852, 1853–1854 (1982).

40. 16 U.S.C. §§ 1853–1854, 1856 (1982).

41. Most of these areas were in the Gulf of Mexico; *see* House Report (Outer Continental Shelf Committee) No. 95–590, Aug. 29, 1977 (to accompany H.R. 1614), at 65.

42. ENVIRONMENTAL QUALITY, *supra* note 10, at 333–34.

43. *See* California v. Watt, 16 ERC 1561 (D.C. Cir. 1981) (remanding the 1980–85 plan); *Outer Continental Shelf: Interior Correcting Flaws in OCS Plan Due to Recent Appeals Court Decision,* ENV'T REP., Oct. 30, 1981, at 818–19 ("Industry will not be able to keep up with the pace of the plan, which offers 875 million acres of OSC lands within five years, compared to the 20 million acres leased during the entire 280 year history of the program, Panetta charged."); *Interior Dept. to Modify Offshore Drilling Plans,* N.Y. Times, Oct. 8, 1981, at 15, col. 1 ("a billion acres"); COASTAL ZONE MGMT., Oct. 7, 1981, at 3–4 ("the department never intended to 'lease 200 million acres. . . .'"). *See also* Shabecoff, *Watt Presses Offshore Leasing Despite Opposition,* N.Y. Times, Nov. 25, 1981, at 1, col. 2. Secretary Watt subsequently issued a memorandum directing that leasing be focused upon only those offshore tracts with the greatest resource potential. Shabecoff, *Watt Alters Offshore Plan, Ordering Curb of Lease Sites,* N.Y. Times, Thurs., Dec. 24, 1981, at 10, col. 1.

44. The current five-year plan, approved in July of 1982, ends in June 1987. Plans are under way for the 1986–91 plan. Current area summaries of outer-continental-shelf oil and gas activities are available under the Outer Continental Shelf Oil and Gas Information Program through the Department of the Interior's Mineral Management Services. For accounts of the controversy surrounding and changes in the leasing program, *see, e.g.,* COASTAL ZONE MGMT., Vol. 14, No. 40, October 27, 1983; ENV'T REP., Jan. 6, 1984, at 1524; COASTAL ZONE MGMT., Vol. 15, No. 1, Jan. 5, 1984; *id.* No. 19, May 10, 1984; *id.* No. 27, July 19, 1984. A useful source of current information is also provided by NOAA's Office of Ocean and Coastal Resource Management: CZM Information Exchange (D. Clark, Coordinator).

45. THE FEDERALIST No. 46, *supra* note 29, at 317 (J. Madison).

46. 92 Stat. 629 (1978) (codified in scattered sections of 16, 30, & 43 U.S.C.). It is interesting to note that until 1978 the OCSLA had not been substantially amended since its passage in 1953.

47. 43 U.S.C. §§ 1340, 1344–1345, 1351–1352; *see* California v. Watt, 520 F. Supp. 1359, 1383–86 (D.C. D. Cal. 1981).

48. *Current Developments, Industry Groups Urge "Fast Tracking" of Environmental Reviews for Port Plans,* 11 ENV'T REP. (BNA) 285 (1981). *See also Current Developments, Port Expansion Problems Include Dredge Disposal, Reviews Panel Told,* 11 ENV'T REP. (BNA) 2094 (1981).

49. *See* 46 Fed. Reg. 58,264 (1981) (to be codified at C.F.R. § 3300); COASTAL ZONE MGMT., Dec. 9, 1981, at 1.

50. LIBRARY OF CONGRESS, CONGRESSIONAL RESEARCH SERVICE, EFFECTS OF OFFSHORE OIL AND NATURAL GAS DEVELOPMENT ON THE COASTAL ZONE, (1976) (interleaved between pp. 98 and 99). The chart was prepared by T. D. Hewitt of CONOCO and L. E. Mark of the American Petroleum Institute. It was designed to show the additional reviews and procedural steps caused by H.R. 6218.

51. The National Petroleum Council "sees many coastal and environmental policies as impediments to 'timely energy resource development.'" COASTAL ZONE CONSERVA-TION—THE OIL AND GAS INDUSTRY: AN OVERVIEW (1981).

52. See CHRISTO: RUNNING FENCE (Gorgoni photographs, Tomkins chronicle, Bour-don narrative 1978); Coffelt, Running Fence: A Drama in Wind and Light, ART NEWS, Nov. 1976, at 84.

53. See CHRISTO: RUNNING FENCE, supra note 52.

54. Alfred Frankenstein, the dean of San Francisco art critics, wrote an article in the San Francisco Chronicle in which he said Christo's going to the ocean without a permit "had destroyed the conceptual integrity of his own creation."

In Frankenstein's view, "the whole idea was to use the machinery of American law on behalf of an unprecedented idea. When Christo took the law into his own hands, his entire conceptual structure collapsed." Christo felt that Frankenstein had missed the point: "'Illegality is essential in American system, don't you see?' he said to me the day after the Frankenstein article appeared. He was sitting on an oil drum in the Bloomfield back lot and leaning forward in his intense way. 'I completely work within American system by being illegal, like everyone else—if there is no illegal part, the project is less reflective of the system.'" CHRISTO: RUNNING FENCE, supra note 52, at 34–35.

55. Id. at 24, 34. "What I learn here—the American system, society, the way the whole big machine works—I find perfect to use for my projects. To grab American social structure and make it work, this is what I learn in America."

56. Id. at 35.

57. Id. at 152.

58. H. GROTIUS, DE JURE BELLI ET PACIS, bk. 2, ch. 3, pt. ix, at 210.

59. Professor John Bonine notes about environmental permits that they "might be seen (1) as a means of promulgating regulatory requirements, (2) as a means of trans-lating broad requirements into terms applicable to individual pollution sources, or (3) as an enforcement device which makes it simpler to achieve compliance with regula-tory requirements." 1 J. BONINE & T. MCGARITY, THE LAW OF ENVIRONMENTAL POLLU-TION, pt. 3, at 112 (1980).

60. 16 U.S.C. § 528 (1982).

61. A thorough treatment of the subject is to be found in Stewart, The Reformation of American Administrative Law, 88 HARV. L. REV. 1669 (1975). Stewart notes that "[i]ncreasingly, the function of administrative law is not the protection of private au-tonomy but the provision of a surrogate political process to ensure the fair representa-tion of a wide range of affected interests in the process of administrative decision. Whether this is a coherent or workable aim is an open issue. But there is no denying the importance of the transformation." Id. at 1670. My principal reservation about Stewart's work is his self-imposed limitation of viewing the political process as the representation of interests instead of the representation of people. See M. BALL, THE PROMISE OF AMERICAN LAW (1981). For a sampling of opinion on the general subject, see Friendly, Some Kind of Hearing, 123 U. PA. L. REV. 1267 (1975); Gellhorn, Public Par-ticipation in Administrative Proceedings, 81 YALE L.J. 359 (1972).

For some of the articles which examine the general phenomenon as it has developed especially in reference to environmental issues, see Tribe, *Ways Not to Think about Plastic Trees: New Foundations for Environmental Law*, 83 YALE L.J. 1315 (1974); *Symposium: Environmental Decisionmaking*, 62 IOWA L. REV. 637 (1977), and sources cited therein.

62. Sax, *The (Unhappy) Truth about NEPA*, 26 OKLA. L. REV. 239 (1973).

63. *See infra* text at notes 87–106. *See also Current Developments, Massachusetts Gives State Approval of Offshore Oil Drilling on Georges Bank*, 12 ENV'T REP. (BNA) 287 (1981).

64. 16 U.S.C. §§ 1431–1434 (1982).

65. *See supra* note 60.

66. The Council on Environmental Quality noted: "As significant new activities commence on the OCS, competing agency objectives may well increase. Within certain geographic limits, deepwater port operations, nuclear powerplants, and oil and gas development and associated pipelines are obviously incompatible. The same is true with respect to those activities and more traditional uses of OCS areas, such as commercial fishing and recreation. Moreover, there are potential conflicts between many of these uses and environmental objectives." 1 Council on Environmental Quality, OCS OIL AND GAS—AN ENVIRONMENTAL ASSESSMENT: A REPORT TO THE PRESIDENT 179 (1974).

I formerly viewed this conflict among agency missions as a fault to be remedied. *See* M. BALL, LAW OF THE SEA: FEDERAL-STATE RELATIONS (Dean Rusk Center Monograph No. 1, 1978). I herewith recant.

67. Rodgers, *Benefits, Costs, and Risks: Oversight of Health and Environmental Decisionmaking*, 4 HARV. ENVTL. L. REV. 191, 212–13 (1980).

68. *Id.* at 212 n. 146.

69. *See, e.g.*, W. RODGERS, HANDBOOK ON ENVIRONMENTAL LAW 16–23 (1977); Stewart, *The Development of Administrative and Quasi-Constitutional Law in Judicial Review of Environmental Decisionmaking: Lessons from the Clean Air Act*, 62 IOWA L. REV. 713 (1977). *Cf.* Strycker's Bay Neighborhood Council, Inc. v. Karlen, 444 U.S. 223 (1980); Vermont Yankee Nuclear Power Corp. v. Natural Resources Defense Council, Inc., 435 U.S. 519 (1978)(narrowing the scope and content of NEPA obligations both procedurally and substantively); *see* Rodgers, *A Hard Look at Vermont Yankee: Environmental Law under Close Scrutiny*, 67 GEO. L.J. 699 (1979); Stewart, *Vermont Yankee and the Evolution of Administrative Procedure*, 91 HARV. L. REV. 1805 (1978); *See* Leventhal, *Environmental Decisionmaking and the Role of the Courts*, 122 U. PA. L. REV. 509 (1974).

70. Greater Boston Television Corp. v. Federal Communications Comm'n, 444 F.2d 841, 851–52 (D.C. Cir. 1970), *cert. denied*, 406 U.S. 950 (1972).

71. 347 U.S. 483 (1954).

72. The seminal essays on this subject were Chayes, *The Role of the Judge in Public Law Litigation*, 89 HARV. L. REV. 1281 (1976), and Fiss, *The Supreme Court, 1978 Term: Forward: The Forms of Justice*, 93 HARV. L. REV. 1 (1979).

73. Massachusetts v. Andrus, 594 F.2d 872, 886 (1st Cir. 1979).

74. *Id.* at 838.

75. On the question of judicial protection of powerless minorities, *see* M. BALL, THE PROMISE OF AMERICAN LAW (1981).

76. *See* 9 WEEKLY COMP. PRES. DOC. 1312, 1317 (Nov. 10, 1973); 10 WEEKLY COMP. PRES. DOC. 72, 83–84 (Jan. 26, 1974).

77. County of Suffolk v. Secretary of the Interior, 7 ENVTL. L. REP. (ENVTL. L. INST.) 20230 (E.D.N.Y. 1977).

78. 434 U.S. 1064 (1978).

79. There have been 27 exploratory wells drilled with 22 dry holes; 12 natural-gas zones and a small oil zone have been found in five wells on three adjacent blocks. COASTAL ZONE MGMT., Oct. 21, 1981, at 3.

80. *See* McQuiston, *Shell Wins 41 Offshore Oil Tracts,* N.Y. Times, Dec. 6, 1981, at A29, col. 6; *id., Offshore Oil Plan Stirring Opposition,* N.Y. Times, Nov. 13, 1981, at A14, col. 4; *Mid-Atlantic Bids Rejected,* N.Y. Times, Dec. 24, 1981, at A10, col. 3. *See generally,* DEP'T OF INTERIOR, MMS, MID-ATLANTIC SUMMARY REPORT 2 (1982); DEP'T OF INTERIOR, USGS & BLM, ATLANTIC INDEX (1981).

81. National Environmental Policy Act of 1969, 42 U.S.C. §§ 4321–4369 (1982). While this Act does not specifically provide for state involvement in federal decision making, it nevertheless has been a major instrument used by the states, and by citizens, for having their interests taken into account.

82. 42 U.S.C. § 4332 (2)(C) (1982).

83. *See, e.g.,* County of Suffolk v. Secretary of the Interior, 562 F.2d 1368 (2d Cir. 1977); Natural Resources Defense Council v. Morton, 458 F.2d 827 (D.C. Cir. 1972); Massachusetts v. Andrus (I), [1978] 8 ENVTL. L. REP. (ENVTL. L. INST.) 20187 (D. Mass. 1978); California v. Morton, 404 F. Supp. 26 (C.D. Cal. 1975).

84. Breeden, *Federalism and the Development of Outer Continental Shelf Mineral Resources,* 28 STAN. L. REV. 1107, 1130 (1976).

85. *See* RODGERS, *supra* note 64.

86. For example, federal regulatory guidelines for the preparation of environmental impact statements call for "scoping." 40 C.F.R. § 1501.7 (1980). *See also* the definition of "scope" at 40 C.F.R. § 1508.28 (1980). This sterile-sounding bureaucratic term means that there "shall be an early and open process for determining the scope of issues to be addressed and for identifying the significant issues related to a proposed action." *Id.* § 1501.7. For this purpose, the agency is to "[i]nvite the participation of affected Federal, State, and local agencies, any affected Indian tribe, the proponent of the action, and other interested persons (including those who might not be in accord with the action on environmental grounds). . . ." *Id.* § 1501.7 (a) (1). Furthermore, "scoping" and consideration of environmental impacts are a roving commission, for "environment" is to be "interpreted comprehensively" in that when "economic or social and natural or physical environmental effects are interrelated, then the environmental impact statement will discuss all of these effects on the human environment." *Id.*

87. A good summary of the features of Georges Bank geology and exploration activities is to be found in R. Dorrier, NORTH ATLANTIC SUMMARY REPORT: OUTER CONTINENTAL SHELF OIL AND GAS ACTIVITIES IN THE NORTH ATLANTIC AND THEIR ONSHORE IMPACTS: A SUMMARY REPORT (U.S. Geological Survey Open-File Report, July 1981) 81–601.

88. COASTAL ZONE MGMT. Oct. 21, 1981, at 3. *Cf.* Dorrier, *supra note* 87, at 9 (U.S. Geological Survey estimates as of April 1981 showed estimates of undiscovered resources at one billion barrels of oil and 3.2 trillion cubic feet of gas).

89. *See* Massachusetts v. Watt, 12 ELR 20893 (1st Cir. Sept. 16, 1983).

90. *See* Massachusetts v. Andrus, 12 Env't Rep. Cas. (BNA) 1801, 1803–4 (1st Cir. 1979).

91. *Id.* at 1804.

92. *See* Council on Environmental Quality, OCS Oil and Gas Drilling on Georges Bank, ENV'T REP. (BNA) 287 (June 26, 1981). Subsequently, it was announced that no site on Georges Bank would be listed as a candidate for designation as a marine sanctuary at least until 1983. 46 Fed. Reg. 58136 (Nov. 30, 1981); *Georges Bank Will Not Be Considered Active Candidate for Marine Sanctuary,* ENV'T REP. (BNA) 962 (Dec. 4, 1981).

See generally OFFICE OF TECHNOLOGY ASSESSMENT, COASTAL EFFECTS OF OFFSHORE ENERGY SYSTEMS (1976); Library of Congress, Congressional Research Service, supra note 50.

93. Friedman, Oil Drilling in Georges Bank, N.Y. Times, July 27, 1981, at A17, col. 3.

94. Georges Bank Settlement Reached by State, Environmentalists, Governments, 11 ENVTL. REP. (BNA) 1347 (1981).

95. Id.

96. Id. See Massachusetts v. Andrus, 8 ENVTL. L. REP. 20187 (D. Mass. 1978); Conservation Law Foundation v. Andrus, 14 Env't Rep. Cas. (BNA) 1229 (1st Cir. 1980); Conservation Law Foundation v. Andrus, 14 Env't Rep. Cas. (BNA) (1st Cir. 1979); Massachusetts v. Andrus, 594 F.2d 872 (1st Cir. 1979), Massachusetts v. Andrus, 11 ENVTL. L. REP. (ENVTL. L. INST.) 20203 (D. Mass. 1980).

97. Massachusetts v. Andrus, 594 F.2d 872, 886 (1st Cir. 1979).

98. See Massachusetts v. Andrus, 11 ENVTL. L. REP. (ENVTL. L. INST.) 20203 (D. Mass. 1980); Massachusetts Gives State Approval of Offshore Oil Drilling on Georges Bank, 11 ENV'T REP. (BNA) 287 (1981).

99. At the time plaintiffs filed suit, Congress was considering the amendments, a fact that figured prominently in the first court action enjoining the sale. For the amendments, see 92 Stat. 629 (1978)(codified in scattered sections of 16, 30, & 43 U.S.C.).

100. 43 U.S.C. § 1802 (4) (1982).

101. See 43 U.S.C. §§ 1334, 1337, 1340, 1344, 1351 (1982).

102. 43 U.S.C. § 1344 (1982).

103. Id. §§ 1346, 1340.

104. Id. § 1351.

105. Id.

106. North Slope Borough v. Andrus, 642 F.2d 589, 606 (D.C. Cir. 1980).

107. Some idea of the grounds for California's opposition may be gathered from one California congressman's observation that the state's coastal communities depend upon $11 billion per year from the tourism industry and $1 billion per year from the fishing industry. See California Congressman Faults Watt for Reopening California Lease Sale, 11 ENV'T REP. (BNA) 2088 (1981). It should also be noted that the controversy centered on tracts not far north of the Santa Barbara Channel.

This case was not the first resistance to drilling off the California coast. See, e.g., Get Oil Out, Inc. v. Andrus, 468 F. Supp. 82 (C.D. Calif. 1979). See also, DEP'T OF INTERIOR, MMS, PACIFIC SUMMARY REPORT 1982.

108. 16 U.S.C. §§ 1451–1464 (1982).

109. Id. §§ 1454–1456(c) (1982). 16 U.S.C. §§ 1451, 1454–1456(c) (1982). See generally ENVIRONMENTAL QUALITY, supra note 10, at 498–515; Hildreth, The Operation of the Coastal Zone Management Act as Amended, 10 NAT. RESOURCES LAW. 211 (1977).

110. 16 U.S.C. § 1456 (c) (1), (2).

111. Breeden, supra note 84, at 1151.

112. Secretary of Interior v. California, 52 U.S.L.W. 4063 (1984).

113. A spokesman for the Department of the Interior, Frank K. Richardson, is reported to have said that "'federal supremacy prevails and we need not'" go as far as Clark has in negotiating with the coastal states since the departure of Secretary James G. Watt. Richardson added menacingly: 'If the crunch point comes we will be vigorous . . . but we would like to resolve' any OCS conflicts before they reach the courts. He did credit both the states and environmentalists with 'legitimate interests.'" COASTAL ZONE MGMT., Nov. 22, 1984, at 3. The same report goes on to note: "Part of the reason the OCS sales seem so little open to conflict resolution is the single purpose character

of the OCSLA, several coast planners in the audience felt. Interior's OCS process is in itself an adversarial situation to begin with, one source commented, because a single use of the OCS is the overriding purpose of the legislation. Other uses of the OCS receive secondary recognition and are in the position of responding to first claims by the oil interests. One lawyer in the audience thought that conflict resolution techniques have little place in the Interior/OCS scheme of things, while a planner privately called for the replacement of the OCS leasing process with a multiple use scheme for the OCS and the U.S. Exclusive Economic Zone.

"Eldon V. C. Greenberg of Galloway & Greenberg in Washington DC led two other prominent OCS lawyers in a discussion aimed to answer the question: are there ways to improve conflict resolution on the OCS? A bit of a cynic, Greenberg suggested at the beginning that conflicts about oil 'go fundamentally to the psychology of the actors.' Development pits two extreme visions of the coastal zone against each, one of great oil refineries, the other of a pristine environment. And, while there is 'a relatively small risk of a catastrophic accident' in oil activities, it is 'not a zero risk.' Finally, pointed out Greenberg, opponents of offshore drilling perceive themselves as having little to gain personally from OCS development." *Id.*

114. THE FEDERALIST No. 2, *supra* note 29, at 70–71 (A. Hamilton).

115. Romero-Barcelo v. Brown, 643 F.2d 835, 837 (1st Cir.), *rev'd sub nom.*, Weinberger v. Romero-Barcelo, 456 U.S. 305 (1982).

116. *Id.*

117. The district court had found violations of the Federal Water Pollution Control Act, Executive Order 11593, requiring nomination of sites that may be eligible for listing in the National Register of Historic Places, and the National Environmental Policy Act, but it refused to grant the requested injunction. 478 F.Supp. 646 (D.P.R. 1979).

118. 16 U.S.C. §§ 1531–1543 (1982).

119. 643 F.2d 835, 857.

120. *Id.* at 862.

121. 33 U.S.C. §§ 1251–1376 (1982). *See, e.g.,* Smith, *Highlights of the Federal Water Pollution Control Act of 1972,* 77 DICK. L. REV. 459 (1973); Zener, *The Federal Law of Water Pollution Control,* in FEDERAL ENVIRONMENTAL LAW 682, 692–93 (E. Dolgin & T. Guilbert eds. 1974).

122. 33 U.S.C. §§ 1311, 1342, 1362 (7), (8), (12), (14) (1982). The states may be authorized to administer permits.

123. 643 F.2d 835, 861.

124. Weinberger v. Romero-Barcelo, 456 U.S. 305 (1982).

125. *See, e.g.,* Rosenbaum, *Wisconsin v. Weinberger: The Chancellor's Foot and NEPA's Good Right Arm,* 14 E.L.R. 10402 (Nov. 1984).

126. 10 WEEKLY COMP. PRES. DOC. 72, 83–84 (Jan. 26, 1974).

127. Council on Environmental Quality, *supra* note 66.

128. Alaska v. Andrus, 580 F.2d 465, 467 n. 6 (D.C. Cir. 1978).

129. Alaska v. Andrus, 580 F.2d 465 (D.C. Cir. 1978).

130. 486 F. Supp. 332 (D.D.C.), *aff'd in part and rev'd in part,* 642 F.2d 589 (D.C. Cir. 1980).

131. One estimate places U.S. Arctic resources at 24 billion barrels of oil and 109 trillion cubic feet of gas. NATURAL PETROLEUM COUNCIL, U.S. ARCTIC OIL AND GAS (1981).

132. *See* North Slope Borough v. Andrus, *supra* note 106; Verges & McClendon, *Inupiat Eskimos, Bowhead Whales, and Oil: Competing Federal Interest in the Beaufort Sea.* 10 U.C.L.A. ALASKA L. REV. 1 (1980); Rosenblatt, *The Federal Trust Responsibility and Eskimo*

Whaling, 7 B.C. ENVTL. AFF. L. REV. 505 (1979); Bliss, *International Whaling Commission Regulations and the Alaskan Eskimo*, 19 NAT. RESOURCES J. 943 (1979); Comment, *Aboriginal Exemption to the International Whaling Convention*, 6 AM. INDIAN L. REV. 249 (1978).

133. International Whaling Commission Meeting on Aboriginal/Subsistence Whaling, Report on the Panel to Consider Cultural Aspects of Aboriginal Whaling in North Alaska (Seattle, Feb. 5–9, 1979), at 3, *quoted in* ENVIRONMENTAL QUALITY—1980, at 23 (Eleventh Annual Report of the Council on Environmental Quality, 1980). For excellent treatment of the subject, see David Boeri's PEOPLE OF THE ICE WHALE (1984).

134. ENVIRONMENTAL QUALITY—1980 *supra* note 133. *See also* North Slope Borough v. Andrus, 486 F. Supp. 332 (D.D.C. 1980). *See generally* S. FROST, WHALES AND WHALING (1978)(report of an independent inquiry conducted by a special commission sponsored by the government of Australia).

135. ENVIRONMENTAL QUALITY—1980, *supra* note 133, at 24. In March 1981, the Department of Commerce, through the National Oceanic and Atmospheric Administration, and the Alaska Eskimo Whaling Commission signed a cooperative agreement to implement this three-year block quota for bowhead whales. *See* 50 C.F.R. §§ 230.70–.77 (1981).

136. 486 F. Supp. 332, 340–41 (D.D.C. 1980).

137. *Id.* at 341.

138. This grim prediction would be so if the Inupiat and their culture did not survive increasing introduction of American culture and technology. Inupiat exposure to American ways began in the last century: "For generations, the Inupiat People relied on subsistence hunting, shaping their cultural traditions, and defining their settlement patterns. Coastal Inupiat hunted sea mammals and traded with inland Inupiat, who hunted caribou, moose, and other land animals. The culture covered the entire arctic region, including parts of Siberia, Alaska, Canada and Greenland. The Eskimos throughout this vast area still speak variations of the same language, have the same basis of living, and depend on the same unique arctic survival skills. However, as described by Alaska Consultants, Inc. (1979), 'The advent of commercial whaling in the arctic Ocean in the 1850's changed traditional settlement patterns. Coastal Inupiats [*sic*] began to cluster at points such as Barrow to trade with the whalers, rather than with the inland Inupiat, which forced the latter group to move to the coast to obtain needed supplies.' Throughout the commercial whaling period, Barrow supplied many men for whaling expeditions in exchange for trade goods. The commercial bowhead whale market collapsed around 1910 and an era in Barrow's past was ended. The disastrous impact on Inupiat population and culture which resulted from contact between the whalers and North Slope Eskimos, however, lasted well beyond 1910. 'The American whalers . . . carried off the fuel and food supplies of the Eskimos, debauching the Natives with liquor and ruining their health by introducing the diseases of the white man.'" North Slope Borough, COMPREHENSIVE PLAN: BACKGROUND REPORT (Draft)(July 1981) at 5.

139. North Slope Borough v. Andrus, 642 F.2d 589, 593 (D.C. Cir. 1980). *See also id.* at 594, 604 n. 83, 606, 614.

140. North Slope Borough v. Andrus, 15 Env't Rep. Cas. (BNA) 1601, 1602 (D.C. Cir. 1980) (MacKinnon, J., concurring in preopinion order).

Control and studies at the site may be limited by budget realities. Also development policy can be implemented under the rubric of budget cutbacks. It is to be noted in this regard that the amount of federal funds available for the Department of the Interior's OCS environment-studies program is uncertain. The Department of Commerce's National Oceanic and Atmospheric Administration, which runs the program in Alaska for the Department of the Interior, has been subject to severe budget cuts. *See* COASTAL ZONE MGMT., October 14, 1981, at 1.

141. The borough is also attempting to provide protection for local people through land-use law by creating a variety of zoning districts along with a local permit system. *See* NORTH SLOPE BOROUGH, COMPREHENSIVE PLAN: BACKGROUND REPORT (Draft) (July 1981); NORTH SLOPE BOROUGH, COMPREHENSIVE PLAN (Draft) (July 1981); NORTH SLOPE BOROUGH, LAND DEVELOPMENT ZONING ORDINANCE (Draft) (Aug. 1981).

142. 642 F.2d 589, 613. The D.C. Circuit has twice rejected arguments based on a federal-trust responsibility to the Inupiat. *Id.* at 611–13; California v. Watt, 16 Env't Rep. Cas. (BNA) 1561, 1588–90 (D.C. Cir. 1981).

143. 642 F.2d 589, 613.

144. *See* P. FUSSELL, THE GREAT WAR AND MODERN MEMORY 335 (1977).

145. *See* Ronald Dworkin's elaboration of rights as trumps in TAKING RIGHTS SERIOUSLY (1977).

146. THE FEDERALIST No. 51, *supra* note 29, at 352 (J. Madison).

147. *Id.* at 353.

148. *Id.* at 352.

149. *Id.* No. 57, at 386 (J. Madison).

CHAPTER 5

1. COUNCIL ON ENVIRONMENTAL QUALITY, ENVIRONMENTAL QUALITY—1979, at 498 (1980). On the question of barrier-island dynamics, see, e.g., JOHNSON, HILLESTAD, STANHOLZER, & STANHOLZER, AN ECOLOGICAL SURVEY OF THE COASTAL REGION OF GEORGIA 11–67 (1974); W. KAUFMAN & O. PILKEY, THE BEACHES ARE MOVING (1979); E. ODUM, FUNDAMENTALS OF ECOLOGY 352–62 (1971); O. PILKEY & J. NEAL, FROM CURRITUCK TO CALABASH (1978); Griffin, *Georgia Barrier Islands: Shaped by the Winds of Change*, Coastlines Georgia, Spring 1983, at 10. *See also* Webster, *Scientists Find Severe Loss of Coastline*, N.Y. Times, Tues., June 21, 1983, at 17, col. 2.

2. U.S. DEP'T OF INTERIOR, DRAFT ENVIRONMENTAL IMPACT STATEMENT: UNDEVELOPED COASTAL BARRIERS AND FEDERAL FLOOD INSURANCE, Appendix at A-23 (1982) (citing Hicks 1972). *See* Titus, Henderson & Teal, *Sea Level Rise and Wetlands Loss in the United States*, National Wetlands Newsletter, Sept.–Oct. 1984, at 3.

3. National Journal, Dec. 9, 1972, cited in LIBRARY OF CONGRESS, CONGRESSIONAL RESEARCH SERVICE, EFFECTS OF OFFSHORE OIL AND NATURAL GAS DEVELOPMENT ON THE COASTAL ZONE 162 (1976) ("[B]y the end of the century, there may be almost as many people in the Nation's coastal zone as there are now people in the entire United States." *Id.* at 21).

4. U.S. DEP'T OF INTERIOR, ALTERNATIVE POLICIES FOR PROTECTING BARRIER ISLANDS ALONG THE ATLANTIC AND GULF COASTS OF THE UNITED STATES AND DRAFT ENVIRONMENTAL IMPACT STATEMENT vii–viii (1979). *See also* U.S. DEP'T OF INTERIOR, *supra* note 2, at A-76 to A-78.

5. *See* Chapter 3, notes 63, 157.

6. The Court has based its conclusion variously upon the commerce clause (Cooley v. Board of Wardens, 53 U.S. 299 (1851); Hughes v. Oklahoma 1441 U.S. 322 (1979)), the supremacy clause (Douglas v. Seacoast Products, 431 U.S. 265 (1977)), and the privileges and immunities clause (Toomer v. Witsell, 339 U.S. 385 (1948)).

7. *See generally*, A. CASNER & W. LEACH, CASES AND TEXT ON PROPERTY 221–23 (2d ed. 1969); J. CRIBBET, PRINCIPLES OF THE LAW OF PROPERTY 27–65, 442–45 (1975).

8. I have depended upon WILLIAM CRONON, CHANGES IN THE LAND: INDIANS, COLONISTS, AND THE ECOLOGY OF NEW ENGLAND (1983).

9. *Id.* at 53.

10. *Id.* at 137–38.

11. *Id.* at 56–57, 63.

12. *Id.* at 130.

13. *Id.* at 138.

14. The public land not taken by railroads and homesteaders was subject to the General Mining Law of 1872; "all valuable mineral deposits in lands belonging to the United States . . . shall be free and open to exploration and purchase, and the lands in which they are found to occupation and purchase. . . ." 30 U.S.C. § 22 (1982). Under this law, claims could be preserved after the work totaled $500 by paying the government $2.50 per acre.

"[M]any persons," wrote Justice Lamar, "availed themselves of the provisions of the statute." United States v. Midwest Oil Co. 236 U.S. 459, 466 (1915). In fact, there were so many persons and such exploitive intensity that a real version of the "tragedy of the commons" was produced. As Justice Lamar went on to observe, petroleum was located under large areas of California, and "as the flow through the well on one lot might exhaust the oil under the adjacent land, the interest of each operator was to extract the oil as soon as possible so as to share what would otherwise be taken by the owners of nearby wells." *Id.* By 1909, it was reported to the Secretary of the Interior that, at the rate the California land was being taken, "it would be impossible for the people of the United States to continue ownership of oil lands for more than a few months. After that the [g]overnment will be obliged to repurchase the very oil that it has practically given away." *Id.* at 466–67. This circumstance was especially dire "[i]n view of the increasing use of fuel by the American Navy. . . ." *Id.*

The response of the president in this situation was to withdraw the land in issue from the operation of the mining law. This kind of withdrawal, or banking of resources against a day of greater need, has been repeated. In addition, some public lands have been set aside for parks. The single-minded commitment to immediate exploitation has also been mitigated in recent years by statutory provisions for multiple uses, including recreation, mineral development, and preservation of millions of acres as wilderness. In most respects, however, the original policy is the continuing policy: extract what is there, get it to market, move on.

15. My own favorite is the "reciprocal negative easement." *See* Sanborn v. McLean, 233 Mich. 227, 206 N.W. 496 (1925).

16. U.S. DEP'T OF INTERIOR, *supra* note 2, at A-99.

17. *See* Harmon, *He Stands to Lose Plush Home to Sea,* Savannah Morning News, July 11, 1980, at 10B, col. 1; Goodyear v. Trust Co. Bank, Ga., 276 S.E.2d 30 (1981).

18. U.S. DEP'T OF INTERIOR, *supra* note 2, at A-106 (citing NOAA Technical Memorandum NWS NMC 7 (1984, as amended 1980)).

19. *See* C. LEAVELL, LEGAL ASPECTS OF OWNERSHIP AND USE OF ESTUARINE AREAS IN GEORGIA AND SOUTH CAROLINA 67–68 (1971).

20. *See, e.g.,* Smith v. Bruce, 244 S.E.2d 559, 241 Ga. 133, 147 (1978).

21. William Aldred's case, 77 Eng. Rep. 816 (K.B. 1610), is credited with the first use in the common law of the principle *sic utere tuo ut alienum non laedas.* I have found related versions as far back as the Code of Hammurabi.

22. *See* p. 110 *infra.*

23. The right to build wharves is discussed in both Shively v. Bowlby, 152 U.S. 1 (1894), and Illinois Central R. Co. v. Illinois, 146 U.S. 387 (1892).

176

Notes to Pages 100–102

24. Pitman v. United States. 457 F.2d 975 (Ct. Cl. 1972).
25. 33 U.S.C. §§ 403, 407 (1982).
26. 33 U.S.C. §§ 1251 *et seq.* (1982).
27. *See* Avoyelles Sportsmen's League, Inc. v. Marsh, 715 F.2d 897 (5th Cir. 1983).
28. *See* Just v. Marinette Co., 201 N.W.2d 761, 56 Wis. 2d 7 (1972). Professor Sax proposes that sensible people come to realize that the public value of wetlands will be protected to the detriment of their value to the owner. Although it cannot be exactly specified, a point is reached when courts "simply cease to be sympathetic to owners' claims that their reasonable expectations are being sharply disappointed. That is, at some point the imposition of such restraints is no longer seen as sharply destabilizing for the land-development industry." Sax, *Liberating the Public Trust Doctrine from Its Historical Shackles,* 14 U.C.D. L. Rev. 185, 188–89 n. 13 (1980). Professor Sax has more recently noted that private-property rights are being transformed so that development of land is declining in favor. We are turning instead to symbols of stability, continuity with the past, and solidarity. One consequence of the change is that courts tend not to find takings of property where preservation regulations severely restrict the private owner's choices. Sax, *Some Thoughts on the Decline of Private Property,* 58 Wash. L. Rev. 481 (1983).
29. Augustine, The City of God, bk. xviii, ch. 2, at 610 (M. Dods trans. 1950).
30. *Id.,* bk. xv, ch. 4, at 881.
31. 2 W. Blackstone, Commentaries 1–2 (3 Tucker ed. 1) (1803).
32. At the direction of President Carter, the Department of the Interior produced a 1979 impact statement on policies protecting barrier islands. U.S. Dep't of Interior, *supra* note 4. Congress took a second major step by mandating the discontinuance of federal flood insurance for new construction on undeveloped coastal barriers after October 1, 1983. Omnibus Budget Reconciliation Act of 1981, Pub. L. No. 97–35, §341 (d) (1), 95 Stat. 357, 419 (codified at 42 U.S.C. §4028 (Supp. V. 1981)). Then in 1982, President Reagan signed into law the Coastal Barrier Resources Act (CBRA), which virtually eliminated all federal financial incentives for development on undeveloped barrier islands. Pub. L. 97–348, 96 Stat. 1653 (codified at 16 U.S.C.A. ch. 55 (West Supp. 1982)).
Books which may have helped to bring these developments about were E. Odum, Fundamentals of Ecology, *supra* note 1, and J. & M. Teal's Life and Death of the Salt Marsh (1969). *See also* A. Simon, The Thin Edge (1978).
33. Hinds, *U.S. Lists Barrier Beaches Facing Ban on Flood Policies,* N.Y. Times, Aug. 17, 1982, at 11, col. 1 (quoting Interior Department study).
34. U.S. Dep't of Interior, *supra* note 4, at vii.
35. Sharma, *Hazard Mitigation on Barrier Islands and Beaches, in* 2 Coastal Zone '80, at 1454 (B. Edge ed. 1980). "In its first 12 years of operation, the National Flood Insurance Program lost about $425 million on $1.1 billion in claims. Much of the loss occurred in coastal areas regularly hit by storms. . . ." Hinds, *supra* note 33.
36. *See* note 32 *supra.*
37. U.S. Dep't of Interior, *supra* note 2, at B-47; *id., supra* note 4, at vii.
38. *See, e.g.,* Statement of Jim Scott, National Association of Home Builders, before the Subcommittee on Environmental Pollution, Committee on Environment and Public Works, U.S. Senate, Oct. 21, 1981.
Support for federal assistance on barrier islands can sometimes produce interesting forms of thought for those who oppose federal assistance. Consider the following from a letter to Laurance Rockefeller of the Americans for the Coast signed by Senator Jesse Helms: "I oppose the [barrier islands] bill because it attempts to further interject the federal government into the business of land management—a function of state govern-

ment—by withholding federal support." Who says "taking out" cannot be made to mean "getting in"?

39. GAO, *Federal Disaster Assistance, What Should the Policy Be?* PAD-80-39, June 16, 1980.

40. *See supra* note 1.

41. In addition to the sources cited in note 1, *supra, see* U.S. DEP'T OF INTERIOR, *supra* note 2, Appendix, at A-37 to A-42.

42. U.S. DEP'T OF INTERIOR, *supra* note 2, at A-41.

43. *Id.* at 32.

44. U.S. DEP'T OF INTERIOR, *supra* note 4, at vii–viii, 92–97.

45. Rockefeller, *The Great Barrier Island Bailout,* NAT'L PARKS & CONSERVATION MAG., July 1980, at 18.

46. *Id.* at 19.

47. *Id.* at 20.

48. U.S. DEP'T OF INTERIOR, *supra* note 2, Appendix, at A-104.

49. *See, e.g.,* CRONON, *supra* note 8. In his poem about Chief Joseph of the Nez Percé, Robert Penn Warren has the Chief reflect (and then quotes from his statement to the Commissioners of the Treaty of 1876):

> "'But then, my heart, it heard
> My Father's voice, like a great sky-cry
> From snow-peaks in sunlight, and my voice
> Was saying the Truth that no
> White man can know, how once the Great Spirit
> That made the earth had drawn no lines of separation
> upon it, and all
> Must remain as He made, for to each man
> Earth is the Mother and Nurse, and to that spot
> Where he was nursed, he must, in love, cling."

> *"The earth, my mother and nurse, is very sacred to me:*
> *too sacred to be valued, or sold for gold or for*
> *silver . . ."*

Warren, *Chief Joseph,* GEORGIA REVIEW, Spring 1982, at 271, 278–79.

50. *See, e.g.,* T. LUND, AMERICAN WILDLIFE LAW 8 (1980); E. THOMPSON, WHIGS AND HUNTERS 239–40 (1975).

51. J. SAX, MOUNTAINS WITHOUT HANDRAILS 72ff. (1980).

52. Ruby, *At The Beach: Ocean City: Urban Life on the Shore,* Baltimore Sun, July 6, 1982, at 20, col. 1.

53. U.S. DEP'T OF INTERIOR, *supra* note 4, at 134.

54. *Id.* at 123.

55. Ruby, *supra* note 52.

56. Property taxes fixed on the basis of the "highest use" of a piece of coastal land promote capitalism, not equality. It is not so much that they drive away the wealthy as that they drive them into the arms of developers. I am not at all sure that taxes are a real factor contributing to the exodus of families who owned whole Georgia islands. In any event, a number of families who ended their ownership placed their islands under some form of public control and preservation. In some instances this was done at substantial financial loss to the former private owners.

57. Madison, *Property,* National Gazette, Mar. 29, 1792, *in* THE MIND OF THE FOUNDER 243 (M. Meyers ed. 1973).

178

Notes to Pages 108–14

58. Letter from Thomas Jefferson to Joseph Cabell, *in* THE LIFE AND SELECTED WRITINGS OF THOMAS JEFFERSON 237 (A. Koch & W. Peden eds. 1944).
59. *Id.*
60. BALL, THE PROMISE OF AMERICAN LAW 29–41, 85–94 (1981).
61. W. LIPPMANN, THE METHOD OF FREEDOM 101–2 (1934).
62. Boundaries might constitute meeting places, for example, as they did for Indian tribes.
63. R. Frost, *Mending Wall, in* COMPLETE POEMS OF ROBERT FROST 47 (1949).
64. 146 U.S. 387, 452 (1892).
65. INSTITUTES OF JUSTINIAN, 2. 1. 5, at 92 (Sandars trans. 7th ed. 1962).
66. There is a considerable literature on the public trust doctrine. *See, e.g.,* Shively v. Bowlby, 152 U.S. 1 (1894); Illinois Cent. R.R. v. Illinois, 146 U.S. 387 (1897); Martin v. Waddell, 41 U.S. (16 Pet.) 367 (1842); National Audubon Society v. Superior Court, 33 Cal. 3d 419, 658 P.2d 709, 188 Cal. Rptr. 346 (1983); S. MOORE, HISTORY OF THE FORESHORE (1888); W. RODGERS, HANDBOOK ON ENVIRONMENTAL LAW §2.16 (1977); *The Public Trust Doctrine in Natural Resources Law and Management: A Symposium,* 14 U.C.D. L. REV. 181 (1980); Sax, *The Public Trust Doctrine in Natural Resource Law: Effective Judicial Intervention,* 68 MICH. L. REV. 471 (1970); Note, *A Tidelands Trust for Georgia,* 17 GA. L. REV. 851 (1983); Note, *The Public Trust in Tidal Areas: A Sometimes Submerged Traditional Doctrine,* 79 YALE L.J. 762 (1970).
67. Selvin, *The Public Trust Doctrine in American Law and Economic Policy, 1789–1920,* 1980 WIS. L. REV. 1403, 1421.
68. Sax, *supra* note 66.
69. *See* RODGERS, *supra* note 66, at 173.
70. *See* National Audubon Soc'y v. Superior Court, 33 Cal. 3d 419, 658 P.2d 709, 189 Cal. Rptr. 346 (1983); Johnson, *Public Trust Protection for Stream Flows and Lake Levels,* 14 U.C.D. L. REV. 233 (1980).
71. *See* Johnson, *supra* note 70, at 241–44; Ball, *Environment, Natural Resources, and Land Use,* 35 MERCER L. REV. 147, 164–66 (1983).
72. For an example of the police power – public trust analogy, see Home for Aged Women v. Commonwealth, 202 Mass. 422, 89 N.E. 124 (1909). For an example of expansion of navigability in the direction of public trust, see State v. McIlroy, 595 S.W.2d 659 (Ark. 1980).
73. National Environmental Policy Act, 42 U.S.C. §4321 (b) (1).
74. Sax, *supra* note 66, at 558.
75. Gould v. Greylock Reservation Comm., 350 Mass. 410, 215 N.E.2d 114 (1966).
76. Priewe v. Wisconsin State Land & Improvement Co., 93 Wis. 534, 67 N.W. 918 (1896).
77. Meunsch v. Public Service Comm., 261 Wis. 492, 53 N.W.2d 514, *aff'd on reh.,* 261 Wis. 515, 55 N.W.2d 40 (1962).
78. 77 Wash. 2d 306, 462 P.2d 362, 162 U. Cal. Rptr. 327 (1980).
79. *See* Johnson, *supra* note 70, at 242 n. 39.
80. Sax, *supra* note 66, at 557–61.
81. *Id.* at 560.
82. *Id.*
83. *Id.*
84. Elsewhere I have presented arguments both about what powerless minorities are (the issue of identification) and reasons for protecting them (the issues of constitutional theory and of judicial review). *See* BALL, THE PROMISE OF AMERICAN LAW 108–

25 (1981); *id., Don't Die Don Quixote*, 59 Tex. L. Rev. 787, 794, 813 (1981). *See also infra* chapter 6, note 32.

85. Sandars, Commentary on Institutes 2.1.2., *in* Institutes of Justinian, *supra* note 65, at 91.

86. Bureau of Land Management, U.S. Dep't of the Interior, Promise of the Land 37 (1979), *quoted in* Wilkinson, *The Public Trust Doctrine in Public Land Law*, 14 U.C.D. L. Rev. 269, 281 n. 44 (1980).

87. Rodgers, note 66, at 182.

88. *See* Selvin, *supra* note 67.

CHAPTER 6

1. Hyde points out that gift exchange is not an isolated phenomenon but belongs to a "'total social phenomenon'—one whose transactions are at once economic, juridical, moral, aesthetic, religious, and mythological, and whose meaning cannot, therefore, be adequately described from the point of view of any single discipline." L. Hyde, The Gift xv (1979). (He adopts the idea from Mauss.) Hyde thinks that "[n]ot only does law tend to shed the emotional and spiritual content of a total social phenomenon, but the process of law requires a particular kind of society—it requires, to begin with, adversaries and reckoning, both of which are excluded by the spirit of gift exchange." *Id.* at 88. By describing law as medium, and by placing it within its proper context, I hope to fashion a language for talking about laws having the emotional and spiritual content of a total social phenomenon.

A very different but equally imaginative book by William Cronon, Changes in the Land: Indians, Colonists, and the Ecology of New England (1983), describes the total social phenomenon that characterized early New England. He shows the interplay of economics, conquest, racist beliefs about Indians, boundaries, and the way people approach their natural environment.

Another recent example of the interrelation of conceptual metaphors and their consequences (although they do not use the language of metaphor) is provided by Douglas and Wildavsky's discussion of how the environmental movement's selection of dangers to the environment is culturally determined and how risk perception is a social process. They note: "No doubt the water in fourteenth century Europe was a persistent health hazard, but a cultural theory of [risk] perception would point out that it became a public preoccupation only when it seemed plausible to accuse Jews of poisoning the wells." M. Douglas & A. Wildavsky, Risk and Culture: An Essay on the Selection of Technological and Environmental Dangers 7 (1982).

I am not now making a point about the sociology of knowledge; I accept the fact that our patterns of thinking are shaped by our social context. I am suggesting that our conceptual metaphors—culturally formed though they may be—are not isolated phenomena but occur together with other, related conceptual metaphors.

2. Coastal Zone Mgmt., Sept. 30, 1982, at 4.

3. *Id.*

4. *Id.*

5. *Quoted in* Colman McCarthy, *James Watt and the Puritan Ethic*, Washington Post, Sunday, May 24, 1981, at L5, col. 1.

6. *Id.* The specific idea of possessing the sea in expectation of the coming of Christ was first and long ago given expression by an English parliament. *See* Chapter 3 text at

note 15. It could be argued that Watt's metaphors are traceable to the Puritan conception of having been sent on an errand into the wilderness. *See, e.g.,* PERRY MILLER, ERRAND INTO THE WILDERNESS (1956).

Recently, calls for protectionist legislation to "build ever higher the wall against imports" are evidence of the current vitality of the Fortress America way of thinking. *See* Greenhouse, *The Making of Fortress America,* N.Y. Times, Sunday, August 5, 1984, Section 3, at 1, col. 2. It has been given concrete expression in the security measures taken in Washington during the Reagan administration with the erection of street barriers around the Capitol and White House. It has been reported that Congress has "found itself in a veritable fortress of its own." Hunter, *Congress: Fortress on the Alert in a Siege by the Unknown,* N.Y. Times, Tues., Jan. 24, 1984, at 10, col. 3.

7. Isaiah 11: 6–9 (RSV).

8. W. ALLEN, WITHOUT FEATHERS 28 (1972).

9. 347 U.S. 483 (1954) (Brown I); 349 U.S. 294 (1955) (Brown II).

10. According to the Brule Sioux story, there were two worlds before this one. The people who inhabited them did not act like humans, and the Creating Power destroyed them, the first by fire and the second by flood. After the flood had destroyed all living things, the Creating Power, floating on the surface, reached into his pipe bag and withdrew four animals known for their ability to stay under water a long time. First the loon was sent to dive and bring up a lump of mud. The loon could not reach bottom and returned with nothing. The same thing happened with the otter and the beaver. At last it was the turtle's turn. After a long, long time, the turtle returned with mud from the bottom. Out of this mud the Creating Power created the world, and then people. "The Creating Power said to them: 'The first world I made was bad; the creatures on it were bad. So I burned it up. The second world I made was bad too, so I drowned it. This is the third world I have made. Look I have created a rainbow for you as a sign that there will be no more Great Flood. Whenever you see a rainbow, you will know that it has stopped raining.'

"The Creating Power continued: 'Now, if you have learned how to behave like human beings and how to live in peace with each other and with the other living things— the two-legged, the four-legged, the many-legged, the fliers, the no-legs, the green plants of this universe—then all will be well. But if you make this world bad and ugly, then I will destroy this world too. It's up to you.

"The Creating Power gave the people the pipe. 'Live by it,' he said. He named this land the Turtle Continent because it was there that the turtle came up with the mud out of which the third world was made.

"'Someday there might be a fourth world,' the Creating Power thought. Then he rested." *Remaking the World, in* AMERICAN INDIAN MYTHS AND LEGENDS 496, 498–99 (R.Erdoes & J. Ortiz eds. 1984).

TURTLE ISLAND was the title chosen by Gary Snyder for a book of his poems. He explained: "Turtle Island—the old/new name for the continent, based on many creation myths of the people who have been living here for millennia, and reapplied by some of them to 'North America' in recent years. Also, an idea found world-wide, of the earth, or the cosmos even, sustained by a great turtle or serpent-of-eternity.

"A name: that we may see ourselves more accurately on this continent of watersheds and life-communities—plant zones, physiographic provinces, culture areas; following natural boundaries. The 'U.S.A.' and its states and counties are arbitrary and inaccurate impositions on what is really here.

"The poems speak of place, and the energy-pathways that sustain life. Each living being is a swirl in the flow, a formal turbulence, a 'song.' The land, the planet itself, is also a living being—at another pace. Anglos, Black people, Chicanos, and others beached up on these shores all share such views at the deepest levels of their old cultural traditions—African, Asian, or European. Hark again to those roots, to see our ancient solidarity, and then to the work of being together on Turtle Island." G. SNYDER, *Introductory Note*, TURTLE ISLAND (1974).

11. Coleman Barks calls my attention to the following: "Mother Earth brings forth an endless variety of individuals 'she carries in her lap the seeds of those specific differentiations that characterize each individual female and her particular law.' The roots of law run deep and varied in our Mother tongue: from *lien*, to be prostrate; *ligger*, footbridge; *leger*, bed, couch, or *lair*—a place where animals put their young, *lager*, stored before use; *laghe*, what is laid down; *litter*, a portable bed, or the recently borne young of an animal (especially a sow), or the straw bedding that tends to become scattered rubbish; *lokhos*, a lying-in, hence childbirth.

"Law, before it is hatched, is held deep within the body of the Mother. Her laws, the-way-she-lays-it-down, are primitive or basic. . . . Unlike the great changing law of the Father, which is based upon consciousness of self, property, and others, the Mother's laws are those of unvitiated nature. . . . The binding factor of such laws is not the threat of punishment or promise of cultural stability, but rather like the binding of electrons or of flesh to flesh—a natural, instinctual binding inherent in being (matter or energy) that lends cohesion, pattern, system, rhythm to the gradual wending of life toward death. Time does not change these universal laws of nature. The bed, as symbol of where the Great Mother's laws come from, is always, everywhere, the place of birth, of sleep and dreaming, of love, and of death." N. HALL, THE MOON AND THE VIRGIN 40–41 (1982).

12. I do not mean for the image of The Peaceable Kingdom to stand for or be confused with nostalgia for what Leo Marx described as "the once dominant image of an undefiled, green republic." L. MARX, THE MACHINE IN THE GARDEN 6 (1964). The contrast I want to achieve is not between the machine and the garden or between urbanization and pastoralism but between a stifling, monolithic politics and a politics of hope and diversity. I intend my elaboration of The Peaceable Kingdom to be one of Marx's "new symbols of possibility." *Id.* at 365.

13. N. FRYE, THE GREAT CODE xviii–xix (1982).

14. Before his imprisonment, Bonhoeffer wrote several substantial, complete pieces. Much of his later development of theological categories and new departures never reached final form. The most thorough study of Bonhoeffer—the definitive work—is E. BETHGE, DIETRICH BONHOEFFER (Mosbacher, Ross, Clarke, & Glen-Doepel trans. 1970). I have relied upon it.

15. Because of the first amendment, lawyers are familiar with the difficulty of defining religion for constitutional purposes—preventing the establishment and protecting the free exercise of religion. *See, e.g. Symposium: The Religion Clauses*, 72 CALIF. L. REV. 753 (1984) (Greenawalt, Johnson, Mansfield, and Brill). *See also* Choper, *Defining "Religion" in the First Amendment*, 1982 U. ILL. L.F. 579. The religion clauses of the Constitution are of utmost importance. However, my present concern lies elsewhere.

Harvey Cox says that religion is reviving in the contemporary world. He is right. He also rightly says that "religion is not always good." H. COX, RELIGION IN THE SECULAR CITY 20 (1984). The biblical sagas are critical of human religiousness. Just now, as Cox says, theology must interpret the biblical story in a time "when the rebirth of religion, rather than its disappearance, poses the most serious question." *Id.*

Cox writes from within a tradition in which the biblical faith and theology are distinguished from religion and religious practices. I concur in that distinction and underscore it.

I am in the process of sketching the principal features of a family of metaphors surrounding and supporting law as medium. Theology—but not religion—is a pervasive component of that family as I am portraying it.

Karl Barth explained very carefully that religion is man's fruitless effort to justify himself before a capricious picture of a highest being of his own imagining, 1 K. BARTH, CHURCH DOGMATICS, pt. 2, at 280–361 (Thomas & Knight trans. 1956), a God who is "the tedious magnitude known as transcendance, not as a genuine counterpart, nor a true other . . . but as an illusory reflection of human freedom, as its projection into the vacuum of utter abstraction." 3 id., pt. 4, at 479 (Mackay, Parker, Knight, Kennedy & Morlies trans. 1961). In this way of thinking, religion is unbelief. Theology is the discipline that tries to state and understand the meaning of the particularities of the biblical Word. It is not concerned with the universalities of religion except critically.

Barth and Bonhoeffer, like Calvin and Augustine before, began at a radically particular point of departure: God's self-revelation in the history recounted in the Bible. From this beginning they were led, as they could be in no other fashion, to radically inclusive affirmation of things human and secular. A "No" is pronounced upon a fallen world. Radical evil is judged. But the "No" is penultimate. It is declared upon the world together with an ultimate "Yes." Indeed, it is the "Yes" that makes the "No" possible. From knowledge of God comes the knowledge of ourselves and our world that finally clarifies how "our very existence is nothing but a subsistence in God alone." 1 J. CALVIN, INSTITUTES OF THE CHRISTIAN RELIGION 478 (Allen trans. 1949). So theology moves from its particular starting point to embrace things secular and worldly. It describes the basis for their fullest celebration. It does so nonreligiously.

16. Natural theology is a way of trying to say what we know about God from nature, proving the existence of God from the created order. I think natural theology is a dead option. There can be no knowledge of God apart from His revelation of Himself. There is no independent line of access. Knowledge of God like knowledge of the creation comes only from the Word of the biblical story.

An example of a natural theologian discussed by Barth is one Friedrich Christian Lesser, who sought "traces of the divine attributes not only in the revealed book of Scripture but also in the great open book of nature. . . ." 3 K. BARTH, CHURCH DOGMATICS, pt. 1, at 296 (Edwards, Bussey & Knight trans. 1958). Lesser wrote an "Insecto-Theologia" laboriously accumulating evidence of God's power and wisdom from insects. Barth judged that Lesser had tried to make "a 'one' out of the greatest number of noughts." Id. at 407. Barth also found that Lesser's constant moralizing and cheerfulness aroused a sense of oppression: "It is hard to conceive that Lesser was not heartily weary of insects when he had finished his Insecto-Theologia." Id.

There are no contemporary insecto-theologians. That brand of piety belongs to an earlier epoch. There are contemporary cosmologists. See generally M. TOULMIN, THE RETURN OF COSMOLOGY (1982). Human responsibility for science and its consequences is one of the outcomes of this contemporary cosmology. That return to human responsibility is to be applauded. However, I seek a fuller and more satisfactory description of responsibility than that afforded by cosmology. I do not think that our only choice is "the Buddha or . . . the Bomb." F. CAPRA, THE TURNING POINT 87 (1983).

Capra's position is illustrative of the weakness I find in modern cosmology. I do not believe human responsibility is likely to be supported or exercised in consequence of what Capra calls spiritual synchrony: "At rare moments in our lives we may feel that we are in synchrony with the whole universe. These moments may occur under many circumstances—hitting a perfect shot at tennis or finding the perfect run down a ski slope, in the midst of a fulfilling sexual experience, in contemplation of a great work of art, or in deep meditation. These moments of perfect rhythm, when everything feels exactly right and things are done with great ease, are high spiritual experiences in which every form of separateness or fragmentation is transcended." *Id.* at 302. Quite apart from my puzzlement over an equivalence between tennis, skiing, and sex (maybe my experience of the first two has been limited), the facile, fashionable value attributed to feeling good provides no substantive content or motive for responsibility.

Paul Davies thinks that science provides a surer path to God than does religion now "that the biblical perspective of the world . . . seems largely irrelevant." P. DAVIES, GOD AND THE NEW PHYSICS 2 (1983). I place upon the church no little responsibility for the failure to state the biblical story clearly and repeatedly in such a way that people like Davies, who seem to have a good grasp of science, would not be allowed to think that their picture of God ("the supreme holistic concept," *id.* at 223) has any relation to the God of the Bible. Science provides not a surer way to God, but a way to a different God. Perhaps the church has been so dilatory—thinking to save some space for God— that it has allowed the name "God" to be robbed of the particular and historically pointed content given it in the biblical sagas.

Although the impulse is altogether different, the theological direction of these modern cosmologists is the same as Lesser's. They are modern scientists and philosophers of science who have come to the conclusion that their views—their views from within their discipline—have religious dimensions. They construe the larger patterns they discern as the traces of God who, as a minimum datum, does not throw dice. The insecto-theologian deals in microcosmic specifics, the cosmologists with macrocosmic patterns. But both move from the place of creature within the natural order to the larger scheme of things to a God.

Neither insects nor patterns, however, give independent evidence of the God of the biblical sagas. The Christian tradition properly has no cosmology. Or, rather, it has many cosmologies. *See* 3 K. BARTH, CHURCH DOGMATICS, pt. 2, at 6–8, 447 (Bromiley, Fuller, Knight & Reid trans. 1960). In the biblical story there is no larger scheme of things, no world view, no ontology of created totality. Consequently Christians have employed various cosmologies (sometimes too gullibly).

Instead of natural theology and its devices for reading God from the book of nature, I use the term "theology of the natural." By it I intend a qualitively different enterprise. A theology of the natural attempts to understand nature Christocentrically. *See infra* note 17. If natural theology tries to prove the existence of God, a theology of the natural tries to prove the reality of man. As Barth said: "it is primarily the creature and not the Creator of whom we are not certain, and . . . in order to be certain of him we need proof or revelation." 3 K. BARTH, CHURCH DOGMATICS, pt. 1, at 6.

When we do not subject it to a tiresome duty to exhibit God, the world provokes spontaneous delight and astonishment. Barth thought that, because there is no master key unlocking the mystery of the universe, the believer "will always be the most surprised, the most affected, the most apprehensive and the most joyful in the face of events." 3 *id.*, pt. 3, at 242 (Bromiley & Ehrlich trans. 1961). Barth goes on to observe that "life in the world, with all its joys and sorrows and contemplation and activity, will always be for [the believer] a really interesting matter, or . . . an adventure, for which he for his part has ultimately and basically no qualifications of his own." *Id.* at 242–43. It is in this context that I understand the tribute Barth paid to Mozart. Creation is good. There is a dark side, a negative side, confrontation with nothingness. But even taking this side into account as part of the totality, creation is good. The goodness of the totality of creation was sounded by Mozart: "in the music of Mozart . . . we have clear and convincing proof that it is a slander on creation to charge it with a share in chaos because it included a Yes and a No, as though oriented to God on the one side and nothingness on the other. Mozart causes us to hear that even on the latter side, and therefore in its totality, creation praises its Master and is therefore perfect." 3 K. BARTH, CHURCH DOGMATICS, pt. 3, at 299.

To disavow worshiping God in nature is not to deny a place to nature but to celebrate it in its own right. My present point is that natural theology is not a fruitful possibility and that I intend a qualitatively different discipline when I speak of the theology of the natural.

17. It was Barth who introduced Christocentric thinking about nature. Near the end of his life, Barth struck up a correspondence with the poet Carl Zuckmayer. In the course of it, Barth had occasion to state the sum of his understanding of the doctrine of creation. In conversation, Zuckmayer had evidently made reference to worshiping God in the presence of Alpine trees "and even in the form of the bark" of a tree. A LATE FRIENDSHIP: THE LETTERS OF KARL BARTH AND CARL ZUCKMAYER 12 (Bromiley trans. 1982). Barth was dubious. Poetic license would not warrant "worshipping God in the Bark of a tree." *Id.* at 13. To worship God in this way, *i.e.,* in nature, may be permissible but not directly or unqualifiedly.

Using Zuckmayer's figure, Barth explained that "God in the bark of a tree is God the Creator." *Id.* God the Reconciler "is certainly one and the same as God the Creator, but he is the God who truly acts and speaks only in Jesus Christ. It is to him and him alone that worship truly belongs . . . and to God in the tree bark only indirectly and inconclusively and mediately." *Id.*

At stake in this distinction are important differences for the understanding of nature, ourselves, and God. What Barth insisted upon then was that the creation—God in the bark—is not an independent source of knowledge or being. The source can only be revelation, the Word who is the subject of the biblical sagas. There is no correspondence or similarity between the being of man and the being of God.

Therefore, I cannot speak of an *analogia entis* as the Roman Catholic tradition does. In the Protestant tradition in the United States, Jonathan Edwards provides the most elaborate theological consideration of nature. It is my own judgment that Edwards's thought generally and his understanding of nature in particular have not received the active attention that they warrant. The finest recent piece known to me is the so-far-unpublished doctoral dissertation of Paula Cooey-Nichols, Nature as Divine Communication in the Works of Jonathan Edwards (Harvard University 1981). Edwards attempted a Trinitarian (as compared with Barth's Christocentric) theology of nature. There is much to commend his attempt and much to learn from it. He found in nature images and types shadowing forth God's providence. I remain finally uncertain whether his understanding of God controlled his understanding of nature or his understanding of nature gave rise to his understanding of God.

Like the biblical sagas, the Apostles' Creed opened with the creation: "I believe in God the Father Almighty, Maker of heaven and earth. . . ." But as Barth observes, what comes first is not creation but the "I believe." The creation is an article of faith. It follows from revelation, not creation. Creation is a Christological subject. The Word is the source of our knowledge of man and nature. Barth puts it this way: "Because man, living under heaven and on earth, is the creature whose relation to God is revealed to us in the word of God, he is the central object of the doctrine of creation. As the man

Jesus is Himself the revealing word of God, He is the source of our knowledge of the nature of man as created by God." 3 K. BARTH, CHURCH DOGMATICS, pt. 3, at 3.

The same point is made in Norman Maclean's short novel *A River Runs through It*. In one scene the author's father sits high on a bank overlooking the river where his family of fly fishermen have been taking trout. He has been reading the New Testament in Greek, the Gospel of John. He tells his son: "In the part I was reading it says the Word was in the beginning, and that's right. I used to think water was first, but if you listen carefully you will hear that the words are underneath the water." N. MACLEAN, A RIVER RUNS THROUGH IT 95 (1976).

18. D. BONHOEFFER, LETTERS AND PAPERS FROM PRISON 58 (Bethge ed. 1967).

19. *Id.*

20. *See* BETHGE, *supra* note 14, at 623.

Bonhoeffer's notion of nature as penultimate is a rejection of both Christian radicalism and compromise. It proscribes radicalism which, "whether it consists in withdrawing from the world or in improving the world, arises from hatred of creation. The radical cannot forgive God His creation." D. BONHOEFFER, ETHICS 87 (Bethge trans. 1955). It also rejects compromise which "always springs from hatred of the Ultimate." *Id.* at 88.

21. BONHOEFFER, *supra* note 20, at 90.

22. Paul Lehmann provides this serviceable definition: "By *natural law* . . . we understand the fact that intrinsic to the human reason, and thus, to the nature of man, there is the capacity to distinguish between what is right or good, and what is wrong or bad. In this basic sense, the terms 'right' and 'good,' 'wrong' or 'bad,' are interchangeable. They denote irreducible judgments of value by which the acts of men are to be adjudged responsible or irresponsible. Accordingly, all men, as human beings, know that there is a fundamental and universal moral (or ethical, the terms are interchangeable) order within which their lives are set. This order claims and limits both the judgments and the acts of men, both the reason and the wills and in this way, undergirds and guides the responsible life." Lehmann, *A Christian Alternative to Natural Law, in* DIE MODERNE DEMOKRATIE UND IHR RECHT 517, 522 (Braucher, Dawson, Geiger & Smend eds.)

There is a massive literature on natural law. Once, in my salad days, I took its very size as a challenge and set out to master the whole. Before wilting, I found the following to be among the useful guides. H. CAIRNS, LEGAL PHILOSOPHY FROM PLATO TO HEGEL (1967); F. FLÜCKIGER, GESCHICHTE DES NATURRECHTES (1954); O. VON GIERKE, NATURAL LAW AND THE THEORY OF SOCIETY, 1500–1800 (E. Barker trans. 1957); L. STRAUSS, NATURAL RIGHT AND HISTORY (1953); E. TROELTSCH, THE SOCIAL TEACHING OF THE CHRISTIAN CHURCHES (O. Wyon trans. 1931).

23. FRYE, *supra* note 13, at 119.

24. E. O. Wilson defines sociobiology as "the systematic study of the biological basis of all social behavior." SOCIOBIOLOGY: THE NEW SYNTHESIS 4 (1975). William Rodgers has usefully related sociobiology to law by showing that biological theory "offers important, and much neglected, partial explanations." Rodgers, *Bringing People Back: Toward a Comprehensive Theory of Taking in Natural Resources Law,* 10 ECOLOGY L.Q. 205, 206 (1982). Rodgers is modest in his use of and claims for sociobiology's relation to law, and he does provide helpful insights. He is more modest and more helpful than some representatives of sociobiology. Rodgers refers to his theory "as biological not because dark human impulses predetermine rules of law but rather because the rules that emerge are explicable in terms of a coherent view of human nature conforming to

contemporary biological theory." *Id.* at 251. It appears to me that once the conversation turns to views of human nature, then either explicitly or implicitly it draws on much more than physical elements, ceases to be a description of biological process, and reenters the general philosophical-theological-political dialogue about what nature and the human are. In this dialogue, biology plays a role but by no means the leading role. I am fundamentally troubled by any theory that yields an ethic of survival.

25. I have addressed this subject in Ball, *Cross and Sword, Victim and Law: A Tentative Response to Leonard Levy's Treason against God*, 35 STAN. L. REV. 1007 (1983); *id., Obligation: Not to the Law but to the Neighbor*, 18 GA. L REV. 911 (1984).

26. This is the core of Critical Legal Studies' attack on liberalism. *See* R. UNGER, KNOWLEDGE AND POLITICS (1975); Tushnet, *Darkness on the Edge of Town: The Contributions of John Hart Ely to Constitutional Theory*, 89 YALE L.J. 1037 (1980).

27. Barth observes that "[i]f it is true that man is more noble than [the] creatures, it is also true that he is just as much in need of them as of all that went before, whereas they for their part have no need of him whatever." 3 K. BARTH, CHURCH DOGMATICS, pt. 1, at 117.

28. White, *The Historical Roots of our Ecological Crises*, 155 SCIENCE 1203 (1967), *reprinted in* THE ENVIRONMENTAL HANDBOOK 12, 25 (G. de Bell ed. 1970).

29. *Id.* at 26, 24.

30. *See* Genesis 1:28. *See also* Psalms 8:4–6, Hebrews 2:8.

31. WHITE, *supra* note 28, at 26.

32. Perhaps religion and politics should not be mixed. Formally it may be well to keep a wall of separation between church and state. However, as I understand theology, it is preeminently political. Therefore in addition to understanding nature in Christocentric terms and distinguishing theology from religion as well as natural theology from a theology of the natural, I find politics to be inseparable from theology.

Of course politics played a prominent role in James Watt's thinking. The difference lies in which kind of politics is compatible with which kind of theology. In most important respects, Watt's conceptual thinking is that of the Moral Majority. I think in terms not of morals or majorities but of ethics and minorities. The difference is quickly and easily identifiable: poor people. The tradition from which I speak is a theology and politics of the poor. It has to do with their liberation.

In this I follow my teacher Paul Lehmann. Lehmann demonstrates that the activity of God is politics and that the activity of politics is authentic human community. As Lehmann points out, the biblical story is told in political images: the gathering of a people, the formation of a kingdom, the coming of a messiah, etc. In this story, God is seen to be doing politics, *i.e.,* "what it takes to make and to keep human life in the world." P. LEHMANN, ETHICS IN A CHRISTIAN CONTEXT 347 (1963). *See also id.* at 74–87. For an exposition of such a politics see P. LEHMANN THE TRANSFIGURATION OF POLITICS (1975). The discernible outcome of this activity is a redeeming community—a polis or *koinonia.*

The chief characteristic of the community is deliverance of the poor. The poor are "all those without status and without power in the world [who constitute] the society that God has called into life for the humanization of human life." P. LEHMANN, THE TRANSFIGURATION OF POLITICS 258. *See also*, G. GUTIERREZ, A THEOLOGY OF LIBERATION 287–306 ("Poverty: Solidarity and Protest") (1973); Cox, *supra* note 15, at 147, 166–67 (God as "el dios pobre") (1984). In his recent Dudleian Lecture at Harvard, Gutierrez explained: "God is the first and the last reason for the preferential option for the poor. The reason is not, first of all, social analysis, or human compassion, or the direct experience of poverty. . . . The beatitudes in the Gospels—Blessed are the poor—are not, in the first instance, a word about the poor, but about God. 'Blessed are the poor' is a revelation of God. God loves the poor by preference, not because the poor are good persons, better than others, or good believers, better than other believers, but because God is God. . . .

"Linked with this first and fundamental reason, there is another. Poverty—and in Latin America and other places in the world, we are more and more conscious about that—poverty means, finally, death. Death from hunger, from sickness, but not only these aspects, because when we talk about poverty in Latin America, and other places, we are speaking about the destruction of individuals and peoples, cultures and tradition. . . .

"Consequently, despite what is sometimes thought, in a spirituality of liberation, a theology of liberation, we are not dealing simply with a social problem. Rather we are confronted with a reality contrary to the kingdom of God, the kingdom of life, the kingdom that the Lord proclaims. Poverty means death." Gutierrez, *Theology and Spirituality in a Latin American Context*, HARV. DIVINITY BULL., June–August 1984, at 4–5.

Writing in the context of the United States, William Stringfellow observes that advocacy of the cause of the victims of society "exemplifies the church's worship of God, an intercession for anyone in need, which exposes and confounds the blasphemy of predatory political authority." W. STRINGFELLOW, CONSCIENCE AND OBEDIENCE: THE POLITICS OF ROMANS 13 AND REVELATION 13 IN LIGHT OF THE SECOND COMING 95 (1977).

The poor are decisive to the authenticity of human community. The believer is a participator in the redemptive community which advocates the cause of the poor.

The Moral Majority has a wholly different agenda. According to Jerry Falwell: "We could never bring the issue of the poor into Moral Majority because the argument would be, Who is going to decide what we teach those people? Mormons? Catholics? No, we won't get into that. As private persons and ministers, we make a commitment if we feel convicted. But for Moral Majority, no! If we go in there, create jobs, raise funds, and get involved with the local pastors, the fundamentalists are gone. If we say the Catholic pastors, the Jews are gone and so forth. We just have to stay away from helping the poor." *Quoted in* Cox, *supra* note 15, at 230. The Moral Majority rejects the poor and avoids conflict. The tradition from which I speak does not shrink from conflict and acknowledges that God's active presence is manifest among the poor.

Also, this tradition of theology rejects the terms of programs as much as those of morals and majorities. The believer's responsibility is always concrete. It cannot be programmatic without ultimately shifting allegiance from the humanizing activity of God to the program. Politics is necessarily episodic. It may take any of a variety of forms, including dissent, opposition, resistance, temporary support for particular measures or officers of the state, and supplication.

In avoiding the Scylla of programs, however, contextual politics runs the danger of Charybdis—the danger of losing sight of the need to address systemic problems. If individuals are to act or to be served effectively, account must be taken of the institutions that shape our lives and thinking. Fitting, theologically based political action does not repudiate programs only to lapse into disengagement and stupefaction.

In this regard, I note the timely warning issued by the church in South America. That church's base communities and liberation theology exemplify the politics I intend. The warning from that quarter is directed to liberal, learned neutrality. José Miguel Bonino differentiates South American from European and American theologies on the ground that the latter are neutral. According to Bonino, while European and American theology is properly political and historical, it has wrongly found "no need to opt for this or that political praxis." J. BONINO, DOING THEOLOGY IN A REVOLUTIONARY SITUA-

TION 95 (1975). He believes it is an unethical luxury to maintain neutral critical freedom and to draw back from particular liberating undertakings of particular oppressed classes in particular countries. When European and American theologians "conceive critical freedom as the form in which God's eschatological Kingdom infringes on the political realm," he says, "they are simply opting for one particular ideology, that of liberalism." *Id.* at 149. He and other South American theologians have opted for Marxism. Bonino observes that their assumption of Marxism is limited and critical for they do not assume it absolutely or with religious fervor but simply as "the best instrument available for an effective and rational realization of human possibilities in human life." *Id.* at 97. For thoughtful, theological assessment of Latin American revolutionaries, see P. LEHMANN, THE TRANSFIGURATION OF POLITICS, *supra*, at 138–62.

I accept the judgment of the liberation theologians in South America that limited, critical alignment with a Marxist movement is a legitimate theological decision in their time and place. I also accept their warning about American temptation to liberalism and to disengagement from real political choices. In the United States, advocacy of the cause of the poor has taken forms in addition to that of Marxism with additional options to draw us out of neutrality.

Theology and politics are inseparable. Politics is properly directed to the communal advocacy of the cause of the poor. This advocacy is not programmatic, but neither is it abstract. It cannot avoid praxis.

33. BONHOEFFER, *supra* note 20, at 102.

34. *Id.* at 60.

35. I would elaborate the natural life narratively rather than in Bonhoeffer's terms of a framework of rights and duties. I am not sure that the language of rights is adequate or even correct.

36. 3 D. BONHOEFFER, GESAMMELTE SCHRIFTEN 477. This statement is made at the end of Bonhoeffer's first attempt at an interpretation of "History and the Good," and reads: "Politische Handeln bedeutet Verantwortung Wahrnehmen. Es kann nicht geschehen ohne Macht. Die Macht tritt in den Dienst der Verantwortung. . . ." I have used the translation of these lines suggested by Paul Lehmann, who called them to my attention.

Of course talk of power must be understood in the light of Bonhoeffer's treatment of powerlessness. Taking responsibility and therefore power seriously requires that we understand the biblical images for the exercise of power, namely the little child of Isaiah or the crucifixion in the New Testament, and those are images of powerlessness, the quintessential images of the natural person.

Here is the way the biblical Book of Hebrews expresses it: "Now in putting everything in subjection to man [God] left nothing outside his control. As it is, we do not see everything in subjection to him. But we see Jesus, who for a little while was made lower than angels, crowned with glory and honor because of the suffering of death, so that by the grace of God he might taste death for every one." Hebrews 2:8–9 (RSV).

The powerless, crucified Jesus is *the* natural person. We see ourselves as we are meant naturally to be. The image given us for a person in command of creation—with nothing outside our control—is a person wholly for others. This is what Bonhoeffer meant when he said that only the suffering God can help us: "God lets himself be pushed out of the world on to the cross. He is weak and powerless in the world, and that is precisely the way, the only way, in which he is with us and helps us. . . . Man's religiosity makes him look in his distress to the power of God in the world: God is the *deus ex machina*. The Bible directs man to God's powerlessness and suffering. . . ." Bonhoeffer, *supra* note 18, at 196–97.

To live the natural life is to be for others. It requires participation in the powerlessness of Jesus. Hence, our "relation to God is not a 'religious' relationship to the highest, most powerful, and best Being imaginable" for this would not be authentic transcendence and would not help us to be natural. *Id.* at 210. Rather, as Bonhoeffer explained, "our relation to God is a new life in 'existence for others,' through participation in the being of Jesus." *Id.*

So Bonhoeffer's reference to power in the service of responsibility does not authorize triumphalist uses of force in the name of God. Another way to address the issue of power is to distinguish the power of love from the love of power. The best treatment of this distinction and the way in which the power of love relates to modern revolutionary politics is Paul Lehmann's *The Transfiguration of Politics*.

37. Like members of a family, related conceptual metaphors undoubtedly interact with each other in complicated ways. This would be true of both the individual's and the culture's constellation of metaphors. I do not know all that is necessary to a full statement of these interactions. My present understanding of the subject is that conceptual metaphors within a family cluster have a certain degree of autonomy but are also mutually affective.

Certainly law as bulwark is relatively autonomous. It serves national security, for example, but there are times when law does not yield to demands made by the majority view of national security, as when law protects freedom of speech and press or other citizen rights over against military or police or bureaucratic ideas of national security. If you think you must have a dam against chaos and erect one, then you foreclose your choices for altering it to suit convenience. By limiting others, you limit yourself. If you think of law as a set of rules, you will think the rules apply to yourself as well as others. You cannot both think of law as a protective edifice and think that it is to be bent or manipulated. Law as adamantine defense against anarchy has served the interest of the powerful to the detriment of the weak, but it has also exhibited relative autonomy. The powerful, too, have found themselves hemmed in by the bulwark to the benefit of the weak.

Law as bulwark has also affected other members of its family. If I carry in my head the metaphor of law as a defense against chaos, then I shall more likely view life as presenting the threat of chaos. Or, to take another example, if my lawyer is a hired gun, then I am more likely to give my social and business relationships a combative color—perhaps in the way that carrying a handgun must affect one's self-image and image of others.

So a conceptual metaphor for law, like any other conceptual metaphor, is a relatively autonomous and affective member of its family. But a metaphor also falls under the influence of the rest of the family. Lawyers like to think that the law is crucially important. I think that conceptual metaphors for law are subordinate members of their families and that law as bulwark is particularly susceptible to influence. (I am not sure about this last point. In general, I understand the interaction of conceptual metaphors no better than I understand the linkage of firing neurons in the brain or thought patterns in a culture.)

38. 2 CALVIN, *supra* note 15, bk. 4, ch. 20, paras. 17–21.

39. *Id.* para. 18.

40. *See* Lohn & Ball, *Legal Advocacy, Performance, and Affection,* 16 GA L. REV. 853 (1982).

41. I take the idea and the examples from G. LAKOFF & M. JOHNSON, METAPHORS WE LIVE BY 4 (1980).

42. *Id.* at 10.

43. *See* BALL, THE PROMISE OF AMERICAN LAW (1981).

44. *The Talk of the Town: Notes and Comments,* NEW YORKER, Mar. 15, 1982, at 33.

45. Turnbull, *The Individual, Community and Society: Rights and Responsibilities from an Anthropological Perspective,* 41 WASH. & LEE L. REV. 77, 87–88 (1984).

46. Abel, *Torts, in* THE POLITICS OF LAW 185 (D. Kairys ed. 1982).

47. *Id.* at 196.

48. *Id.* at 199.

Attorney-client relationships can also be made over to reflect personal care and communal bonds. Gerald Frug, for example, notes that lawyers do not have to require that clients defer to professional expertise. The relationship between lawyer and client "involves—and helps create—both parties' moral and political concerns, both parties' ways of understanding the world, and both parties' sense of self-respect and empowerment. As a result, the lawyer-client relationship can become a training ground in which both parties learn how to engage in a dialogue about their most basic beliefs and values in a context in which concrete decisions about future courses of action need to be made. . . ." Frug, Book Review, *The Language of Power,* 84 COLUM. L. REV. 1881, 1894 (1984). For the task, a new language is needed, one that will "enable those who speak to develop their skills of critical analysis and to develop the capacity to engage in practical reasoning with people of differing views on how to make the world better." *Id.*

49. *See* BETHGE, *supra* note 14, at 782–93; Lehmann, *Faith and Worldliness in Bonhoeffer's Thought, in* BONHOEFFER IN A WORLD COME OF AGE 25, 41–45 (1968).

50. A note by a young staffer on the New Yorker freshly reminds me of the power of narrative to shape our lives. The writer's reflections upon the senseless murders and rapes of several friends or acquaintances was guided by reflection upon *The Brothers Karamazov.* The note concludes by addressing the issue of how one acts in the present and future after confronting atrocity: "The deepest instinct is to gather close around you those you love, and live your life. But the world keeps intruding. I'm afraid that I'll begin to believe this world beyond redemption, not necessarily in a theological sense but in a human one. I don't want to hate the world. At one point in The Brothers Karamazov, Alyosha comes across a gang of schoolboys stoning a pale, sickly classmate, and shields him with his body; with the same aggressive, individual, gratuitous, healing love, he turns a proud lad, Kolya, into a man. No other course of action suggests itself to me." *The Talk of the Town: Note and Comments,* New Yorker, Dec. 17, 1984, at 39, 40. I think it is not an accident that the biblical story lies behind the story which helped to give sense and direction to the events of that young person's life. I have written about these matters with particular emphasis on the role of story in law in THE PROMISE OF AMERICAN LAW, *supra* note 43, at 16–28, where I have tried to show both how theology is done by narrative and how narrative relates to law.

51. P. RICOEUR, TIME AND NARRATIVE x (1984).

52. *Id.* at xi.

53. LEHMANN, THE TRANSFIGURATION OF POLITICS, *supra* note 32, at 258. *See also id.* at 7–8, 10, 24, 248–49.

54. *See* BETHGE, *supra* note 14, at 789–90.

55. *Id.* at 786. Bonhoeffer was also aware of those occasions when proclamation is necessary and silence is wrong. For example, it was necessary for the Confessing Church in Germany to declare her faith over against the total state and to declare her solidarity with the Jews. Bonhoeffer's appreciation of silence did not arise from cowardice or the dodging of ethical responsibility. It had much to do with the issues I discuss in the text and with his commitment to let action speak for itself.

56. *See* BONHOEFFER, *supra* note 18, at 154.

57. *Id.* at 122.

58. BETHGE, *supra* note 14, at 829. After his comrades assured him that they wished him to do it, Bonhoeffer conducted the worship service.

59. *Id.* at 787.

60. *Id.*

61. The center from which "those who interpret Christianity in a non-religious way are maintained, led on and 'spiritually nourished,' cannot be outwardly propagated or demonstrated. And certainly not when circumstances have evolved that have destroyed the automatic relation of the names of these events of life to the world of those around us." *Id.* at 785. For discussion of the secrecy of the Gospel of Mark, see F. KERMODE, THE GENESIS OF SECRECY (1979). On "covert communication" and modern fiction (and their bearing on law), see Richard Weisberg's splendid book THE FAILURE OF THE WORD (1984).

AFTERWORD

1. D. BONHOEFFER, LETTERS AND PAPERS FROM PRISON 155 (Bethge ed. 1967).

2. *Id.* at 196.

3. *Id.*

4. "[O]ur relation to God is a new life in 'existence for others'"; "so the transcendental is not infinite and unattainable tasks, but the neighbor who is within reach in any given situation." *Id.* at 210.

5. 3 K. BARTH, CHURCH DOGMATICS, pt. 4, at 567 (Mackay, Parker, Knight, Kennedy & Morlies trans. 1961).

INDEX

Abel, Richard, 134
Accretion, 98
Alaska: offshore oil and gas, 88–90
Allen, Woody, 123
Alluvion, 98
Analogia entis, 184*n17*
Anselm, 36
Arcane discipline, 135
Argument: and law, 44–45; as theater, 133
Auden, W. H., 19
Augustine of Hippo, 101
Avoyelles Sportsmen's League, Inc. v. Marsh, 175*n27*
Avulsion, 98

Baltimore Canyon, 81–83
Barks, Coleman: Fightingtown Creek, 28–23; weakness of law as medium, 160*n158*; Mother Earth, 181*n11*
Barrier Islands: movement, 103–4; danger, 104–5; privacy, 105–6; private ownership of, 107
Barth, Karl: transformation of thought, 17; priority of theology, 19; and Bonhoeffer's theology, 126; limits, 138; religion, 182*n15*; natural theology, 182–84*n16*; and Zuckmayer, 184*n17*; christocentric creation, 184–85*n17*
Beach nourishment, 103–4
Beaufort Sea, 88–90
Bethge, Eberhard, 136, 181*n14*
Bible: and legal imagination, 125
Black, Hugo, 25
Black holes, 6
Blackstone, William: property ownership, 101
Bonhoeffer, Dietrich: prison and nature, 126; theology of the natural, 126–27; theology contrasted with Watt's, 129; unexceptional, 135; arcane discipline, 135–36; death and boundaries, 137–38; power and responsibility, 188*n36*
Bonine, John, 168*n59*

Bonino, José Miguel, 187–88*n32*
Boundaries: dissolve in darkness, 4; of experience, 5; not lost when absent, 15, 138; territorial sea, 69; and federalism, 74; state and private ownership, 95–99; and death, 138
British seas, 146*n8*
Brown v. Board of Education, 25, 80, 125
Burke, William, 159*n158*

Calder, Alexander: mobile as image of federalism, 73
California: and Coastal Zone Management Act, 85–86
California v. Watt, 85–86, 163*n8*, 167*n43*, 167*n47*, 171*n112*, 174*n142*
Calvin, John: priority of theology, 19; litigation as gift of God, 132
Cannon-shot rule, 41
Canute, King, 37
Case method, 24
Christ: and nature, 129; and politics, 129; second coming, 129; and arcane discipline, 136; and creation 184–85*n17*; powerlessness, 188*n36*
Christo: Running Fence, 77, 108
Clean Water Act, 86–88, 100
Coast: public nature, 110
Coastal urbanization, 93–94
Coastal Zone Management Act, 85–86, 95
Cod War, 49
Commodity: contrasted with gift, 14
Common Heritage of Mankind: Pardo proposes, 50; deep seabed, 52, 55; said to be without legal significance, 154*n114*
Conceptual metaphor: new, summarized, xiii; use by scientists, 6; and transformation of thought, 17; for law, 21–36; in family cluster, 119–120. *See also* Metaphor
Conciliation: complement to consensus, 61

193

198

Index

Thoreau, Henry David, 109
Transformation of thought, 17
Transit passage, 51
Trial: as theater, 23, 133
Truman Proclamations, 46, 47–48, 66, 120
Truth, 8, 9, 32
Turnbull, Colin, 133–34
Turtle: boys, 3; egg-laying, 3; and son, 3, 10, 11, 12, 13; tears, 4; appearance, 5; support for earth, 5; hatcheries, 6; research, 6; and law, 15, 24; and Peaceable Kingdom, 124, 180–81$n10$; and theology, 126, 130; death, 137; and Native Americans, 180$n10$; Island, 180–81$n10$
Tushnet, Mark, 166$n29$, 186$n26$

United Kingdom: Cod War, 49
United Nations Conference on the Law of the Sea (I), 48–49
—(II), 48
—(III): United Nations General Assembly and, 48; treaty summarized, 48–54; difficulties, 50; treaty and law as medium, 56–64; conference itself as medium, 58–64; and metaphors, 120
United States: claims to sea, 47–48; subverts conference and treaty, 50, 55, 57–58

United States Navy, 86–88
United States v. California, 66–67, 68, 70, 161$n4$, 161$n6$, 164$n12$, 166$n24$
United States v. Louisiana, 161$n4$, 161$n6$
United States v. Maine, 68, 161$n4$, 164$n12$
United States v. Texas, 161$n4$

Victims of law, xiv, 16

Walcott, Derek, 46
Watt, James: accelerated offshore leasing, 81; Fortress America, 121; and Marx, 128; contrasted with Bonhoeffer, 129. *See also* Second Coming
Watt v. California. *See* California v. Watt
Weinberger v. Romero-Barcelo. *See* Romero-Barcelo v. Brown
Weisberg, Richard, 191$n61$
Whales: and Eskimos, 89
Wharve out, 99
White, James Boyd, 15, 141$n19$, 142$n5$
White, Lynn, Jr., 128–29
Wife, 12, 34
Wilbour v. Gallagher, 113
Wilderness Act, 7

Zabel v. Tabb, 165$n20$
Zuckmayer, Carl: and Barth, 184$n17$

DESIGNED BY RICHARD HENDEL
COMPOSED BY GRAPHIC COMPOSITION, INC.
ATHENS, GEORGIA
MANUFACTURED BY INTER-COLLEGIATE PRESS, INC.
SHAWNEE MISSION, KANSAS
TEXT AND DISPLAY LINES ARE SET IN PALATINO

Library of Congress Cataloging-in-Publication Data
Ball, Milner S.
Lying down together.
(Rhetoric of the human sciences)
Includes index.
1. Maritime law. 2. Maritime law—United States.
3. Law—Philosophy. I. Title. II. Series.
JX4411.B33 1985 341.4'5 85-40361
ISBN 0-299-10450-8